ROUTLEDGE LIBRARY EDITIONS: PUBLIC ENTERPRISE AND PRIVATIZATION

Volume 8

THE NATURE OF PUBLIC ENTERPRISE

THE NATURE OF PUBLIC ENTERPRISE

Edited by
V.V. RAMANADHAM

Routledge
Taylor & Francis Group

LONDON AND NEW YORK

First published in 1984 by Croom Helm

This edition first published in 2019
by Routledge
2 Park Square, Milton Park, Abingdon, Oxon OX14 4RN

and by Routledge
52 Vanderbilt Avenue, New York, NY 10017

Routledge is an imprint of the Taylor & Francis Group, an informa business

British Library Cataloguing in Publication Data
A catalogue record for this book is available from the British Library

ISBN: 978-0-367-14233-9 (Set)
ISBN: 978-0-429-25929-6 (Set) (ebk)
ISBN: 978-0-367-18199-4 (Volume 8) (hbk)
ISBN: 978-0-429-06011-3 (Volume 8) (ebk)

Publisher's Note
The publisher has gone to great lengths to ensure the quality of this reprint but points out that some imperfections in the original copies may be apparent.

Disclaimer
The publisher has made every effort to trace copyright holders and would welcome correspondence from those they have been unable to trace.

The Nature of Public Enterprise

Edited by
V.V. RAMANADHAM

CROOM HELM
London & Sydney

© 1984 V.V. Ramanadham
Croom Helm Ltd, Provident House, Burrell Row,
Beckenham, Kent BR3 1AT
Croom Helm Australia Pty Ltd, GPO Box 5097,
Sydney, NSW 2001, Australia
Croom Helm, 51 Washington Street,
Dover, New Hampshire, 03820 USA

British Library Cataloguing in Publication Data

Ramanadham, V.V.
    The nature of public enterprise.
    1. Developing countries— Government business
    enterprises
    I. Title
    338.6'2'091724

    ISBN 0-7099-2262-0

Printed and bound in Great Britain

CONTENTS

Part III

Decentralisation of Public Enterprise Control

To my father V. Seshayya Sastry, who
instilled in me intellectual curiosity

PREFACE

This book is comprised of three studies. The first deals with what is to be expected of a public enterprise by virtue of its conceptual significance. One may contrast with it what actually obtains and devise policy measures to bridge any gap between concept and practice.

The second study explores the distinctive problems of public enterprise in developing countries. It ends with the plea that governments of mixed economies should evaluate the comparative advantage that individual public enterprises possess as units of organisation today in their circumstantial context and proceed with any structural changes that the evaluations suggest.

The third is a study of an important aspect of governmental relationships with public enterprise, viz. control, which can have a determinative impact on its performance.

The London Business School has been an excellent academic base for my researches during 1982-83. I have had the opportunity of a continuous dialogue with my Faculty colleagues on the subject matter of this book - in particular with Professors Michael Beesley, David Chambers and John Heath. The weekly seminar on Public Enterprise and the Developing World, which I conducted at the School during March-June 1983, also proved valuable to me in organising the material in these studies.

Sir Norman Chester commented on Parts I and III; Mr. R.W. Roseveare on Part III; Mr. Nick Woodwar on Part II; Dr. Adrian Strain on Part I; and Professor Maurice Garner on the entire manuscript. Their queries and suggestions have helped me in improving the text at several places. I convey my grateful thanks to them.

London Business School   V.V. Ramanadham

TABLES

FIGURES

APPENDICES

PART I

THE CONCEPT OF PUBLIC ENTERPRISE

Chapter One

INTRODUCTION

This study aims at an analysis of the concept of public enterprise. The focus is on what being a public enterprise implies conceptually.

(i) At the minimum it sorts out the wood from the trees and focusses on the conceptual essence of what a public enterprise implies as distinct from symptoms and partial perceptions.

(ii) It enables us to compare an actual public enterprise situation with the conceptual and establish the area in which practice may have to improve in order that the conceptual implications are fully realised. And it suggests the conditions, as derived from the concept, under which the utility of public enterprise is likely to be at a maximum to the nation.

(iii) It throws up the inherent difficulties in creating a situation that closely approximates to the conceptual model of a public enterprise and suggests the existence of certain in-built costs in the evolution of public enterprise as an institution.

Chapter 2 deals with the 'public' element of the concept and Chapter 3 with the 'enterprise' element; and the crucial issue of synthesising the two is covered in Chapter 4.

Chapter 5 looks at taxonomic aspects relevant to the conceptual analysis, limiting itself to highlighting the particular problems or biases that certain categories of public enterprises present in relation to a conceptual element

The last chapter refers to the question of

3

operationalising the concept of public enterprise through a definition. The term <u>public enterprise</u> is employed here in its generic sense and subsumes such terms as state enterprises, nationalised industries, parastatals, statutory boards and decentralised agencies, which we come across in the literature. These are not necessarily homogeneous in every aspect, but the interest of the present study lies in pursuing a matter of commonality, namely, what they all imply as public enterprises.

Chapter Two

THE 'PUBLIC' CONCEPT

Three elements stand out predominantly under the head of the 'public' concept.

(a) Non-private accretion of net benefits

First, the net benefits of the activity under-taken by the enterprise do not go to the enrichment of a private group of individuals standing in the position of owners. The benefits are of two kinds: surpluses, which represent the net revenues realised in the course of operations in a given period and are available for distribution as dividends; and capital appreciation, which results from the accu-mulation of undistributed profits (as reserves or under any other designation), or from the issue of bonus shares, or from a sale of assets. There can also be another source of capital gain which emerges in the event of sale of the business in a new pro-prietor, viz., goodwill.

The reason why these benefits of investment do not reach individuals is simply that the risk capital ranking for such benefits does not originate in them. There may be private lenders but what they get is limited to a fixed rate of interest, or (exception-ally) stockholders but not of the equity kind. As long as the surplus as a rate on capital employed exceeds the rate of interest on loan capital, there is an accretion of a net benefit to the non-private sector even from the use of private funds received as loans.

A similar cause of gain exists in the case of private participation in the equity capital of a public enterprise, if the regulations governing the dividend – over a specified period or indefinitely –

limit it to a level that turns out to be lower than the rate of actual net return derived from the use of such funds. Even where a regulation of that nature does not exist, the same result is possible if the board of directors is so influenced as to declare dividends at a rate lower than the rate of net returns earned from such funds.

At this point it would be of interest to make a reference to the unique case of the 'socially owned' enterprise of Yugoslavia. There is no owner in the case of a 'self managed' Yugoslav enterprise in the sense of one that contributes equity capital. The investment funds are found from bank loans and, as time passes, the business fund of the enterprise itself. The lending banks have no owner-ship rights. Though the enterprise is self-managed and the workers have formal powers of management as well as entrepreneurial decision, none of them, even on retirement, can lay a claim to a share in the capital of the enterprise. In the event of its liquidation, the assets get merged in those of another enterprise or of a community of interest. What is crucial to our context is not the question who owns the enterprise but the fact that no private person owns it; and there can be no net benefit accretion to any private person, subject to the comment on wages in a following paragraph.

The way in which the net benefits of a Yugoslav enterprise get disposed of is simple in one sense: they do not go to anyone outside the enterprise. But the substantive position is somewhat complicated by two considerations, viz., that several governmen-tal agencies receive payments from the enterprise out of what, in other countries, would have ended up as its net revenues, and that there is never a time when the net revenues that stay within the enterprise can be claimed by any insider as his share (1).

It is necessary to introduce two qualifications to the concept of non-private entitlement to net benefits of public enterprise. The first is that a leakage can occur in favour of certain private groups, though not owners, even before the point of net benefits is reached. This process often works in a way which is not readily detected. Three prominent channels of such leakage may be distinguished.

(1) <u>Wage incomes</u>: There occurs a diversion of what could be a net benefit (or surplus) to the category of cost when relatively high wage incomes are secured by the employees of a public enterprise This might take place through relatively high levels of wages or through surplus staff and low productivity – two features found associated with many public enterprises in developing (2) as well as developed (3) countries. The likelihood of such a leakage is the greater, the nearer the enterprise is to the following situations:

(i) The employees have a de jure right to participate in top directoral and management policies. An extreme case is that of an enterprise which is self-managed, as in Yugoslavia, where even at the conceptual level the wage incomes are strictly personal net incomes, or appropriations of net revenue (4), and the workers have the right to determine the levels of what they take out of the net revenue.

(ii) The employees have political strength enough to attract the government's support to their generous wage and staff-number claims, overtly or covertly, and the directors, for various reasons, are too weak to resist them.

(2) <u>Other input policies</u>: If a public enterprise offers contracts for construction works or raw materials under political pressures at inflated levels of cost, or offers inflated compensation for any break in terms of contract on its part, there is, in effect, a conversion of what could have been a net benefit to the category of costs; and this benefit goes to private groups of individuals – not owners, but contractees.

(3) <u>Price concessions</u>: A strong consumer group may extract price reductions (5) that tend to diminish the net benefits otherwise accruable to the owners of the enterprise (6).

The other qualification of the concept of accretion of net benefits to non-private beneficiaries is simple, viz., that net benefits do exist in the first place; in other words, that a surplus <u>is</u> raised by the public enterprise. Or else, the point would be of little moment, as in several cases today.

Reference may be made to a far reaching implication of the non-private accretion of net benefits. It is possible that, on grounds of the surplus reaching a public level, the government may be tempted, in the case of certain public enterprises with a high profit potential, to let them raise extraordinarily high surpluses. But these imply prices that carry the function of taxes. The kind of calculations that underlie (or are introduced in support of) a tax measure are absent in this case; for example, the question of whether the given consumer groups are fit candidates for the indirect tax is not brought into the open. The process ordinarily escapes the attention of Parliament, unless the financial targets, if any, for a given public enterprise are approved by Parliament in the knowledge of their price implications; and the value of a comprehensive debate in Parliament on a given net income accretion in the total context of the revenues of the public exchequer is lost. Basically it would be helpful to keep the public exchequer angle distinct – though co-ordinated – as far as possible, from that of public enterprise pricing and net revenue.

This section emphasised the idea of net benefits (or surpluses) rather than ownership, since that more accurately represents the conceptual essence of public enterprise.

(b) Public decision-making

The second basic element in the 'public' concept is that entrepreneurial and other major decision-making activity shifts from the level of private groups of persons brought together as owners and/or managers to some public level at which no such personal interest exists. There can be several ways of describing such decisions but they relate primarily to three areas: investment, covering the size, technology and location of the activity, and the capital expenditure sequence; surplus goals and the overall price level, as well as any prominent aspects of the price structure; (8) and input policies which have extra-enterprise rather than merely commercial implications. This is a broad statement; admittedly there exist many broader aspects of management, the legitimate preserve of the managers, into which entrepreneurial or major decisions belonging to any of these categories penetrate. For instance, when is a price structure

8

a major decision and when is it to be considered as
a managerial decision?   And when is a product mix
to be considered a major decision and when is it to
be conceded as an appropriate subject for the management to decide?

The shift of entrepreneurial or major decision-
making from private to public or communal levels,
which is implicit in public enterprise, is not just
the product of government ownership or of governmental provision of loan capital in the case of an
enterprise with all loan capital.   The rationale
of the shift is independent of this legal or institutional fact.   We sometimes come across the conten-
tion that the government is entitled to a role in
decision making with reference to a public enterprise,
by virtue of its being the owner.   Such a private
enterprise analogy is superfluous, for the role is
justified squarely by the intrinsic relevance of
non-private criteria in decision making.   Ownership
perhaps renders the government's role in decision
making easy.   It can be seen from the above argument that the essential aspect of a public decision
is not that the government (or a public agency)
makes it but that the decision rests on distinctive
social criteria.   Though the government can try to
facilitate the realisation of certain social returns
even from private enterprise by means of laws, per-
suasion and fiscal policies, it would be easier,
more direct and possibly more economical to aim at
realising them through public enterprise.

Two issues of substance on the concept of non-
private decision-making may be discussed at this
stage: (1) the criteria, and (2) the authorship.

(1)   The criteria of decision-making: It is in
terms of the criteria that public decision-making
is really meaningful.   Different from the relatively simple aim of maximising net revenue, these
have to be understood on lines of the Pigovian distinction of social net returns from private net
returns.   Private decision-making neither takes
necessary note of all external benefits and costs
traceable to an activity, nor adopts, in its calculations, prices other than those that prevail in
the market.   Neither is a commendable basis of
decision making, especially in a developing country
with intense market imperfections.   The object of
non-private decision-making has to be 'to maximise
social gains' or 'to contribute most to the ultimate

9

objectives of the country' - to borrow phrases from the cost benefit UNIDO Guidelines (9). In fact, the literature on cost-benefit analysis of public sector projects is of relevance in the present context. It brings out the nature and complexity of the project-decisions, since the whole attempt is to move from financial profitability to economic profitability or to social or 'total national profitability' (10). The analysis can be envisaged as a five-stage process (11):

(i)   calculations of financial profit at market prices;

(ii)   shadow pricing of resources to obtain the net benefit at economic (efficiency) prices;

(iii) adjustment for impacts on savings and investment;

(iv)   adjustment for impacts on income distribution:

(v)   adjustment for merit goods.

Three categories of problems complicate the exercise, viz.,(a) the establishment of shadow prices for outputs and inputs such as wages and foreign exchange as distinct from market prices, and for investment reflecting the value of savings; (b) the determination of distributional and other goals of the country; and (c) the attribution of weights to them. While sophisticated techniques can deal with part of problem (a), the parts relating to the social rate of discount and to (b) and (c), involve 'value parameters' reflecting 'ethical judgements' (9).

Obviously there is need for precision in respect of these aspects of non-private decision making, if the concept of 'public' enterprise is, genuinely, to internalise in decision-making various items left out as externalities by private decision making. In practice, this may turn out to be difficult; and there emerge costs of public decision-making in any of the following ways: (a) some decisional criteria are set but not all;   (b) the weights attached to different criteria are controversial; and (c) the exercise may often boil down to seeking criteria and weights that support an already favoured decision.

The idea is, not that a financial analysis is unnecessary, but that it is neither sufficient nor conclusive in public decision-making. There is an important caveat, however. Given the goals, a particular decision vis-à-vis a public enterprise is but one instrument in the arsenal of policy decisions open to the government. For example, as against a pricing decision or a location decision in favour of certain identified interests, there is the possibility of direct-budget policies designed to transfer the self-same income benefits to those groups. The decision maker ought not to rush to the public enterprise medium without analysing its comparative efficiency.

(2) Authorship: In whom does the decisional power rest? The bulk of thinking on this question, as well as practice, has been in favour of the government. The Guidelines terms the government as 'guardians of public policy' (9): and the White Paper of 1967 (UK) on Nationalised Industries, while arguing that 'significant costs and benefits can occur which are outside the financial concern for the industry', observes that 'it is the special responsibility of the Government to ensure that these social factors are reflected in the industries' planning' (12).

The grounds on which the assumption of decision making by the government seems not only natural but justified are as follows:

(i)   it is simple and carries with it the authority of the government:

(ii)   the government has the constitutional prerogative of representing the decisional will of the nation;

(iii)   any other arrangement may at some point call for final arbitration by the government, subject only to the alternative of the appellate verdict of a court of law.

However, problems can arise in the context of maximising overall social or national benefit.

(i)   The government of the day has a short-run view of the criteria of decision, whereas a far longer perspective is implicit in the case of such criteria as concern the social rate of discount and the growth-equity conflicts (13).

(ii) The government has a tendency to so formulate the criteria as to suit its political forum and benefit the groups and regions that are essential to please in its political interest (14). For instance, the closure of an inefficient plant may be put off by overweighting its employment benefits if that suits the government at the polls (15).

(iii) The government may not possess adequate expertise within the departments for the sophisticated computations needed at times on alternative assumptions as to weights or adjustment factors in the evaluation of social costs and benefits. If the bulk of the exercise is undertaken outside the government on the basis of broad guidelines and on diversely postulated hypotheses, the government's ultimate choices from among the results can be minimally partisan and the public can gain confidence as to the reasonableness of their appropriateness.

It is therefore to the advantage of the concept of non-private decision making that it is appropriately shared between the government and outside (public) agencies in the interest of expertise and impartiality (16). There can then be some check on the political party in office in wielding the decisional power.

The decision process may run on the following lines: (a) the Acts may incorporate broad criteria that govern public decision making; (b) expert agencies such as a Price Commission, Public Investment Board and Monopoly Control Commission may be established with functions relevant to the application of social criteria to public enterprise behaviour (17); and (c) different levels of government - central, state and local - may be entrusted with responsibility for different aspects of the decision-making, the more justifiably in respect of social costs and benefits significantly associated with sub-national levels (18). There is one (rather difficult) requirement in this exercise of decentralisation: all the pieces have to fit into a co-ordinated national decisional system.

This discussion may be concluded with the observation that the idea of non-private decision making is conceptually superior to that of non-private ownership. For, the concept is essentially one of <u>how</u> the entrepreneurial and major decisions are made both at the level of investment and at the level of using the assets set up. Even in private enterprise importance attaches to those in positions of decision making as distinct from those that just own the enterprise. The essence of 'managerial revolution' is precisely that (19).

It is interesting to note in this connection the emphasis on the decisional aspect which the European Economic Community laid down while defining 'a public undertaking' as 'any undertaking over which the public authorities may exercise a dominant influence by virtue of their ownership of it, their shareholdings in it, or <u>the rules which govern</u> it; any undertaking in which one or more of the undertakings defined above may do the same, either directly or indirectly' (20).

(c) Social Accountability

The third distinctive element in the 'public' concept is that the enterprise is accountable to the public for its performance. It is of primary importance that the nature and degree of accountability are verifiable; or else the concept ends up as a subjective idea. The accountability requirement is closely linked with the element of public decision discussed in the preceding section and has to be established in relation to the criteria that underlie the relevant public decisions. It transcends the major goal of ownership interest, namely, net revenue, and introduces difficult problems of specification.

The inter-relationship between the decisional structure and accountability is of great significance from two points of view. The first is one of sheer logic: if a set of decisions have governed the working of an enterprise, it has to be held accountable in terms of the implications of those decisions, i.e. in consonance with the aims reflected in those decisions and the resource (and other) constraints that the decisions have involved. What is needed is that the canons of accountability have to be laid down consistently with the decisional parameters. This is not easy, of course. For experience suggests that the decisional parameters are not clearly visualised by the deciding agencies, nor are they transparent; and establishing indi-

cators whereby accountability in terms of the decisional criteria can be verified becomes, therefore,
a complex exercise.

The exercise gets complicated as the levels at
which decisions originate are not exactly the same
as those that are involved in accountability adju-
dications. In a general way it can be said that
it is the 'government' that is involved in both
cases. But this is an over-simplification. For
two reasons. First, its direct role at the accountability end is unlikely to be as substantial as at
the decision end; several agencies such as consumer
councils, monopoly control commissions, and the
audit agencies (with gradually extending remits)
are also substantively concerned with the accountability process. Second, there is no single
point in the name of government, which sits in
exclusive judgement of accountability. It is
composed of various parts, each of which has its
own angle; and their angles may turn out to be
mutually conflicting at times. What makes accountability a meaningful concept is that the criteria
of accountability are specified. It is not enough
to identify the agency, e.g. government, to which
accountability is to be rendered by the enterprise.

One may come to this conclusion by another
route: and this takes us into the anatomy of the
concept of accountability. This is really in two
parts - first, there is the accountability of the
managers provided with certain powers and privi-
leges, responsibilities and duties, objectives and
targets, resources and directives. Very simply,
the managers must render an account of their behaviour, operations and net results in terms of all
these conditions. Then there is the other part,
viz., the accountability of the enterprise to
society. Here enterprise is a comprehensive term
and, in the context of the public sector, covers
both the managers and the outsiders who play a role
in the decisional process. The government departments that participate in the latter, if not dominate it, are, therefore, an integral section of
the agencies whose 'derived' accountability as
reflected in the consequential actions of the managers also deserves notice, scrutiny and adjudication. This is basic to the concept of public
enterprise. The idea is not that the government
men concerned should be held personally accountable,
except in cases of corruption, fraud or personal

negligence. In fact the turn-over of ministers
(21) and senior civil servants in a given department may be so great as to make the person-oriented
approach unmeaningful. What is needed is the accountability of the decisions taken by, or at the
instance of, the government. Once again, the way
to go about it is by setting up the criteria by
which the decisions may be judged; in fact the
process is two-fold; first, the premises of a
decision and the consistency of the decision with
the premises have to be reviewed; and next, the
nature of results that ensued from the implementation of the decision has to be appraised. Thus
the teeth of the accountability process lie in its
criteria.

It would be relevant at this point to introduce
the term 'social' accountability - a term coming
into vogue. Hair splitting apart, the term seems
to have special significance in emphasising that
the concept is not one of accountability to the
government - if the more traditional term 'public'
accountability was supposed to signify that alone -
but that it extends to the totality of the operations of the enterprise, whichever source have
decisional bases have been derived from, from the
multiple angles of the consumers, the workers, the
public exchequer, economic growth and social transformation.

Inevitably the relevance of Parliament in
this entire exercise surfaces at this point. (Here
Parliament (22) is understood as a formal institution which under the country's constitution represents the will of the people; and the term covers
all decentralised versions of it.) Even if the
accountability of the managers can, in a limited
sense, be adjudicated by the executive wings of
the government, the accountability of the enterprise as a whole has to be adjudicated at the level
of Parliament, even if by appropriate delegation
(23). The most obvious reason is the constitutional one, viz., that the executive branch of
government has to be accountable to the legislative branch for its actions and omissions

More substantively, there is the need for
Parliament's scrutiny (24) so as to ensure that
nothing is done by the Government through its decisional influence on public enterprise policies,
that ought to be done normally through budget

policies open to the parliamentary process, that
any substitution of enterprise for budget policies
rests on proven grounds of superior efficiency (or
effectiveness), and that such enterprise policies
attract adequate adjudication in point of results
at the hands of Parliament or a Parliament-inspired
agency in due course. This prevents the possibility of public decisions not sufficiently justified
by social criteria (25).

To conclude: the concept of social accountability has both a positive and a negative connotation. In the positive sense its focus is on ensuring that the enterprise has delivered to the nation
the maximum economic or social profitability possible
within its circumstances. In the negative sense
it focusses on ensuring that no group of persons
enjoying a decisional role has so acted as to
induce the enterprise into providing for private
or partisan gains.

NOTES

1. For a detailed discussion of the substantive
aspects of the Yugoslav enterprise's finances, see
V.V. Ramanadham, The Yugoslav Enterprise (ICPE,
Ljubljana, 1980).
2. This fairly general feature may be illustrated with reference to Food Corporation of India.
There was a 'surplusage' of 8,319 workers in 1974
as against the total number of employees of 48,757.
That is, 17 per cent of the employees were surplus.
(Report of the Comptroller and Auditor General of
India, 1976, Part IV, (New Delhi), pp.57 and 65.)
3. The steep reductions in the numbers employed by British Steel Corporation, National Coal
Board and British Railways over the recent decade
illustrate the extent of surplus manpower that had
existed. The reductions are not merely occasioned
by closures of capacity.
4. This is reflected even in the accounting
presentations, in which there is no item of wages
under costs; but 'personal income' ranks as one of
the claimants of 'net income', the others being
reserve fund, common consumption fund, and business
fund. Also, see The Associated Labour Act (Belgrade).
5. Not such price reductions as raise net
revenues because of elastic demands and decreasing
costs.

6.   A recent instance is that of price in-
creases having been rescinded by the Government of
Thailand due to strong public pressures, in the case
of the State Railways and Bangkok Mass Transit
Authority.   (Maurice Garner 'Public Enterprise in
Thailand', Seminar on Public Enterprise and the
Developing World, London Business School,1982).

7.   The pricing and profits policy of
British Gas Corporation in recent years illustrates the point.

8.   Just to illustrate from a developing
country context: the Kuwait Government observed
that the tariffs of electricity, water, telecommunications, etc. 'must be subject to state control
and are finally determined by the State'.   The
Planning Board, The First Five-Year Development Plan,
1967/68-1971/72 (1968), p.171.

9.   Guidelines for Project Evaluation, pp.27
and I.   (United Nations, New York, 1972) (E.72 II
B.II).

10.   Ibid, p.28.

11.   Guide to Practical Project Appraisal:
Social Benefit-Cost-Analysis in Developing Countries
p.3 (United Nations, New York, 1978, E.78.IIB.3).

12.   National Industries, A Review of Economic
and Financial Objectives, p.4 (London, HMSO, 1967,
Cmnd. 3437).

13.   The NEDO study in the UK refers to 'the
difficulty of reconciling the different time scales
of politicians and industries' and to the fact that
enterprise plans may be for periods 'which far extend well beyond the life-time of a single Parliament'.   (National Economic Development Office,
A Study of UK Nationalised Industries: Their Role
in the Economy and Control in the Future (London,
HMSO, 1976) p.9.

14.   Statutory disqualification of Members
of Parliament (and Ministers) for membership of public enterprise boards or the convention of not ap-
pointing them has a merit in the context of the
present argument.   For example, in UK being a
member of the House of Commons is a disqualification for board membership under most nationalising
Acts.   D.N. Chester, The Nationalised Industries,
A Statutory Analysis (London, 1948), p.9.   In
Canada the general practice has been not to appoint
Members of Parliament to the boards.   Don Gracey,
Public Enterprise Management and Training, Commonwealth Secretariat (London, 1980), p.106.

15.   'Government itself is part of the class
and interest struggle.   Representing a single

interest (or alliance of interests), their weighting
of social objectives does not represent some sort
of attempt at synthesis of the national interest,
but rather primarily the interests on which they
depend for their power.' Frances Stewart, A Note
on Social Cost Benefit Analysis and Class Conflict
in LDC's (World Development, Vol.3, No.1, January
1975, p.36).

16. See Part III for a full discussion on
the role of non-government agencies in public enterprise matters.

17. Where an agency set up to deal with all
enterprises is entrusted with a function appertain-
ing to public decision making - e.g. price determination, it is necessary to provide it with
guidance on the criteria to be specially kept in
mind while dealing with a public, as against a
private, enterprise question. For instance, the
British Government has asked the Price Commission,
when it investigated price proposals by a nationalised industry, 'to take account of any financial
target which the Government had set' (The
Nationalised Industries, London, HMSO, 1978, Cmnd.
7131, p.27).

18. There is a skilful use of the guidelines strategy in Yugoslavia, which conspicuously
decentralises public decision making. The Associated Labour Act, which governs the self-managed
enterprises, provides for social compacts and self-
management agreements of various kinds which have
the force of introducing non-private decision into
the working of the enterprises. The direct assignment of decisional power to the Federal Government
or even the Republic level Government is minimal.

19. James Burnham, Managerial Revolution
(New York, 1941).

20. Article 2, Commission Directive on the
Transparency of Financial Relations between Member
States and Public Undertakings. European Econo-
mic Community (Brussels).

21. For example, during Sir Peter Parker's
tenure of seven years as Chairman of British Rail
there have been five Ministers. Over the last 25
years there have been fourteen Ministers dealing
with this enterprise.

22. Lloyd D. Musolf terms Parliament 'the
ultimate guardian', with the obligation of holding
the corporations 'ultimately accountable' (Public
Ownership and Accountability), (Havard, 1959), p.102.

23. A recent instance of governmental appreciation of the concept of its own accountability is

available from British experience.   The White Paper,
The Nationalised Industries, observed: 'When the
(financial) target has been settled for the
industry, the Secretary of State will announce it
to Parliament.   He will indicate the main assumptions on which it is based: for example, any particular social or sectoral objectives which the
Government has set the industry, and which may
have affected the level of the target, the broad
complications for the pricing policy; and any other
important factors of which Parliament and the public should know when they subsequently judge the
industry's performance against the target.   (Cmnd.
7131, 1978, p.26).

24.   This is illustrated by a recent recom-
mendation contained in the Final Report of the Royal
Commission on Financial Management and Accountability,
Canada, March 1979.

25.   In this context the observations of
Frances Stewart on social cost-benefit analysis
are interesting: 'Governments do not represent
the "social" interest, but their own class interests and yet wish to appear to represent the
"wider   social interests".'   World Development,
Vol.3, No.1, January 1975, 'A Note on Social Cost
Benefit Analysis and Class Conflict in LDCs', p.38.

Chapter Three

THE 'ENTERPRISE' CONCEPT

An analysis of the 'enterprise' concept has a two-
fold purpose. It helps in distinguishing public
activities that may be considered as enterprise
from those that are not; and it suggests what
essential implications of 'enterprise' need to be
preserved while giving effect to the 'public' concept - an issue to be pursued in the next chapter.

It is difficult to be precise on what constitutes the core of an enterprise. Two inter-related
ideas suggest themselves, viz., financial viability
and the cost-price equation.

(a) Financial viability

The first is financial viability. This is
best understood as an expression, in brevity, of a
conscious effort on the part of the enterprise towards raising a net revenue. It is on the size
of the net revenue that some annotation is required.
The goal, in theory, can be net revenue maximisation;
but in practice several qualifications exist, (1)
even in the private sector. Only such a size of
net revenue is sought as (i) does not damage the
long-term financial interests of the enterprise;
(ii) does not encourage powerful competitive
threats; (iii) does not provoke labour unrest;
(iv) does not cause such consumer protests as
invite price controls restrictive of prices and
revenues and (v) does not arouse public antipathy
towards the enterprise in respect of its output
(restriction) policies. And then there is another
qualification derived from the conditions of modern
corporate working, viz., that the professional managers have enough power to subject the net revenue
policies to their own interests of personal finan-

cial benefit and public image through employment and other input policies and through output and price policies that reduce the net revenue below the theoretical maximum.

These are all powerful qualifications to the text-book delineation of net revenue maximisation, Nevertheless, if a purposive direction of behaviour is to be attributed to the enterprise, it is that, within the constraints enumerated above, there is an effort towards increasing the net revenue. 'How high' is the point for controversy.

It is interesting to note Posner's formulation that 'in the private sector growth of ouput is maximised subject to the rate of profit attaining a minimum satisfactory level' (2). The profit condition is basic, the output condition being supplementary; where a given net revenue can be raised from two or more of output options, the option of maximum output is worth choosing (3). The 'minimum satisfactory return' may be interpreted as the net revenue that is inferred as reasonable in the face of the qualifications mentioned above. In fact once this is set as a goal there already is an implicit impact on the output size.

The 'viability' feature has to be spelt out as viability <u>by intention</u> and <u>in the long run</u>. This helps in explaining any occasional deviations from viability experienced by an enterprise. For instance,there may be little viability during its gestation period; it does not achieve viability during periods of bad business; and its viability may be disrupted under conditions of managerial inefficiency. But the intention is viability in the long run (4); or else it is not an enterprise and, in the public sector context, may be deemed as a non-enterprise activity of a governmental agency.

Another implicit element of the viability feature is risk-taking, right from the point of investment decision. Ideally, the most profitable risk decisions are called for in respect of investments; prices, costs, outputs and net revenues are in the nature of variables, in whatever terms the profit is envisaged. It is true that a decision on certain items preempts decisions on certain other items. For example, given the cost decisions, a decisional choice on output is possible but the price and size of the net revenue will follow as results and are not again subject to the enterprise's decisional choice. Or, given the cost conditions, a decisional choice on price is possible, but the sizes of output and net revenue follow as a sequel and are not again amenable to simultaneous decisional choice on the part of the enterprise. Subject to such internal limitations on decision freedom, the enterprise is characterised by the impulse of risk taking so as to maximise the net revenue or, where this is under some insuperable constraint, to maximise some other value for which the enterprise is responsible. Ordinarily it can regulate the magnitudes of costs and outputs or revenues so as to achieve this end. A non-enterprise in the public sector does not possess this kind of decisional flexibility derived from risk taking.

(b)   The cost-price equation

The 'enterprise' concept strictly goes beyond financial viability, and is concerned with the way in which the viability is achieved. It is realised from the sales activity, no doubt; but significance attaches to the relationships that prices bear to costs (5).

The following versions of revenue raising illustrate how an enterprise differs from a non-enterprise. The enterprise does not operate at a uniform fee, like a park authority. It does not levy a charge in relation to the clients' income or wealth status, like a government hospital or house allotment department. It does not seek income through contributions, suggested but not insisted upon, like certain museums or art galleries. As an enterprise it goes by cost considerations in determining the payments that customers are to make.

Let us look at this in some detail. Ordinarily an output is not offered if it does not meet the cost involved; and extreme caution is needed before a disproportionate excess of price over cost (or shortfall below cost) in the case of a given output is practised, for it is open to challenge by the consumers adversely affected. (The 'disproportion' needs definition, after allowing for the overall revenue-cost relationship implicit in the financial viability aimed at; besides, cost allocations within the market totality of the enter-

23

prise assume importance.)

The last idea needs some explanation. It
refers to cross-subsidisations among different
markets, whose costs can be isolated for comparison with the prices charged. The question now
shifts to the unit of the market to which cost
ascertainment should apply. It can be each individual consumer, at one extreme. But this is
rarely done, except in such cases as ships, whose
buyers usually have their own specifications, or
housebuilding contracts for a similar reason.
Ordinarily a market may be so demarcated that the
output supplied to it is characterised by cost
jointness, implying that the non-sale of a unit
of the product in that market has the effect of
raising the net incidence of (fixed) cost on the
remainder of the market, i.e. on the average cost
level in that market. The aim should be to go
as far down as possible in the demarcation of markets for cost-price comparisons, without reaching
the point of cumbersome cost allocation that becomes
an extra cost in itself - sometimes for the very
purpose of convincing the consumers or control
agencies of its reasonableness and desirability.
For example, to distinguish electricity markets
by time, place and nature of consumption is desirable; so is the distinction among letter mail,
parcels, telegrams and telephones, offered by the
post office. One may go somewhat further too -
e.g. first class and second class mail; and charg-
ing on foreign mail on the basis of distance.

It is not suggested here that cross-subsidisations do not exist in practice. The proposition
is that an enterprise, implicitly, has to be concerned with how it relates its prices to costs; or
else challenge is to be expected from competitors,
consumers and control agencies. Where competition
is effective, an enterprise cannot hope to work on
prices that deviate from costs in the market vulnerable to competition; and where monopoly prevails,
this is possible but monopoly control agencies catch
up with the 'unfair' practice (6).

It is the two ideas underlying the concept of
enterprise, viz., financial viability and the cost-
price question, that help in distinguishing a public enterprise from a public activity in such fields
as education, public health, sanitation and environment protection. In these cases the idea of long

term viability has little force.   Further, the availability of an output to a client is not strictly
governed by his ability to pay towards the cost of
the supply to him.   And the fine analysis of cross-
subsidisations does not apply here either.

At this stage let us refer to the view that
legal autonomy (7) is what makes an enterprise.
This is a formal view but not a substantive one.
Autonomy is a helpful condition but not a sufficient condition and is implicit in the foregoing
description of viability and the cost-price equation.   Further, it does not explain how certain
autonomously organised activities in the public
sector are non-enterprises (8), or how certain
non-automonously (i.e. departmentally) organised
activities (like Indian railways) should be considered as enterprises nevertheless.

The Federal Industrial Development Authority
(in Malaysia) set up under an Act in 1965 has predominantly non-enterprise functions, and its revenues are mainly derived from 'the funds ... provided
by Parliament' (9).   Many Latin American countries
have a large number of non-departmentally organised
public activities – entitled decentralised agencies,
statutory authorities etc. (10), but not impelled
by calculations of financial viability.   The
Investment Advisory Centre of Pakistan, which has
an 'autonomous board of directors' is a 'non-profit
organisation'; the Fata Development Corporation has
non-viable functions in the federally administered
tribal areas of Pakistan; similarly, the Pakistan
Broadcasting Corporation is autonomous under an
Act of 1973, but has most of its income through
a government subsidy (11).   The United Kingdom
has a large number of 'quangos' – independent
entities but not 'enterprises'.

Another inconclusive idea is that an activity
is an enterprise when in industry and commerce but
not when in the field of social services.   While
certain broad examples are possible, like textiles
and retailing in the former category and sanitation
and parks in the latter, it is not easy to define
the two categories; and what appears to be a relatively social service in one country or at one time
may appear to belong to the other category in another
country or at another time – e.g. housing, agricultural finance and broadcasting.   Perhaps the idea
rests basically, but not explicitly, on the require-

ment of viability in one case and the lack of it in the other.

In concluding this chapter, we may note four points relevant to the 'enterprise' concept.

First, a whole activity entrusted to an under-taking may not necessarily be of the enterprise type (12). A segment of it may be an enterprise while the rest may be a non-enterprise. Such a bifurca-tion is conceptually necessary, even if on grounds of convenience both kinds of activity are unified in a single apex. This method is not meticulously followed in all cases where it ought to be (13) and doubt arises as to whether the undertaking as a whole is to be treated as an enterprise or not.

Second, an enterprise (or an enterprise segment) may not necessarily be in that position for all time; more commonly, a non-enterprise or a non-enterprise segment of an activity may not remain in the same position for ever. As the public thinking changes as regards the financial rationale of its operations and slides towards viability, its identity alters into an enterprise. For instance, warehousing, rural electrification and industrial estates may start as non-enterprise activities; but as the con-ditions of demand improve and the social justifica-tions for output and price policies weaken, the price-cost equation gains in emphasis and the beha-viour of the activity, by public intention, may tilt towards financial viability. Now it becomes an enterprise.

Third, on grounds similar to those set out above, an activity considered an enterprise in one country may not necessarily be similarly considered in another. For instance, postal service is con-sidered as far more of an enterprise in Britain than it is in a least developed country. Thus, it is not so much the industry classification of the activity as its financial rationale in the local context that underlies the enterprise concept.

One final point, the Act governing the estab-lishment and working of an enterprise does not neces-sarily spell out its financial rationale in explicit terms so as to make it an enterprise. In some cases it does, as illustrated by the 'not-less-than' pro-visions of public corporation Acts, not only in the UK (14), but in several other countries (15). There

are many instances, however, of the Acts being
silent on this kind of stipulation (16). And in
the case of most government companies neither the
Companies Act nor any specific incorporation docu-
ment is found to contain a positive stipulation in
favour of financial viability. In all such cases
one has to go beyond the governing legislation -
too thin in many cases - to establish the intention
on the financial rationale of the undertaking.

NOTES

1. For a full discussion, see R.J. Hall and
C.J. Hitch, 'Price Theory and Business Behaviour',
Oxford Economic Papers, No.2, May 1939.
2. Michael Posner, Public Enterprise in the
Market Place, Nationalised Industries' Chairmen's
Group, Occasional Papers No.1 (London, 1979), pp.2-3.
3. Subject to social constraints on resource
use.
4. Qualifications to this proposition applicable to a public enterprise are part of the synthesis of the 'public' concept with the 'enterprise'
concept and will be the subject of Chapter 4.
5. The identity of costs - full or marginal
- is a secondary matter at this point of the discussion.
6. An interesting illustration may be drawn
from a recent investigation by the Monopolies and
Mergers Commission into the London Electricity
Board's retailing of electric appliances. Losses
have been made in this business conducted in competition with private enterprises; and the Board has
the advantage of making up from the profits of its
main business, viz., supply of electricity. The
Commission declared it an 'anti-competitive practice'
and recommended that the Board's 'sales of appliances
account should be monitored' and that 'to facilitate
this a separate and fully detailed profit and loss
account should be published as part of the annual
accounts'. The Monopolies and Mergers Commission,
London Electricity Board (Cmnd. 8812, London, HMSO,
1983) pp. 35-38.
7. As implied by such incorporating phrases
as 'with a perpetual succession', and 'able to sue
and be sued in its said name'. For example, see
Selangor State Development Corporation Enactment
1964, Section 3 (Kuala Lumpur, Malaysia).
8. The reason why certain non-enterprise
activities are organised autonomously is to ensure

effectiveness of operations, relatively free from
departmental codes and rigidities. Tema Development Corporation in Ghana may be cited as an interesting example. The Minister mentioned among the
reasons for setting up this activity as a Corporation
the following: 'to provide enough staff for the
planning and building of a town' which 'over-worked
and under-staffed' Government Departments could not
shoulder; the public corporation would provide a
better framework for developing the town than the
many Departments of the Government under different
Ministries which would make delays inevitable and
co-ordination difficult, if not 'impossible'.
Robert C. Pozen, Legal Choices for State Enterprises
in the Third World (New York,1967).
     9.   Federal Industrial Development Authority
(Incorporation) Act 1965, Section 6(i) (Kuala Lumpur).
     10. For example in Guatemala - Instituto
Nacional de Transformación Agraria and Consejo Nacional para la Protección de Antigua Guatemala; in
Honduras - Partimonio Nacional de la Infancia,
Junta Nacional de la Infancia, Instituto Nacional
de Formación Profesional and Federación Nacional
Deporte Extraescolar; in Panama-Instituto Nacional
de Cultura; in Costa Rica - Instituto de Tierras y
Colonización and Instituto de Fomento y Asesora-
miento Municipal; and in Venezuela - Caja de Tra-
bajo Peniterciario. Instituto Agrario Nacional,
and Compania Anonima Administrativa del Parque del
Este.
     11. Government Sponsored Corporations 1980-81
(Islamabad, 1982).
     12. The Royal Commission on Financial Manage-
ment and Accountability (in Canada, 1979) refers to
'marketing agencies which, while they are commer-
cially oriented, perform an important regulatory
or advisory function'.
     13. For example, a distinction is maintained
between the 'promotional and developmental' and the
'commercial' functions of the National Small Industries Corporation Ltd. (in India) and the former
are financed by the Government of India 'by way of
grants'. Bureau of Public Enterprises, Annual
Report on the Working of Industrial and Commercial
Undertakings of the Central Government, 1976-77,
Vol.II (New Delhi), p.173.   Contrast this with
the Majlis Amanah Ra'ayat (in Malaysia). With
its duty 'to provide, stimulate, facilitate and
undertake economic and social development ... and
more particularly in the rural areas thereof', it
has some 'enterprise' functions and many non-enter-

prise functions.   The Act does not call for their
specific bifurcation; on the other hand MARA's duty
is stipulated as: 'to secure that the total revenues
... are sufficient to meet all sums properly chargeable to its revenue account'.   And the total revenues are comprised of sums provided by Parliament
and from loan funds, revenues from projects, properties, etc. (Majlis Amanah Ra'ayat Act 1966, sections
14 and 13).

14.   For instance, the British Steel Corporation
are required 'so to exercise and perform their functions ... as to secure that the combined revenues
of the Corporation and all the publicly-owned companies taken together are not less than sufficient
to meet their combined charges properly chargeable
to revenue account, taking one year with another'
(Iron and Steel Act 1967, Part IV, section 16 (II))
(London).   Similar wording is adopted in the case
of the British Airports Authority which 'shall so
conduct its business as to secure that ... its revenue is not less than sufficient for making provision
for the meeting of charges properly chargeable to
revenue, taking one year with another'.   (Airports
Authority Act 1965, Section 3/I), (London).   The
Gas Act 1972 goes a little further in requiring
that the revenues shall also 'enable the Corporation
... to make such allocations to reserve as the Corporation considers adequate ...' (Gas Act 1972,
Section 14) (London).

15.   The Electricity Ordinance 1957 of Guyana
requires the Electricity Corporation 'so to exercise
and perform its functions ... as to secure that the
total revenues ... are not less than sufficient to
meet its total outgoings properly chargeable to
revenue account ... taking one year with another'
(Section 19).

The Water and Sewerage Ordinance of 1970 of
Belize (British Honduras) requires the Water and
Sewerage Authority to 'so exercise and perform its
functions as to ensure that its revenue is not less
than sufficient to (a) cover operating expenses ...
(b) meet periodic payments on long term indebted-
ness to the extent that any such repayment exceeds
the provisions for depreciation, (c) create reserves
for the purpose of future expansion ...' (Ordinance
No.16 of 1970, Section 24).

The Ghana Industrial Holding Company was entrusted
with 'the establishment and the operation ... of
manufacturing and commercial enterprises in or outside Ghana in an efficient and profitable manner.'
GIHOC Decree, 1967, Section 2.

    16.   For instance, the Belize Telecommunications
Authority Ordinance 1972, does not include any pro-
vision of the 'not-less-than' variety.
To cite another example, the Industrial Development
Ordinance (chapter 517 of the Laws of Kenya, 1962)
does not stipulate any specific provision concerning
the financial viability of the Industrial (and, now
Commercial) Development Corporation.

Chapter Four

SYNTHESIS BETWEEN THE 'PUBLIC'
AND THE 'ENTERPRISE' CONCEPTS

Now we come to a rather difficult part of the discussion, concerning the most appropriate way of synthesising the two concepts - 'public' and 'enterprise' - in practice. An excessive shift towards
the former brings the activity near a public non-
enterprise, while an excessive shift towards the
latter brings it near a non-public enterprise.
The problem of balance is a delicate one.

The term 'synthesis' between the two concepts
is preferred here to 'superimposition' of the 'public' concept over the 'enterprise' concept, in order
to emphasise the idea of achieving a judicious balance between the two concepts.

The idea of synthesis applies essentially to
public decision making on one side and viability on
the other, in the sense that the former has the implication of adversely affecting the latter. There
may be a revenue reduction or a cost enhancement -
for example, when the government decides that electricity be supplied everywhere by a public enterprise
below the cost level. Or, there may be a disruption
of the price-cost relativities which the enterprise
intends to implement under its supply and demand
conditions - for example, when the government
decides that electricity be supplied in a given
area or to a group of consumers - e.g. those taking
less than a specified kwh - at prices below costs.

There can also be indirect channels of compromise with viability. The system of public decisions
or the channels of accountability may be such as to
weaken the risk taking initiative of the managers of
the enterprise and the end consequence may be a reduced net revenue. Here no specific decision is

31

identifiable as the cause of a revenue diminution or a cost increase, but the causal relationship between 'public' elements and the enterprise results can be construed through careful analysis.

A prefatory observation worth noting is that there is no suggestion in this discussion that the 'public' concept ought not to intervene in the manifestation of the 'enterprise' concept. That it must is the essence of the concept of public enterprise (1). How it does is the problem - the problem of synthesis.

The problem may be analysed under three heads: (a) the approach to synthesis; (b) the substance of synthesis; and (c) the sanction for synthesis.

(a)   The approach to synthesis

There can be two apparently opposite approaches to the task of synthesis. The first is that the enterprise may proceed in terms of maximal financial viability (2), but a diminution may be worked out for every social or extra-enterprise obligation that is placed on it. It is difficult to assert, in the case of any enterprise, the amount of net revenue that can be considered as the maximum possible; however, experience, coupled with forecasting competence, can suggest a reasonable range of the figure, towards which managerial effort can be purposefully directed. Whenever a social obligation is entrusted to it, an attempt can be made to compute its effect on the net revenue, and the actual figure to be considered as a satisfactory net return (range) can be derived by deducting it from the notional potential. Where the external benefits of an activity are estimated to be substantial and across the whole range of markets served by the enterprise - e.g. electrification or finance for small scale industry, the enterprise may be allowed to reflect the deduction in correspondingly low prices, i.e. prices lower than the possible levels.

It is difficult to state how far the relatively low financial targets established in the case of certain public enterprises in the UK are the result of the procedure outlined above; and it is not certain that specific calculations have been made of the net revenue consequences of each element of public decision - e.g. non-closure of a steel plant,

a coal pit or a railway line - on the net revenue
of the enterprise concerned. But the suggestion
in favour of such a broad approach is implicit in
the White Paper of 1978 (3).

> 'The level of each financial target will be
> decided industry by industry. It will
> take account of a wide range of factors.
> They will include ... social or sectoral
> objectives.' The Secretary of State
> will indicate to Parliament 'the main
> assumptions on which it is based: for
> example, any particular social or sec-
> toral objectives which the Government
> has set the industry, and which may have
> affected the level of the target'.

No wonder that (additionally for other reasons such
as depressed markets) the financial targets set for
British Railways, British Steel Corporation, and
National Coal Board have been relatively low (4).

The other approach is to start at the other
end - of stipulating each social or extra-enterprise
obligation sought to be realised from the operations
of the enterprise, treating as residual the figures
of net return. The net outcome, in theory , can be
similar to that in the above case, if equal managerial efficiency is assumed in both cases. But there
are practical reasons why the former approach may be
considered to be superior. It makes necessary the
computation of the financial consequence of every
externality enjoined on the enterprise. To that
extent caution develops in the assignment of external obligations to the enterprise and in proceeding with the synthesising exercise; or else, the
tendency develops of 'super-imposing' a public
decision on the enterprise. Besides, it keeps
the enterprise alert to realising a fairly defined
figure of net revenue, once it has accepted to
shoulder a given set of extra-enterprise obligations; and everyone knows what it is expected to
earn. Under the residual net-return approach,
the impulse towards managerial efficiency weakens
and becomes passive; and the pressure to earn is
mellowed. The assumption of equal efficiency
under both the approaches proves hardly correct
in practice.

There is another approach - quite common in
many countries: neither the first nor the second

33

approach is consciously adopted. The enterprise
operates neither with set targets nor under clear
public-decision interventions. Two possibilities
exist: the government over-extends itself in exer-
cising its prerogative of public decision such that,
apart from not being specific on what the 'public'
content of the intervention is, it trespasses into
the area of managerial decisions. The enterprise
elements are thereby too heavily subdued. Alternatively, where the government or public agencies
fall short of conveying the extra-enterprise purposes of an activity, the managers tend either to
ignore them totally and aim at maximising the net
revenue or begin to interpret them in their own
way and work towards achieving them. The latter
is more likely in developing countries (and for
the managers' own public image); but it is ques-
tionable: for, how are they in a position to
interpret the extra-enterprise purposes of the
enterprise they are appointed to manage?

(b)   Substance of synthesis

    The substantive aspect of the synthesis concerns
the formulation of the decisions to be applied to an
enterprise such that they represent the most appropriate compromise with, or intervention in, the 'enterprise' elements. There are two major issues to
reckon with.

    First, multiple forces underlie the public de-
cisions; and different government agencies may look
at questions of enterprise investments and operations from their respective angles. For instance,
the Treasury may emphasise the financial return,
the parent ministry may look for technological excellence, the labour ministry may underline the
employment potential, the trade ministry may place
a premium on export earnings, a ministry concerned
with the affairs of a region may be keen on the
benefits of the enterprise for the region in particular, and so on. A prior problem of synthesis
is that of a sub-synthesis among such different
extra-enterprise criteria of decision (5). What
is essential is to determine the best combination
among these in the light of the following considerations.

    (i) There should be the minimum of conflict -
preferably no conflict - among the decisional forces
applied to the enterprise.

(ii) Where different combinations of extra-enterprise obligations to be assigned to the enterprise involve about the same effect on its net revenue, the problem of choice among them rests almost wholly in the government's court.

(iii) In the more likely case of the different combinations involving different effects on the net revenue, the choice is in need of a judgement on what net revenue ought to be considered as satisfactory in respect of the enterprise in question.

While most public decision interventions are of a net-revenue reducing nature, there can be some, occasionally, which are neutral in this respect. If the government directs an enterprise to concentrate, on a priority basis, on certain markets as against others and those markets do not necessarily involve it in net revenue reductions, what takes place is a distribution of the product according to public priorities, without a comprise with the viability concept of the enterprise (6).

Second, before the enterprise is exposed to an external element of decision making, serious thought has to be given to whether it is self-defeating in any way. For instance, a decision to control the capital expenditures of an airline enterprise with the object of saving foreign exchange may no doubt help in saving some foreign exchange but its operations may be so restricted that it loses more foreign exchange through loss of international traffic. Another example may be given of a slightly different nature. An output of price measure expected to benefit a given class of consumers - e.g. poor people or pensioners - may in fact permit of a leakage of benefit to unintended groups of consumers. It is probably better not to interfere with the output and price policies of the enterprise but offer a subsidy exactly to the intended group of persons - through the government budget.

(c) Sanction for synthesis

Since the public-decision intervention represents an abridgement of the market forces that ordinarily determine 'enterprise' behaviour, the question arises: what is the sanction for it in a given case, from the standpoint of society as a whole? The question has two parts:
(i) First, as far as the enterprise is con-

35

cerned, does it derive a decisional-directive from an external source that has the authority to issue it?   In other words, is it 'openly' received?

(ii) Second, does the decisional externality possess the element of the widest necessary acceptability?   Or, does it represent a limited vested interest of the intervening agency, e.g. the minister (7) or a political group (8)?

Ideally, a public decision on intervention should be transparent and open to Parliamentary attention in some way.   Besides, its propriety is to be examined, not on the unilateral basis of whether the decision in itself has substance, but in the relative context of its appropriateness vis-a-vis the net-revenue effects it entails.   That the latter aspect does not secure the necessary attention can be deduced from the generality of public decisions on price non-enhancements in public enterprise; very often the deciding authority does not have before it for consideration full facts on the effects of varying decision options on net revenue and, eventually, on the public exchequer.

Let us look at an entirely different kind of problem.   The managers of a public enterprise may, of their own volition, visualise certain values as desirable from the extra-enterprise point of view and make decisions, as far as these can be managerially made, in favour of, say, high bonus to workers, price concessions and charity expenditures. To the extent that the justification is not derived directly from the supply and demand conditions of the enterprise, the managers are virtually introducing, through internal decisional processes, extra-enterprise considerations.   It is strictly not their business to do so; and it is appropriate for some public agency to be empowered to watch such elements of managerial discretion in enterprise calculations.   This is also an aspect of the problem of synthesis.

The discussion has so far brought out the complexities of public-decision interventions that have the effect of compromising the enterprise elements.   Let us refer to an almost opposite aspect. Do the managers adequately strive towards the viability potential of the enterprise and is the price-cost equation adequately wielded in achieving the viability goals, subject to whatever implications public decision interventions, if any, have? Ensuring positive answers to these questions is also a part of the problem of synthesis between the 'public' concept and the 'enterprise' concept, and there is need for a well-designed system in this respect, for helpful market disciplines are probably lacking.

The concept of synthesis is thus double-edged: for one thing, it is to take place so as not to let the public elements eclipse the enterprise elements; and for another, it has to ensure the maximal manifestation of the enterprise elements, within the constraints of the public elements.

The discussion on synthesis between the 'public' and the 'enterprise' elements may be concluded by introducing the idea of the intrinsic costs of such synthesis, arising from inefficient applications of public decision to the enterprise. Here the reference is not to a diminished net return that certain public decisions consciously accept as an implicit result, but to the conditions of implementing the synthesis which tend to have the unanticipated effect of reducing the revenue or increasing the costs of the enterprise. The costs of synthesis, as understood here, are the costs of public-decision interventions that do not satisfy the criteria implicit in the preceding discussions of approach, substance and sanction of synthesis. Besides, net revenue reductions can occur when managerial efficiency is curbed by such forces as the following: (i) the accountability element may operate rather as a bundle of control instruments that inhibit initiative; (ii) the stress of accountability appraisals may be disproportionately concentrated on the managers to the exclusion of the civil servants that are also, if not prominently, responsible for the enterprise's state of working; and (iii) the pressures on the managers to raise a well defined net revenue at a challenging level may prove to be minimal in most situations, the more truly the greater the 'public' content in the decisional parameters (9). The moral, at the minimum, is that a review of managerial efficiency – ubiquitously alleged as low in the public enterprise sector – should be accompanied simultaneously by an analysis of one of the major determinants of it, viz., the inefficient synthesis of the 'public' with the 'enterprise' elements.

The implications of the synthesis may be presented diagramatically (see Fig.1). The X-axis represents the rates of return that different enterprises can earn if left free from public decision impacts; and the Y-axis represents the rates of return that are likely under such impacts.

Figure 1 : <u>Rates of Return</u>

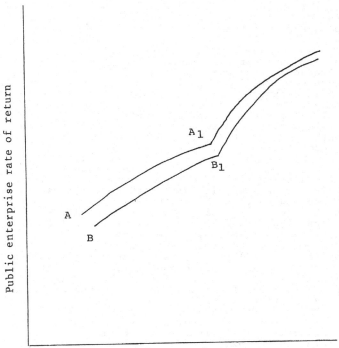

Enterprise rate of return

Curve A thus indicates that for a possible enterprise rate there is a lower public enterprise rate. The difference between the two roughly represents the trade-off for the extra-enterprise returns expected to be realised through the public decision interventions in enterprise performance. It is possible that certain enterprises capable of earning high rates of net revenue by virtue of their market conditions attract nominal public-decision compromises, so much so that Curve A may experience a bulge in such cases (say, from point A1), the public enterprise rates of return approaching parity with the enterprise rates. The so-called revenue monopolies illustrate this phenomenon.

Now we come to the point of inefficient synthesis. This lowers the curve to B. It may not be exactly parallel to A. Its shape depends on the exact costliness of public-decision interventions in enterprises standing at different rates of return (it may be nearer A beyond B1 than before it as the interventions are, by assumption, fewer). The gap between B and A is not an extra-enterprise trade-off but a cost of synthesising the public and the enterprise concepts.

This is almost intrinsic to the process and can be the larger, the less uniform and predictable the public-decision implications are from year to year, for these are an additional source of costs sustained by unsteady managerial responses to changing public decision interventions.

A concluding observation. A cost to society is implicit in the synthesis between the public and the enterprise elements. But for a proper perspective, we have to remember that private enterprise has its own costs to society. If the costs of public enterprise arise from its relative neglect of 'enterprise' elements, the costs of private enterprise arise from its relative neglect of externalities. Neither social costs are borne in its books, nor does it aim at contributing to social returns, except as an incident of its profit-orientation. Besides, it can aggravate the conditions of concentration and distributional inequity. It is to internalise such neglected externalities that public enterprise is resorted to.

The costs of inefficient synthesis are a different matter (as reflected in Curve B). They have little justification and call for a strict watch.

NOTES

1. As illustrated in the preamble of the

Statutory Instrument 51 of 1948, enacted as Law 561 of 1956 concerning IRI in Italy: 'It is the responsibility of the Council of Ministers to lay down the general guidelines to be followed by the Institute in the public interest.'

2. An interesting example is provided by Israel whose Company Law provides that 'a government company shall act in accordance with the business considerations by which a non-government company is normally guided, unless the government with the approval of the (Finance) Committee (of Parliament), prescribes other considerations for acting'. (Cited by Yair Aharoni in 'The State-owned Enterprise: An Agent without a Principal', Second BAPEG Conference on 'Public Enterprise in Mixed Economy LDCs', Boston, April 1980).

3. The Nationalised Industries, Cmnd. 7137 London, HMSO, 1978), p.26.

4. For National Coal Board: break-even after interest and social grants by 1983-84: for British Steel Corporation: break-even after historic cost depreciation and interest (1980-81); for British Railways Board: break-even after receipt of grant of pre-determined level (by 1982).

5. An illustrative device, at least in theory, may be cited from Italy. A special Standing Committee was provided for by Law No. 1589 of 1956, 'to co-ordinate the general guidelines for the various sectors controlled by the Ministry for State Holdings', and 'to ensure that they are in line with action taken by the other Ministries involved: this Committee shall be comprised of the Minister for State Holdings, and the Ministers for the Budget, the Treasury, Trade and Industry, Labour and Social Security'.

6. An interesting instance is provided by Pakistan Industrial Credit and Investment Corporation Ltd. which is required to encourage 'investment in less developed regions of the country ... in alignment with the national development plans' in industries 'covered by the Industrial Investment Schedule which indicates the Industries that in Government's view deserve priority in promotion' and yet 'every proposal' has to pass the test of viability'. The assumption underlying this citation is that the Corporation earns from its financial assistance operations in the less developed regions no less than it might from any other operations. (Government Sponsored Corporations 1980-81), Islamabad, 1982), p.38.

7. For instance, reviewing the working of

Tema Development Corporation in Ghana, whose rent-collecting functions were interfered with by the Government, Robert C. Pozen concludes that the Corporation constituted 'an additional source of patronage not bound by the well developed rules for the Civil Service'. Legal Choices for State Enterprises in the Third World (New York, 1976), Ch.6.

8.   It is interesting to refer at this point to a recommendation of the Chiarelli Commission (in Italy) in 1975 that 'the powers of ministers to intervene for purposes of ante facto control be clarified by the issue of specific authorisations, these to be made public in the same way as the decisions of the CIPE (Inter-ministerial Economic Planning Committee) and those of the collegial organs of government'. Cited in Giorgio Stefani, 'Control Mechanisms of Public Enterprise', Annals of Public and Co-operative Economy, January-June 1981.

9.   Describing the political decisions that constrain public enterprise managers to take high risks in Italy, Franco A. Grassini observes: 'Managers of public enterprises are able to expand into new areas and new fields without fear of losing profits or their positions', and 'Managers of public enterprises are less threatened by their companies' performance than are managers of private enterprises. The Italian Enterprises: The Political Constraints' in State-Owned Enterprise in the Western Economies, edited by Raymond Vernon and Yair Aharoni (London, 1981), p.84.

Chapter Five

TAXONOMY AND THE CONCEPT
OF PUBLIC ENTERPRISE

The taxonomic purpose of this chapter is limited to
the delineation of any particular aspects of the
conceptual elements of public enterprise associated
with each of the major categories into which public
enterprise may be classified. The classification
can be undertaken on the basis of a large number of
criteria (1), but we shall confine ourselves to five:

I   Ownership: subdivisible into

     (i)   Full ownership by government
     (ii)   Majority ownership by government
     (iii) Minority ownership by government

     (A subsidiary aspect of this criterion refers
     to the nature of the 'public' composition of
     ownership, e.g. by different governments or
     levels of government (the federal government,
     the state governments and local governments);
     by governments and public enterprises; and
     by public agencies or public enterprises
     themselves.)

II   Legal form; Subdivisible into

     (i)   Departmental organisation
     (ii)   Public corporation
     (iii) Corporation

III Activity coverage: In two broad senses

     A.   Public share in a given sector (2):
            subdivisible into

     (i)   Full share
     (ii)   Major share

(iii)   Minor share

B.   Public enterprise organisation within
         a given sector: subdivisible into

(i)   Monolithic (i.e. the entire public
         activity in a given sector is organi-
         sed under one statutory apex unit –
         e.g. National Coal Board and British
         Steel Corporation UK)

(ii)   One holding company (i.e. the entire
         public activity in a given sector is
         organised under one holding company,
         which has legally constituted sub-
         sidiaries – e.g. National Bus Company
         in the UK.   National Transport Corpo-
         ration in Zambia, and Cement Corpora-
         tion of Pakistan).

(A significant secondary aspect common to both
(i) and (ii) above is that the one unit may be
national or regional – e.g. Electricity Boards
in the UK and the State Electricity Boards in
India.)

(iii)   Multiple units (i.e. the entire public
         activity in a given sector is organised
         under several legally distinct units;
         some of them may be very large or hold-
         ing companies – e.g. chemicals, steel
         and banking in India).

IV   Objective mix: subdivisible into

(i)   Activities with significantly non-
         commercial objectives (more akin to
         the non-enterprise description)

(ii)   Enterprises with predominantly commer-
         cial objectives.

V   Nature of emergence: broadly subdivisible into

(i)   Enterprises established in the public
         sector

(ii)   Enterprises nationalised or taken over
         into the public sector

(There can be other bases of classification
relevant to the activity concerned, e.g.

By industrial category: e.g. transport, steel,

banking, trade and tourism

By monopoly proneness or size (e.g. electricity).

By labour intensity

By capital-output ratio

While the focus of the classification chosen here is apparently institutional or organisational, it does cover consideration of substantive issues at several points. The following presentation simply aims to indicate the unique considerations, if any, that are associated with a given category of public enterprise, over and above the comments contained in the preceding chapters. Where no special consideration suggests itself the chart contains a blank.

Table 1

Category and concept of public enterprise

Type of public enterprise (1)	Net benefits (2)	Public decision (3)
I. Public ownership		
(i) Full	Dividend decisions or restrictions are a secondary matter.	Bias develops for centralising the decisional authority in government.
(ii) Majority	Regulations regarding dividend (l) declaration, the issue of bonus shares, the marketability of shares, and the distribution of assets on liquidation assume importance.	The constitution of the board of directors, the proportionality of decisional powers with ownership, reservations of decisional matters to government, and provision of veto power for government, assume importance.
	The degree of emphasis on non-private accumulation of net benefits depends on the exact purpose of government investment in a given case: e.g. to encourage private enterprise?	
(iii) Minority	Emphasis on non-private accretion of net benefits is the less, the smaller	This gets restricted to the purposes of public investment, unless the

the public investment

possibility of decisional non-proportionality with investment is explicitly agreed upon.

Inter-government-public enterprise

There can be concealed attempts by certain participating governments to promote leakages in favour of given regions or vested interests.

Both decision and social accountability may turn out to be spread out as a sequel to multiple ownership: whereas, in the absence of any special considerations or approved sectional interests, a 'total' approach to the enterprise is desirable.

47

Category and concept of public enterprise (cont'd.)

Type of Public enterprise (1)	Social accountability (4)	Financial viability (5)	Cost-price equation (6)
I Public ownership			
(i) Full			
(ii) Majority	Are all channels of accountability, e.g. audit by Auditor General, applicable exactly as in the case of full ownership? Is there a differential approach towards accountability to the government and the non-government segments of ownership and decision-making?	Qualifications call for explicit enunciation.	Similar to (5).
(iii) Minority	What minimal channels are necessary to maintain in order to realise the precise purpose of relatively small public investment?	Qualifications, if any and minimal, have to be related to the precise purpose of public participation in ownership.	
Inter-government public enterprise			Diverse regional interests can seriously affect this; any resulting cross-subsidations call for rigorous scrutiny.

Type of public enterprise (1)	Net benefits (2)	Public decision (3)
II Form		
(i) Departmental organisation		Bias exists for nearly exclusive centralisation in government.
(ii) Public corporation		The Act may not adequately spell out its distribution as between government and others; hence a given decision may not necessarily be taken by, or originate in, the right agency.
(iii) Government company		The situation is broadly similar to (ii) above; it is possibly more complex because the Companies Act does not generally deal with the substantive issues even to the extent that a specific Corporation Act may; and the Articles of Association hardly attract Parliament's attention. A major problem is that there is the least clarity, of all forms of organisation, on how exactly a decision has been authorised.

Type of public enterprise (1)	Social accountability (4)	Financial viability (5)	Cost-price equation (6)
II Form			
(i) Departmental organisation	A paradox is deducible. While totally accountable to Parliament, whether this adequately represents social accountability depends on how representative the government is of the long-term interests of the nation, and, essentially, on whether criteria of accountability are indicated as explicitly and extensively as in (ii) and (iii).	Is this element suppressed by the automatic link with, if not absorption in, government budget? There is the danger of the activity being treated as a non-enterprise.	The rights of consumers to protest on this ground, and the jurisdiction of price or monopoly control agencies to cover the enterprise, are likely to suffer serious restriction. It is doubtful if such fine issues as the price-cost equation adequately attract Parliament's time and attention.

(ii) Public corporation

If the Act is used for the formal escape of accountability of the Minister, is this fact verifiable? And is the real actor's accountability verifiable?

Where the Act does not indicate the financial targets and pricing principles, specific guidelines are necessary.

(iii) Government company

The Companies Act does not provide much help in this respect. A framework of accountability, outside the Act, has to be built up.

The situation is similar to (ii) above.

Type of public enterprise (1)	Net benefits (2)	Public decision (3)
III Activity coverage		
A. Public share in a given sector		
(i) Full		In the absence of the influence of market disciplines, the need for evolving helpful criteria of decision is great.
(ii) Major		Some commonness of decisional criteria is to be developed as between the public and the private segments.
(iii) Minor		The role of public decision is to have specific relevance to the precise purpose of the relatively small public ownership.
B. Public enterprise organisation		
(i) Monolithic		Two possibilities exist. The enterprise may be availed of as a delegatee of government in respect of certain decisions; or it may be wielded as a single point for decision imposition. An unintended, third possibility is that, instead of helping public decision making, the monolithic unit may build itself into an exclusive decisional agency.

Type of public enterprise (1)	Social accountability (4)	Financial viability (5)	Cost-price equation (6)
III Activity coverage			
A Public share in a given sector			
(i) Full	How correctly are substantive criteria formulated, in the absence of market guidance on indicators of performance?	To establish potentialities of financial viability is rendered difficult.	As comparisons with non-public activity are not possible, the cost basis of price and elements of cross-subsidisations call for special exercises of detection.
(ii) Major	A rigorous scrutiny of performance, wherever inferior to the non-public level, is needed, constructively and not for explaining away.	The danger exists of financial inefficiencies leading to price rises; yet the private segment catches windfall profits; these need being syphoned off into the public exchequer.	Similar structures are necessary in the public and the private segments, unless there is an open or concealed market sub-division.

Type of public enterprise (1)	Social accountability (4)	Financial viability (5)	Cost-price equation (6)
(iii) Minor	The market probably provides the criteria of performance by which to seek accountability.	It is possible that the purpose of the public segment des-tines it into specific sub-markets needing softness. If so, this has to be established.	
B Public enterprise organisation			
(i) Monolithic	This becomes complex, depending on the decisional actuality. Where the unit assumes the position of a parallel exclusive decisional agency de facto, special measures of ensuring accountability are needed	Liquidation of inefficient plants may not receive due attention.	Ample opportunities of manipulation regarding the cost-price equation and of cross-subsidisation exist.

Type of public enterprise (1)	Net benefits (2)	Public decision (3)
(ii) One holding unit		The situation is similar to that in (i). Further, a new problem arises, viz., the nature of direct government involvement in decision making concerning the subsidiaries (the operating units) and of its co-ordination with the decisional exercise by the holding apex.
(iii) Multiple units		The benefits of comprehensive decision and economies of decisional scale for the sector as a whole have to be preserved. Decisions concerning one unit ought not to be in conflict with those concerning another, from the social point of view.

Type of public enterprise (1)	Social accountability (4)	Financial viability (5)	Cost-price equation (6)
(ii) One holding Unit	A unique need is to establish the accountability of the enterprise for any non-enterprise functions delegated to, or undertaken by, it. Is the accountability of the subsidiaries left to be judged by the holding apex? A diversified holding structure calls for disaggregated scales of judgement on accountability. If there exists a holding apex for each region in the country accountability adjudications have to take into account their results on the kind of regional balance contemplated by the government.	The situation is similar to that of (i). Specifically, inter-subsidiary transfers of resources, inputs, etc. need scrutiny (2). Where the holding structure ranges over diverse activities rather than relating to a single sector, the problems of viability and cost-price equation have to be disaggregated suitably.	
(iii) Multiple Units		Do the several units, de facto, maintain conditions of healthy competition? Do inter-firm comparisons lead to any reorganisations and liquidations, if need be? Basically, are the several units individually optimal or is an individual unit's deviation from optimality the conscious result of the total sectoral interest of the public enterprise?	

Type of public enterprise (1)	Net benefits (2)	Public decision (3)
IV Objective mix		
(i) Significant non-commercial objectives		Open channels of public decision-al intervention have to be evolved.
(ii) Significant commercial objectives		Specific guidance on the assumption of non-commercial objectives, if any, is necessary.
V Nature of emergence		
(i) Enterprises established in the public sector		There is no benefit of a precedent in decisional criteria.
(ii) Nationalised enterprises		The history of the enterprise and the special factors that caused nationalisation condition public decisions.

Type of public enterprise (1)	Social accountability (4)	Financial viability (5)	Cost-price equation (6)
IV Objective mix			
(i) Significant non-commercial objectives	The room for public decision being wide, the need for ensuring its accountability is great. There is a temptation for 'more' control rather than 'right' control. A discerning system of verification on the realisation of the non-commercial objectives is necessary; and special need exists for ensuring the accountability of the exact authors of a decision.	It is preferable to scale down the financial target suitably; or else, substantial and too many specific compensations will be necessary.	Do the price discriminations reflect the social criteria of output supply?
(ii) Significant commercial objectives		There is the danger of letting price discrimination take care of the non-commercial objectives. Instead, specific compensations have to be worked out.	

V Nature of emergence

(i) Enterprises established in the public sector		Net revenue potentialities and cost-price relationships have to be designed de novo.
(ii) Nationalised enterprises	There exists a structure of established interests (3) which conditions, unless revised, the canons of accountability	Established enterprise elements are both a help and a problem: the latter because special effort is needed if a change is desired.

Footnotes

(1) For example, the Bank for Housing and Construction Decree, 1972, of Ghana, places certain restrictions on dividend declaration. (Sections 8 & 10) The Act provides for the Government taking 'fifty centum' of the share capital.

(2) For example, ENI (in Italy) took over a number of losing companies following a government directive, offsetting 'the losses sustained by one company against the operating profits earned by another, simply because they both happened to belong to the same financial holding company'. Giorgio Stefani, 'Control Mechanisms of Public Enterprises', Annals of Public & Co-operative Economy, January-June, 1981.

(3) For example, a salary-and-prerequisites structure inherited from the pre-nationalised time.

NOTES

1.   For extensive information on the classifi-
cation, see Leroy Jones' paper and the Report of the
Expert Group Meeting held by ICPE at Tangier in
December 1980.
2.   For example, recent data from Sri Lanka
suggest that: Category (i) includes Central Freight
Bureau, Sri Lanka Ports Authority – Service, Ceylon
Steel Corporation (in certain products), Parantham
Chemicals Corp., Ceylon Plywood Corp., National Salt
Corp., State Films Corp. (hire of films), State Rub-
ber Mfg., Ceylon Electricity Board (generation),
Ceylon Petroleum Corp.,(LP Gas), Colombo Gas and
Water Co., Ceylon Oxygen Co., Ceylon Insurance
Corp., Sri Lanka Export Credit Insurance Corp.
Category (ii) includes State Jute Industries Corp.,
Ceylon Ceramics State Pharmaceuticals Corp., Buil-
ding Materials Corp., and Sri Lanka State Trading
(General) Corp. and
Category (iii) includes Sri Lanka Timber Corp., Sri
Lanka State Plantation Corp., J.B. Fishing and
National Textile Corp.
Commonwealth Secretariat, <u>National Policies and Pro-
grammes for Public Enterprise Management and Training</u>
(London, 1980), pp.231–245.

Chapter Six

THE DEFINITIONAL ISSUE

(a) The need for a definition

We have so far been concerned with an analysis
of what a public enterprise conceptually involves.
There is the practical problem of identifying an
organisation as a public enterprise to which the
public and the enterprise elements, duly synthesised, are to apply.   Hence the need for a definition that operationalises the concept and covers
all enterprises to which the public elements are
to apply and all public agencies to which the enterprise elements are to apply.   The definition can
be so formulated as to widen or restrict the coverage.

The need for an operational definition of public enterprise is obvious in a wide range of circumstances, as illustrated below:

(i)   Where the Auditor General is given
       the authority or responsibility to
       audit public enterprises (1).

(ii)   Where certain overall features of
       the organisation and working of
       public enterprises are sought to
       be brought into a pattern (2); or
       where certain statistical purposes
       are involved (3).

(iii) Where a price preference or purchase
       preference is accorded to the products
       of public enterprises (4).

(iv)   Where a special financial institution
       is set up for providing funds to public

61

enterprises (5).

(v)   Where a regulatory agency is set up exclusively for public enterprises (6), e.g. to concern itself with their personnel or purchase activities.

(vi) Where the government or Parliament wishes to exercise rights of review- ing the working of public enter- prises, or receiving annual or any reports from them (7).

(vii) Where public enterprises are required to submit their budgets for govern- ment approval.

(viii) Where the government promulgates an industrial policy that involves the reservation of certain sectors of activity to public enterprise (8).

There are two points to note at this stage. First, the definition of a public enterprise may vary from one purpose to another (9). Second, a clear definition may not always be provided; but where a public purpose is sought to be achieved in relation to certain enterprises, the prac- tice may be adopted of naming the enterprises to which it applies (10).

The particular utility of a definition in the context of statistical work and inference may be outlined as follows:

(i)   In respect of generalisations such as: public enterprises have, in the aggre- gate, earned x per cent of net revenue in a given year (11); the net return rate increased from x to y from a certain year to another; the number of public enterprises or investments in public enterprises changed from x to y during a given period; and pub- lic enterprises accounted for x per cent of the nation's savings or capital formation.

(ii) In making inter-firm comparisons: for example, public enterprises in sector A have earned a higher net revenue than

those in Sector B; and public enterprises in a given sector have done
better - by net revenue - than private
enterprises.

(iii) In making inter-country comparisons:
for example, public enterprises constitute x per cent of the national
economy, by some criterion, in country
A and y per cent in country B (12);
and public enterprises in country A
have done better than those in country B.

(b)   The problems of defining

We shall conclude the present study with a few
comments on the problems encountered in defining a
public enterprise.   The definition has to be satisfactory both conceptually and operationally.   This
is not easy.

Let us look, first, at the aspect of ownership.
There is little difficulty in defining a wholly publicly owned (13) enterprise as a public enterprise.
But problems arise as we begin to deal with the
phenomenon of a 'continuum' in respect of ownership.
Governments have varying proportions of ownership in
different enterprises in most countries.   The familiar definitional device has been: 'an enterprise
in which there is a majority public ownership'.
This has been operationalised in several countries
- e.g. in India and Tanzania as earlier cited - in
terms of 50 per cent of the equity or more in the
context of certain governmental purposes.   There
is a statistical convenience in such a step, no
doubt.

But what is the position from the conceptual
angle?   The essential significance of ownership
lies in its being a window for control.   From the
institutional circumstances of the corporate sector
with which we are familiar, we deduce that for control to be possible there ought to be an ownership
interest, in the first place, of a majority nature.
(Actually we have to substitute the term 'control
potential' for 'control', for we find that in the
real world the owners of most big enterprises do
not exercise so much effective control as they are
entitled to.)(14)   Two qualifications merit notice.
For one thing, ownership of a 49 per cent block (or

even 40 or 30 per cent) is almost certain to vest
in the hands of that owner de facto powers of control, assuming that the rest of the shares are dispersed in ownership. For another, even a smaller
than 50 per cent ownership on the part of the government has a practical implication of control potential out of proportion to ownership. Apart from
the scrupulous respect that the other owners pay
to the view of the minority owner, the government,
it is possible that the articles of association or
other regulations are so drafted as to reserve certain major issues (see Chapter 3) for government
decision, or give a veto power to the government
directors on the board, or oblige the enterprise
to seek government's approval for certain board
decisions, or introduce similar other clauses that
effectively convey the spirit of government control
irrespective of its minority status as owner. What
is of importance here is the role the government
seeks to play in the entrepreneurial and major decision making – not as just owner but as government.

In terms of this conceptual argument, we can
even question the operational conclusiveness of
majority public ownership in the definition. For,
if the government has de facto potential for control despite minority ownership, or if it wants to
bring the enterprise concerned under some form of
public control – e.g. as regards the budgets, major
distribution contracts, purchase procedures, employee recruitment and retrenchment and closures of
units, the operational definition has to cover
lower than 50 per cent ownership too. The cut-
off point will, no doubt, be arbitrary (15). It
is even conceivable that the definition is set in
terms of different percentages of ownership in
respect of different control purposes such as
audit by the Comptroller and Auditor General,
budget submissions to the government, public
sector borrowing limits, current cost accounting conventions, the determination of financial
targets, and personnel administration. (Where
the definition is not so meticulously devised,
the procedure may be adopted of naming the enterprises or categories intended to come within a
given regulatory context.)

The usual phrasing of definitions in terms
of 'majority ownership or control' on the part of
the public has to be re-appraised in the light of
these observations. In any case, the 'control'

element, unlike the ownership element, cannot be operationalised in terms of a statistical norm.

Difficulties exist in operationalising the 'enterprise' component of the definition also. Conceptually it is featured by 'viability' by intention through the price-cost basis. Analogous to this is the 'marketedness' criterion used by Leroy P. Jones. He operationalises it in terms of the proportion that sales revenues constitute out of costs (16). (Neither the definition of 'costs' nor the exact figure depicting the proportion is material to the main argument pursued here. These, no doubt, are material in expanding or contracting the area netted under the caption of public enterprise.)

While the 'marketedness' idea underlying Jones's approach is unquestionable and approximates, in some ways, to the feature subsumed by the concept of viability through the price-cost basis, discussed in Chapters 3 and 4, operationalising it in terms of the sales revenues as a proportion of costs does not adequately take note of situations in which a low proportion of sales revenue to costs is the result of enterprise inefficiency or poor business conditions.

Further, given a norm, the proportion might move above or below it from time to time in the case of certain enterprises; so that they become enterprises in some years and non-enterprises in others. Then the chief merit of an operationalised definition is weakened. To get over this problem a five (or seven) year period may be proposed for judging the purport of the sales revenue as a proportion of cost for deciding on the enterprise identity of an activity. Even then the judgement would be difficult in the first five (or seven) years of the activity; besides, the activity is subject to the prospect of being considered an enterprise or a non-enterprise from year to year, as the moving average of the norm moves up or down.

The sales-revenue-cost-proportion criterion raises two further problems, from the conceptual angle. By itself it does not say much about the price-cost basis of enterprise operations. More fundamentally, it makes an activity an enterprise if it earns 'well'; and makes it a non-enterprise if it earns poorly; whereas the basis ought to be whether it is 'publicly' intended to be an enterprise or not. What proportion of the cost it earns through sales is a function not only of efficiency and business conditions but of the public decision interventions, which may cause a serious reduction in net revenues. This by itself does not deflect the enterprise from its enterprise character.

In practice, however, the public intention that an activity be viable and subject to the price-cost basis is not always adequately explicit from the governing statute or any other governmental directions. This raises the problem of the lack of clarity regarding the financial objective of the activity, and demands attention from law makers and policy makers.

To conclude: a public enterprise may be understood to be an activity in which the majority ownership and/or control is non-private and which is intended to be viable through sales activity on the basis of price-cost relationships. This is a conceptual statement, of which we are familiar with several versions (17). It is when we begin to operationalise it that problems arise.

NOTES

1. For example, the Indian Companies Act, which empowers the Comptroller and Auditor General to audit a government company, defines it as one 'in which not less than 51 per cent of the paid-up share capital is held by the Central Government or any State Government or Governments or partly by the Central Government and partly by one or more State Governments'. Indian Companies Act 1976, Sec. 617. It may be noted that ownership by public enterprise is not bracketed with that by the Central or State Governments in computing the 51 per cent.
Another example in the area of audit, may be cited from Ghana, where the State Enterprise Audit Corporation was set up to audit 'industrial and commercial enterprises established by the State; joint enterprises and other enterprises which the President, the Investment Bank or any other organ of Government requires to be investigated by the Auditor General or the Corporation '. Instrument of Incorporation of the State Enterprises Audit

Corporation, Part III.
       Likewise the Act establishing the Tanzania
Audit Corporation in 1968, which was empowered to
audit all parastatals, defined 'a parastatal' as:
'(a) a local authority;
 (b) any body corporate established by or under
       any written law other than:
       (i)   the Community:
       (ii) any corporation within the community;
       (iii) any company registered under the
             Companies Ordinance other than a
             company to which para (e) applies;
 (c) The Tanganyika African National Union, any
       organ of the Tanganyika African National
       Union and every body of persons whether
       corporate or unincorporated, which is af-
       filiated to the Tanganyika African National
       Union;
 (d) a trade union registered under the Trades
       Union Ordinance;
 (e) any company registered under the Companies
       Ordinance not less than 50 per centum of
       issued share capital of which is owned by
       the Government or a parastatal organisation
       or, where the company is limited by guarantee,
       a company in respect of which the amount that
       the Government or a parastatal organisation
       which is a member of such a company has under-
       taken to contribute in the event of the com-
       pany being wound up is not less than 50 per
       centum of the aggregate amount which all the
       members have undertaken to contribute; and
       references in this paragraph to 'Parastatal
       Organisation' include references to any such
       company;
 (f) any body of persons, whether corporate or
       unincorporated, which the Minister may by
       notice in the Gazette, declare to be a para-
       statal organisation for the purposes of
       this section.'
       2.   As is implicit in the classification of
crown corporations in Canada into Departmental,
Agency and Proprietary Corporations, each coming
under a distinctive pattern of government supervision.
       The Statutory Corporations, etc. (Special
provisions) Decree 1969 in Nigeria provides for
common structures of board constitution.   However,
instead of defining the corporations to which it
applies, it specifies them (in the opening section).
       3.   For example, a definition is provided in

the UK for National Income and Expenditure purposes:
'Public corporations ... can be defined as public
trading bodies which have a substantial degree of
financial independence of the public authority –
generally the central government – which created
them ...' (National Accounts Statistics – Sources
and Methods, C.O.S., 1968)
    Note, however, that 'companies in which govern-
ment has a significant shareholding' are not treated as part of the central government or public
corporation sectors, but are included in the company sector 'for national income and expenditure
purposes'. (National Economic Development Office,
A Study of UK Nationalised Industries – Appendix
Volume (London, HMSO, 1976) p.8.
    'There is no legal definition of a nationalised
industry ... The criteria used by the Treasury relate to control as well as ownership. Thus the
British Petroleum Company has always been excluded
from the public sector figures, because of the self-
denying ordinance under which the government had
declared that it would not intervene in the management of the Company.' Sir Leo Pliatzky, Getting
and Spending: Public Expenditure, Employment and
Inflation (Oxford, 1982).
    4.   For example, in India 'the public enter-
prises and Government organisations ... were advised
in 1971 to make direct purchases from the public
enterprises and also to extend price preference of
up to 10%, subject to quality standards and deli-
very schedules'. (This was withdrawn in later
years.) Bureau of Public Enterprises, Annual
Report of the Working of Industrial and Commercial
Undertakings of the Central Government, 1976-77,
Volume I (New Delhi, 1978) p.163. The preference
was re-introduced recently.
    5.   For instance, National Development Finance
Corporation (in Pakistan) is set up to give financial assistance to public enterprises wholly or
partly owned by the Federal Government and to
any others declared by it as eligible.
    A demarcation in lending activity – by the
Bangladesh Shilpa Rin Sanstha for public enterprises
and by the Bangladesh Shilpa Bank for private enterprises – was contemplated in Bangladesh at one time,
though not implemented. R. Sobhan and M. Ahmad,
Public Enterprise in an Intermediate Regime (Dacca)
p.507.
    6.   Illustrations are available from Nigeria:
The Corporation Standing Board 'to which shall be
transferred all the powers of any statutory corpo-

ration to which this Decree relates as to supervision of award of contracts' (The Corporations Standing Tenders Board Decree, 1968); and the Statutory Services Commission in which 'power to appoint ... dismiss and exercise disciplinary control ... shall vest'. (The Statutory Corporations Services Commission Decree 1968, Section 4). However, without defining the corporations, these Decrees name the corporations and companies to which they apply.

7.   The Government Control Act (1945) of the USA aims to bring 'under annual scrutiny by the Congress' and 'provide current financial control thereof', wholly owned government corporations and mixed-ownership government corporations; but these are named and not defined. (Public Law 248, 79th Congress, Ch.557).

The Tanzanian Act 17 of 1969 simply defines a public corporation for the purpose of that Act as one 'established by an order under this Act'.

Some definition has been necessary in the UK, of 'public corporations' for purposes of National Accounts Statistics or for the Government's Financial Statement and Budget Report, and of 'nationalised industries' for determining the remit of the Select Committee on Nationalised Industries. (As cited in NEDO, A Study of UK Nationalised Industry: Their Role in the Economy and Control in the Future (Appendix Volume, pp.1-5) (London, HMSO, 1976).

8.   For example, the Industrial Policy Resolution of 1956 in India; likewise in Trinidad and Tobago.

9.   For example, the definition of a parastatal organisation (in Tanzania) for the purposes of the Presidential Standing Committee on Parastatal Organisations is different from the one found in the context of the State Enterprises Audit Corporation, cited earlier. 'For the purposes of this notice a parastatal organisation is a body which is not an integral part of the Government but is an institution, organisation or agency which is wholly or mainly financed or owned and controlled by the Government. The criterion of such public enterprises would be the ownership and control by the Government of 50% or more of the capital shares or other forms of Government participation and effective influence in all aspects of management of the enterprises and includes any company whose whole or at least 50% of the share capital is owned and controlled by the Government or any parastatal organisation (including such company).' General Notice No.1286 (Official Gazette, 24 September 1976 (Tanzania).

69

10. As in the Nigerian Decrees already cited.

11. For instance, overall percentage figures of returns from public enterprises in India suffer from the complication that they (possibly) do not cover departmental enterprises like the railways, the Port Trusts, State Government enterprises and several 'mixed' enterprises.

12. For example, in using the figure of 11 per cent reflecting the share of UK public corporations in the total output of the economy (in 1975), one has to note that the coverage is not as comprehensive as the very postulate of NEDO suggests as regards 'publicly owned enterprises'. (National Economic Development Office, A Study of UK Nationalised Industries – Appendix Volume (London, HMSO, 1976), pp.11 and 1.

A glance at the data on 'non-financial public enterprises' cited in Table 4 of Government Finance Statistics Year Book 1979, published by the International Monetary Fund, brings out the quite diverse coverages in different countries: e.g. ports, mint and ordnance factories are found in the case of the UK but not of India; and the table for Tanzania includes national parks but not the post office.

13. This term may be re-expressed as 'non-private' ownership so as to cover the Yugoslav enterprises as well as enterprises with all loan capital as in the UK.

14. Adolf A. Berle and Gardiner C. Means, The Modern Corporation and Private Property (New York, 1932).

15. Leroy P. Jones considers as public ownership 'more than ten per cent of outstanding equity' in his studies on Korea. Public Enterprise and Economic Development (Seoul, 1975), p.23.

16. Leroy P. Jones suggests an enterprise 'if sales cover more than half of current costs'. op. cit., p.23.

17. For example, L. Musolf 'Public Enterprise is used here to refer to governmental activities operated exclusively or primarily on the economic model.' Organisation and Administration of Public Enterprises, p.111.

United Nations: 'Publicly owned and/or controlled enterprises ... incorporated public corporations, i.e. by virtue of company acts or other public acts ... or large unincorporated units (government enterprises) that sell most of the goods ... they produce to the public.' A System of National Accounts, 1968, United Nations E.69, XVII 3, p.78.

V.V. Ramanadham: 'The term "public enterprise" may be understood to signify an economic activity of which the majority ownership or managerial control vests in the government and/or other public agencies ... we shall limit the term "enterprise" to signify an activity whose costs, primarily, are expected to be financed from the sale proceeds – generally and in the long run.' Commonwealth Secretariat, <u>The Role and Management of Public Enterprises</u> (London, 1977) p.29.

L.P. Jones: 'A public enterprise is a productive activity which is owned and/or controlled by public authorities and whose output is marketed.' <u>Public Enterprise and Economic Development: The Korean Case</u> (Seoul, 1975) p.23.

PART II

PUBLIC ENTERPRISE IN DEVELOPING COUNTRIES

INTRODUCTION

This study analyses certain basic aspects of public enterprise in developing countries with a view to improving understanding of its performance. (No ideological observations are intended.)

The theme is broadly three-fold:

(a)   that public enterprises in developing countries are characterised by problems and costs that distinctly stem from the development context and the organisational circumstances;

(b)   that their financial performance, on the whole, has been unsatisfactory and has disquieting effects on the public exchequer; and

(c)   that it is time that governments of mixed economies examined the degree of comparative advantage possessed by individual public enterprises, with an openness in policy decisions on entrepreneurial arrangements.

A detailed plan of the study is as follows.

Chapters 7, 8, 9 and 10 correspond to the first part of the theme.   Chapter 7 considers the development   context and brings out its impact on the genesis and evolution of public enterprises. Chapter 8 examines the relevance of the processes through which public enterprise has come into being in a country, for its performance situation. Chapter 9 looks at a distinctive and crucial problem of many public enterprises in developing countries – monopoly.   Chapter 10 considers the implications of the wide sectoral coverage attained by public enterprise in the developing world.

The second part of the theme is covered in Chapters eleven, twelve and thirteen. Chapter eleven analyses the concept of financial and social returns and reviews the nature of deficits and severe losses of capital sustained by many public enterprises in developing countries. Chapter twelve suggests that, while public enterprises in many developing countries have been exposed to conditions of high cost, the real costs are probably higher than the costs shown in their accounts. The impacts of public enterprise performance on the public exchequer are analysed in chapter thirteen.

Chapter fourteen addresses the last part of the theme and brings out the intricacies of the concept of comparative advantage of public enterprises from the angle of policy decision.

The aspects of study have been chosen to reflect the element of uniqueness attached to the institution of public enterprise in the circumstances of developing countries. Ideas on desirable public policies have been included at appropriate places and their conceptual implications brought out.

Despite many commonalities, developing countries range over a wide spectrum of development status. It would be interesting to look at this for its possible connection with public enterprise performance. Chapter fifteen undertakes some classifications of the countries from this point of view.

The focus of the study is analytical, in the light of global experience. The intention is neither to be descriptive nor to cover every aspect. Many familiar topics such as form, boards, control and accountability, and direct discussions of pricing and investment have been omitted.

One obvious caveat: it is inherent in studies such as this that exceptions exist to almost any observation.

Chapter Seven

THE DEVELOPMENT PERSPECTIVE

The emergence of public enterprise in developing countries has coincided with initial stages of
industrialisation and modern economic development.
It has even seemed to be a necessary condition for
the latter; and governments have felt that they had
'little choice in this respect' (1). The merits
of such policy choice are outside the present discussion; it is the implications for public enterprise with which we are concerned, looking essentially at three aspects of the facts of history.

(a) The development status

First, the development status of several countries was so low that the first efforts towards development involved them in heavy costs which were
analogous to overheads of national economic development. A significant proportion of these devolved
on public enterprises which happened to be the
vehicle of the development strategy.

How serious the costs must have been may be illustrated briefly by data on select indices reflecting the structural disadvantages in which a wide
cross-section of developing countries were placed
some twenty years ago. Data for 1960 are examined
in respect of (i) manufacturing as per cent of gross
domestic product, (ii) energy consumption per capita
(as kilograms or coal equivalent), (iii) urban population as per cent of total population, (iv) labour
force (as a percentage) in agriculture, and (v)
adult literacy (as a percentage). The frequency
of the least favourable figures under these heads
in the case of each country is indicated in Appendix 1. (The values considered as the least favourable are, respectively for the five indices, (i)

below 10, (ii) below 50, (iii) below 10, (iv) above
80 and (v) below 20.) Constraints of space rule
out a detailed discussion of how such values aggravate the costs of gestation of national economic
development; but it may be surmised that they raise
the costs of technology acquisition and absorption
(2), entail inordinate costs of technical and managerial training, occasion expensive (expatriate) arrangements for skills, saddling the countries with
expensive foreign collaboration (3), and cause uneconomical sequences of capital expenditure on projects
(4).

These are really costs of national gestation,
though, in several cases, carried in the books of
the public enterprises concerned. In countries
where private enterprises heralded (industrial)
development, such costs were borne:

(i)   through bankruptcies of some enter-
        prises;

(ii)   by virtual enjoyment of monopoly
        power by enterprises over a span
        of time sufficient to compensate
        their initial high cost and losses;

(iii)   by subsidies offered by the govern-
        ment - e.g. the grant of free land
        to railway companies in India in the
        last century; and/or

(iv)   through multi-national operations
        which either proportioned the manu-
        facturing content in local activity
        to suit gradual diminutions in struc-
        tural diseconomies over time or
        brought the benefits of their global
        economies to bear on local activity,
        with a view to some kind of eventual
        advantage.

In most developing countries, such costs tended
to devolve squarely on public enterprises. Without
an understanding of this historical perspective one
may derive inaccurate judgements on their performance.

An empirical word on the message of Appendix 1.
Of the 89 countries for which data are available,
nearly half - all low- and middle-income developing

countries - are marked by one or more of the unfavourable indices with 32 of these in Africa and none in Latin America. Five, all in Africa, are badly placed in respect of all five indices - Chad, Niger, Mauritania, Tanzania and Upper Volta; and these are among the countries with high, if not dominant, proportions of public enterprises - e.g. Tanzania. Of the eight countries badly placed under four indices, six are in Africa - Central African Republic, Somalia, Uganda, Toga, Mali and Mozambique - and two are in Asia - Yemen Arab Republic and Papua New Guinea. That these again are dominantly public enterprise economies with the exception of the last, supports the theme of this section.

(b) National gestation

The second aspect of the development perspective is that the costs of national gestation, though applicable to private enterprises as well, are disproportionately associated with public enterprises. For, most of the countries have development plans which are based on macro preferences that work towards the emergence of public enterprises almost without choice. Definitive reservations of certain sectors of activity for public enterprise, as illustrated by industrial policy enunciations in India, Bangladesh, and Trinidad and Tobago (since 1948) are but the end result of governmental preference such as the following:

> unrestricted location of activity is not permitted; only locations conducive to regional balance in development are;

> it is not necessarily technologies that permit of immediate profit but such technologies as sustain long term self-reliance in development that are to be chosen;

> the choice should not be for a rate of growth that might satisfy individual entrepreneurial motivations of profit, but for rates designed to compress development into as short a span as possible (5);

> and entrepreneurial entry is generally not unconditional.

The last condition cuts out foreign inflow of capital and skills except under restrictive provisions of government policy. The development plans which incorporate such preferences, including large doses of promotional rather than profit-oriented pricing policies, tend to restrict local private entrepreneurs to residual areas. Here they can pick and choose business activity but will remain uninterested in or incapable of entering the main stream of developmental activity. Such policy statements as the following, referring to certain developing countries, effectively say that private entrepreneurship is a function of (restrictive) macro preferences in development. This, naturally, turns out to be so low as to oblige public enterprise to assume a large measure of the costs of gestation of national development.

> The place of government investments is 'where the risks were too great for private capital, or too much capital was needed and private enterprise was unable or unwilling to provide it, or the returns appeared too low for private enterprise but the project was nevertheless necessary in the national interest'.(6).

> Government invests in 'industries that had little attraction to the private sector, that is, industries that would be characterised by small profits and heavy burdens, or whose investment could not be split up'. (7).

The inevitability of public enterprise is not unqualified in theory; for foreign private enterprise can come in. But the choice (8), generally, is such as to restrict it so meticulously that either the inevitability of public enterprise is reinstated or it operates through investment in a joint venture.

(c) Recent independence

A third historical fact, which intensified the burdens of national costs of development borne by public enterprises, is that the latter, representing the beginnings of national development efforts, came into being in the early years of national (political) independence in many cases. This occurred in the sixties in many countries of Africa and as recently as in the last five to ten years in more than 25 countries.

Appendix 2, which indicates the recency of independence of developing countries as reflected in
their membership in the United Nations, provides
empirical support for the proposition that there
must have been heavy costs or diseconomy for public enterprises in a wide cross-section of the
developing world, on the following grounds:

(i)   It takes time and effort for a newly independent country to make amends for certain structural legacies of colonial subjugation.   These
include a disproportionate bias of the community for
trading rather than for manufacturing, foreign trade
orientation of the economy in terms of primary exports and manufactured imports, and excessive localisation of economic activity on the coast line
rather than in a more balanced manner.   Even a
big country like India experienced these problems
(9); so did Algeria (10).   Such structural imperfections (viewed from a national perspective) have
entailed high costs through ameliorative actions of
public policy.

(ii)   Governments are under the disadvantage
of inexperience - especially in two respects -
economic administration and negotiations with foreign governments and collaborators.   The larger
and the more rapid the exodus of expatriates, the
more serious the disadvantage.

(iii) Rapid programmes of indigenising government and economic services have a cost tag (11).
In the process initiative can pass into the hands
of civil servants out of proportion with their
capability.

(iv)   The position deteriorates as a result
of a common feature found in several newly independent developing countries, viz. over-zealous political and parliamentary interferences with enterprise matters.   Politicisation, sometimes to a
serious degree - as in Ghana (12) and Nigeria (13)
- takes place.

It is not difficult to appreciate that the diseconomy flowing from these factors impacts public
enterprises far more heavily than it affects private
enterprises.   (Some interesting evidence on the
proposition may be derived from a comparison of the

degree of economy in the governmental background
enjoyed by certain public enterprises set up in the
colonial times in East Africa and that relating to
public enterprises set up immediately after independence   or to the Community enterprises' performance
in the seventies.)

The actual impact of the 'new independence' on
public enterprises in developing countries is unlikely to be uniform across all of them.   Important qualifications exist.   For example, the gra-
vity of the development indices discussed earlier
is a material consideration (and the countries
which featured the least favourable indices
must have been most handicapped) (14).   Further,
the legacies of colonialism are not similar in the
Anglophone, Francophone, Belgian, Dutch and Portu-
guese cases.   And a few colonies did possess a
strong administrative framework at the time of
independence – e.g. India; whereas many others,
especially in Africa – e.g. Congo, lagged disas-
trously behind in this respect.   But in every
case new independence was a source of costs that
developed significantly on public enterprises.
Of course, there could be no escape from this
phenomenon.

In brief, this chapter suggests that the development perspective enables us to appreciate the
existence of certain 'givens' that conditioned the
genesis and evolution of public enterprise in developing countries, and that attempts at the appraisal
of their performance without reference to the impacts
of the development context are unlikely to be fruitful.   Few developed countries have initiated public
enterprise in their early stages of development or
in their infancy as independent nations.

NOTES

1.   It was observed in the course of a study
by the Centre for Development Planning, Projections
and Policies of the United Nations that 'in some of
these countries that are at a relatively early stage
of industrialisation but wish to expand manufacturing
output rapidly, the underlying current of thought
in policy making is that there is little choice in
this respect: only through large investment outlays
of public authorities will it be possible to achieve
the goal of industrialisation'.   Journal of Develop-

<u>ment Planning</u>, No.8 (1975) (New York, 1975), p.83.
       2.   Indian Drugs and Pharmaceuticals Ltd. was
seriously exposed to problems of technology for a
long time in respect of its surgical plant unit in
Madras.
      Afghanistan aptly illustrates the problem, with
'virtually no domestic engineers with a knowledge of
electronics, electro-technology, automation and
other modern techniques'. <u>Industrialisation of the
Least Developed Countries</u> (UNIDO, ID/WG/234/13)
(Vienna, 1977), p.28.
      A relevant excerpt from a recent UNCTAD study
is as follows: The existing juridical and legal
environment of technology transfer 'has served to
distort the priorities in production, prevent an
appropriate choice of technology and increase the
degree of packaging, and inhibit the maximum use
of domestic inputs of intermediate products, capital goods and skills'. <u>Towards the technological
transformation of the developing countries</u> (TD3238,
p.40 and TD/238/Carr.1).
      Also see Fund for Multinational Management
Education, <u>Public Policy and Technology Transfer</u>,
Vol.3 (1978), p.7.
      3.   Two examples may be cited from Nepal.
A Danish loan tying high-priced procurement to
Denmark was not used by the private sector, but
a public sector enterprise, Nepal Livestock Company, came into being; likewise a Japanese loan,
with procurement tied to Japan, was used, not by
any private enterprise, but by a public enterprise
- Transport Corporation of Nepal. <u>Performance of
Public Enterprise in Nepal</u> (Macro Study), HMG Office
of Corporation Co-ordination Council, and Industrial
Services Centre (Kathmandu, 1977), p.54.
      4.   Several instances are available in the
reports of Parliamentary Committees in the sixties
in India.
      5.   It is said of Ghana that 'too many indu-
stries were created in too short a time with too
little or no proper planning'. R.A. Quarshie,
GIHOC, <u>Ghana's Industrial Complex</u> (Accra), p.5.
      Further, notice the observation of the Centre
for Development Planning, Projections and Policies,
United Nations, that 'irrespective of whether the
target is high or low, a comparison of the annual
rate of increase in manufacturing output planned
for the early years of the 1970s with that achieved
in a period immediately preceding the current plan
period shows that a large majority of the developing countries have projected a <u>significant accele-</u>

ration in manufacturing activity'. (Underlining mine). Journal of Development Planning, No.8 (New York, 1975), p.65.

6.   K.D. Kaunda, Zambia's Economic Revolution (Lusaka, 1968), p.48.

7.   Comparative Study of Development Plans of Araba States, UNIDO (Vienna, 1977), p.178, concerning Libya.

8.   A convincing illustration of the trend comes from Tanzania.   'The pragmatist in Africa ... will find that the choice is between foreign private ownership on the one hand and collective ownership on the other.'   President Julius K. Nverere,'Economic Nationalism' in Uhura na Umoja (Dar Es Salaam, 1968), p.264.

9.   For evidence on the nature of colonial impacts of railway rates policies on development, see N.B. Mehta, Indian Railways: Rates and Regulations (1927); and R.D. Tiwari, Railway Rates in Relation to Trade and Industry in India (Calcutta, 1937).

10.   (In the colonial regime the entire economy of Algeria was subordinated to the metropolitan authority, namely France, and all economic activities were so designed as to support the development of the metropolis ... Secondly, practically all economic activity and productive enterprises were in the hands of the French colonists and there was virtually no local entrepreneurship. Thirdly, there was an imbalance in regional development with very heavy concentration on the coastal belt. Findings based on Mahfond Ghezale's paper presented at the Regional Meeting of Arab and Mediterranean Countries on the Role of the Public Sector in Developing Countries (Ljubljana, 1979). See Report of the Meeting.

11.   For comments on the 'rapid and haphazard Africanisation programmes' adopted in certain countries, see The Twelfth Inter-African Public Administration and Management Seminar (Ibadan, 1973), p.126.

12.   For some striking evidence, see Robert C. Pozen, Legal Choices for State Enterprises in the Third World (New York, 1976).

13.   The Reports (in the sixties) of the Tribunals of Inquiry into the affairs of Nigerian Ports Authority, Nigerian Railway Corporation, Electricity Corporation of Nigeria and Nigerian Airways are replete with evidence on this point (Lagos, 1967-68).

14.   For further evidence see Chapter 15.

This chapter was presented at the Seminar on Public

The Development Perspective

Enterprise and the Developing World, at the London
Business School, in March 1983.

Chapter Eight

THE GENESIS OF PUBLIC ENTERPRISE

The genesis of public enterprise and the processes
through which major segments of it have emerged in
a country have a material impact on the nature of
its performance. Developing countries do not present a uniform picture from this point of view.
This chapter is devoted to a review of the diverse
nature of impacts that flow from nationalisation of
existing enterprises and creation of new enterprises
in the public sector. Comments will be made on the
problems associated with the nationalisation of
foreign holdings. The consequences of holding company
structures for the performance of public enterprises
will also be indicated.

A public enterprise comes into being either
through nationalisation of an erstwhile private enterprise or through creation by the government of an
enterprise de novo, or through governmental investment in what comes to be termed a mixed enterprise
or a joint venture. On the whole, nationalisation
has been a more important means than creation de novo
in developed countries; even the latter has generally
taken the shape of subsidiaries being established
by existing public enterprises.

On the other hand, developing countries, while
showing a variety of mixes of the two measures, have,
by and large, attained their public enterprise sectors more substantially through fresh creation than
through nationalisation. This may have been because
in most of them there has not been much to nationalise; besides, governments believing in a mixed
economy would rather use their resources for establishing new activities than for buying up existing
enterprises (1). (Exceptions, by way of large-
scale nationalisations, do exist and will be refer-

red to in due course. Even in such cases the eventual proportion of new creations in the totality of the public sector is pronounced.)

This point is of substantive interest, in that new creation lacks certain merits of nationalisation from the standpoint of organisation, management and operation. There is no structure to build from in any of these respects; nor are there 'former' managers who, even if with exceptions, can continue to run the enterprises. (Contrast the position with the nationalised electricity or steel industry in the UK, where the fund of managerial capability that had existed before nationalisation was readily available for the public sector corporations.) The governments of countries creating public enterprises anew are exposed to decisional costs of inexperience in the sectors concerned. This, as was argued in the previous chapter, is aggravated by their underdevelopment status.

Such new public sector creations as exist in developed countries, present a favourable contrast. Where these incorporate existing technologies, few insurmountable problems occur, as with ENI's energy enterprises in Italy. Where they represent technological advances involving risk, as with British National Oil Corporation, the activity is really built on stable foundations of technological excellence that already exist. And where a fairly new technology or activity is sponsored, such as television in the UK, the current technical basis is already there, awaiting commercial development.

In contrast, India, though it does not rank among the 46 countries of Appendix 1, illustrates the problems experienced in enterprise initation. While there has been nationalisation in a few sectors like banking, insurance, transport and coal, most of its public sector enterprises were created de novo. Many of the problematic and costly decisions relating to location and technology, size and product mix, and capital expenditure sequences experienced in connection with the large number of enterprises (covered in the central government's list of some 200) can be shown to belong to the category of new-venture incidentals. (Specific examples include Heavy Engineering Corporation Ltd., Indian Drugs and Pharmaceuticals Ltd. and Hindustan Photo Films Manufacturing Co. Ltd.)

The Genesis of Public Enterprise

Even where public enterprises came from nationalisation, developing countries, which practised it
suddenly and extensively have experienced certain
disadvantages. Excessive compensation may be ruled
out, on the whole, as a major problem. Large-scale
nationalisations have been carried out in countries
like Zambia, Tanzania, Somalia, Ethiopia, Sudan,
Egypt, Iraq, Syria, Pakistan and Bangladesh on some
form of socialist ground, and exorbitant compensations were most unlikely here. But the hurried
emergence of an extensive public enterprise sector
over-night reflected the handicaps of unprepared-
ness. Whatever advantages nationalisation could
have preserved at the operating and managerial
levels have been overshadowed by organisational
structures hastily created to take charge of the
enterprise. These generally took the shape of
giant apex bodies (2), within which were incorporated many similar - sometimes quite dissimilar -
enterprises, unleashing a new series of costs - of
over-centralisation in decision-making. The Board
of Industrial Management which was set up in Pakistan in the wake of the Economic Reforms Order of
1972 as the managerial apex for a large number of
nationalised industries, illustrated the multi-tier
problems in the management of the public enterprises
so impressively that it was abolished in 1979 (3).
Large scale nationalisations have not been accompanied adequately by precise enunciations of the targets of performance sought for individual enterprises,
unlike selective pieces of nationalisation - e.g.
insurance or coal in India; hence governmental involvement and over-centralisation have evolved as
values in themselves. But as means to enterprise
performance these arrangements have proved an almost
permanent disadvantage, with their tendency, even if
unwittingly, to stand constantly in the way of introducing economical managerial logistics. An exception may be claimed in the case of a holding company or a monolithic apex that scrupulously decentralises managerial decisions to the plant levels
below (4), reserving to itself major policy matters.
While acceptable in theory, this process does not
seem to be in wide vogue; and the so-called policy
matters to which the apex limits itself tend to
expand very widely in practice.

It is worth noting that there exists a wide
range of structural diversity within the domain of
a holding company, and that the costs of such an
organisation vary with its precise nature. Thus

a development corporation set up with the limited
function of promoting industrial enterprises may,
in fact, confer economies of scale on the promotion
activity; whereas an enterprise which just holds
shares in operating companies, promoted by it or
otherwise acquired, may be a source of diseconomies.
The following chart analyses the heterogeneity of
the holding company structure and includes some
examples.   (The processes listed in column 1 are
not mutually exclusive; the chief feature is high-
lighted in the title.)   The chart helps to suggest
that the problems and costs of a holding company
structure vary among developing countries according as the structure belongs to one category or
another presented in columns (2) to (5) and the
genesis and process borders on one kind or another
presented in the first column

On the whole it is noteworthy that most countries whose public enterprise sectors were not a
result of, or did not witness, (sudden) large-scale
nationalisations, have not gone in for any specta-
cular holding-company type of apex organisations.

India, Thailand, Nepal, Indonesia, Philippines
and Nigeria illustrate this point.   Not that there
is no holding-company structure in these countries,
but it is not a basic feature of their public enterprise organisation.

Public enterprises which are significantly a
product of nationalisation of foreign capital, in
terms of either large numbers or lumpiness in point
of occurrence, are marked by distinctive problems.
The nationalisations need not have implied public
enterprise except for two reasons, valid in most
developing countries.   The first is that the sectors concerned are too 'basic' in the government's
view to be left to private entrepreneurs, even if
domestic.   (The sectoral distribution of the aggregate number of 1,369 take-overs during 1970-76
reflects the pre-eminence of banking and insurance,
followed by petroleum, agriculture and manufacturing.)
(5)   The other reason is that the purchase prices
are too large for the local investor capacity.
That the bulk-cases of nationalisation have occurred in countries known to have large public enterprise systems is, therefore, not accidental.   For
instance, about an eighth of the 71 developing
countries where take-overs of foreign enterprises
occurred during 1970-76 had each taken over more

than 50 enterprises - Algeria, Angola, Egypt, Ethiopia, Uganda, Tanzania, Sudan, Sri Lanka and Indonesia. All these have large public enterprise sectors.

An immediate consequence of the nationalisations was the loss of managers; for many foreigners must have left - particularly in the case of enterprises under foreign ownership of 96-100 per cent (6). In several cases management contracts were entered into, which allowed some continuity of these managers or other foreign talents. But, by and large, the developing countries have been the weaker party in the negotiation and the enterprises suffered from a variety of disadvantages - e.g. excessive payments for management, loss of foreign exchange, doubtful practices of repatriation, inadequate training of local staff, and difficulties in exportation. Further, some of the enterprises were formerly successful as parts of the global strategy of a multinational. Once the latter was removed from the scene the operating and marketing deficiencies of the parts stood out, and the methods of rendering them into 'complete' economic units were neither easy nor inexpensive. The immediate diseconomies were greatest where the enterprise had been part of a multinational vertical integration - e.g. in iron mines. Once removed from the integration, they were exposed to inexperience in export markets, the more so when the foreign buyers had some degree of monopsony power.

The deficiencies in the performance of such enterprises are strictly not those of public enterprises but of nationalisation of foreign holdings. So remedies have to focus on such substantive lines as the formation of cartels or other kinds of combinations among such public enterprises in the affected developing countries, and the acquisition of technical skills (to replace former foreign skills) under helpful international technical assistance - e.g. from UNCTAD or UNTNC. Equally worth serious exploration is the prospect of the technically better placed among the developing countries going to the rescue of their less well placed brethren - perhaps at inter-governmental or inter-public enterprise level.

Another aspect of nationalisation which, as a process, has uneconomic legacies for public enterprise, relates to the take-over of sick enterprises (7). Such cases are not confined to developing

Table 2

Holding company structures

Genesis and process	No private sector; but other public units exist	Private sector exists	The whole Sector	Multi-sectoral (possibly with monopoly in certain sectors)
(1)	(2)	(3)	(4)	(5)
1. On nationalisation		National Textile Corporation Ltd.(India)	Sector Corporation (Egypt	Board of Industrial Management (1) Pakistan ENI (Italy)(2)
2. On creation		Kenya Tourist Development Corp.		
3. On organisational reform	Steel Authority of India Ltd. Coal India Ltd.	National Fertiliser Corporation Ltd. (Pakistan)	Leather and Associated Industries Ltd. (Tanzania)	GUYSTAC (Guyana)

4. Through promotional activity (including shareholding)	Agricultural Finance Corp. (Kenya)		Industrial and Commercial Development Corp. (Kenya) Uganda Development Corp. (Uganda) PERNAS (Malaysia) INDUPERU (Peru)
5. De facto status (3)	Hindustan Machine Tools Ltd.(India)	Bharat Heavy Electricals Ltd. (India)	GIHOC (Ghana)

(1) In de facto terms, analogous to a holding company.

(2) Essentially in the energy sector, ENI today has a fairly diversified coverage. For instance, it includes textiles and chemicals.

(3) Though with no subsidiaries in the eyes of the law.

93

countries. Italy's IRI and ENI and the UK's National Enterprise Board offer us interesting examples from the developed world. The disadvantage that developing countries suffer probably rests on the ineffectiveness of interest in inducing the enterprise managements to adopt prompt measures of physical and financial reorganisation, including closures, with a view to reaching the point of viability and attaining needed competitiveness expeditiously. Hospitalisation takes the upper hand over rehabilitation. What developing countries have to provide against is institutionalising inefficiency under recurrent public subsidy and developing permanent, complacent acceptance of the enterprises sickness.

Joint ventures in which the government and foreigners participate can enjoy the economies of the latter's managerial skills. But experience shows that in not a few cases the management agreements have been so drafted as to benefit the foreign partner at the expense of the enterprise (8). This has been facilitated by the inability or ineffectiveness of control by the government on the cost-raising practices of the management in respect of purchases, maintenance, technology and marketing.

We conclude this chapter with a tabular presentation illustrating the genesis or process through which a public enterprise has come into being and the major heads under which the degree of economy or diseconomy varies 'accordingly'. The method adopted here is to assign a symbol - A, B or C - reflecting diseconomy in a descending order. A genesis or process against which a large number of As are entered is, in theory, likely to have given rise to severe diseconomies for the enterprise. At the other extreme a process with the fewest As, or with many Cs, may have caused the least severe diseconomy. (The attribution of the symbols represents hypothesising. It would be interesting to illustrate the argument empirically).

The purpose of the chart is to provide not a conclusive or precise statement, but a methodological tool in understanding the probable differences in public enterprise situations in developing countries from the angle of the genesis and process in the enterprises.

Table 3

The impact and genesis of public enterprise

Genesis (1)	Investment decision (2)	Technology choice (3)	Managerial skills (4)	Governmental involvement (5)	Legacies (6)	Politicking (7)[1]
Nationalisation						
Domestic	B	B	C	C	B	B
Sick	A	B	B	A	A	A
Foreign	B	B	B	B	B	B
Creation						
Existing sector	B	B	B	B	–	B
New sector	A	A	A	A	–	B
Joint venture						
Domestic						
Nationalisation	C	C	C	C	B	A
Creation	B	B	C	B	–	B
Foreign						
Nationalisation	C	C	B	C	B	B
Creation	B	C	B	B	–	B

1 The actual symbol is really unpredictable.

'Investment decision' includes decisions on size, location(s), product mix, sequence of capital expenditures, and welfare expenditures (e.g. housing). 'Technology choice' refers not only to choice of technology but also to the foreign source of technology. 'Managerial skills' cover both availability and cost. 'Government involvement' denotes the role of the government in project formulation, negotiations with any foreign or other collaborators, decision-making at the board of directors level, and managerial processes within the enterprise. 'Legacies' refer to the impact of past events in the life of the enterprise – e.g. arrears in modernisation, poor industrial relations, excess capacity, surplus staff and inefficient technology. 'Politicking' covers all actions on the part of the politicians, including ministers and members of Parliament, overt or covert, having the effect of deflecting a decision from the efficiency criterion of the enterprise.

The attribution of a symbol to a process-and-head is a matter of judgement on the basis of global observation. It is just possible that an extreme disadvantage under a single head outbalances the rest of the symbols against a given process. For example, a bad management contract under the head of government involvement can upset 'C' values in the rest of the columns in the case of a joint venture (foreign); or distinctly unfavourable 'legacies' or politicking can affect the net fortunes of a process out of proportion to the values of its several symbols.

Subject to these qualifications, creation of an enterprise in a new sector is under the greatest potential disadvantage, followed by the nationalisation of sick units. (The former has particular relevance to many developing countries).

NOTES

1. For example, in Kenya, 'the government believes that its primary duty is to use the limited financial resources it can command to build up the stock of national assets by new investment, rather than merely purchasing existing assets leading to no net increase in the total stock of national capital'. Mwai Kibaki, Minister for Finance and Economic Planning, Budget Speech, 17 June 1971.

2.   For example, Zambia set up INDECO, MINDECO, FINDECO etc., Tanzania set up National Development Corporation, Sudan set up sector corporations, Pakistan set up the Board of Industrial Management, Bangladesh set up sector corporations, Iraq set up State organisations, and Syria set up Unions.

3.   The experience of Iraq and Syria may be cited as well.   A comment on the Iraqi creation of six State organisations (for spinning and weaving; clothing, leather and cigarettes; chemicals and food; construction; engineering; and planning and industrial construction) was that 'The Iraqi system of management is quite centralised ... Decisions tend to be referred to one level higher than necessary for 'approval' and 'confirmation', where they may be vetoed even though they are within the jurisdiction of the lower management levels.' Review and Appraisal of the Process of Decision-Making and Management in the Public Industrial Enterprise of Iraq.   Expert Group Meeting on Review and Appraisal of Progress in the Implementation of the International Development Strategy for the Second Development Decade, Beirut, 1973.   (UN Economic and Social Office in Beirut).

Similar is the position in Syria with its three Unions (for textile industries, food industries, and chemical and engineering industries).   'At the firm level little autonomy is retained ... The functional basis of the control system is reflected in the multiplicity of decision-making and control agencies issuing directives and controlling various functions of the enterprise ... This ... serves to strain and confuse the director of the enterprise who no longer knows to whom he should report.' (The same Meeting).

4.   To cite an example, though from a developed country, British Steel Corporation has been aiming at effective decentralisation as this minimises the costs of statutory, single-apex, sectoral organisation in the public sector.   The following excerpts from Report on Organisation, 1980, British Steel Corporation, are interesting in this context. 'The Corporation has concluded that the achievement of ... improvements in performance calls for its activities to be organised into a series of discrete businesses, each oriented towards separate product markets and each acting as profit centre linking the manufacturing and commercial responsibilities for that product under a single individual ...'   'This will enable responsibility for profitability and capital employed to be delegated to the

maximum and thus enable the efforts of management to be directed most effectively towards the objectives of achieving competitive costs and performance.'

5.   Transnational Corporations in World Development, United Nations Centre for Transnational Corporations (New York) Table III - 28.

6.   Such cases accounted for four-fifths of all cases of nationalisation during 1960-74.   Permanent Sovereignty over Natural Resources (Report for the Economic and Social Council, United Nations, A 19716, 20 September 1974).

7.   For instance, the Sick Textile Undertakings (Nationalisation) ordinance of 21 September 1974 nationalised 103 sick textile undertakings in India and vested them in the National Textile Corporation Ltd.

8.   To illustrate from Kenya: 'Many management and consultancy contracts are negotiated at really high prices and on terms in which the rewards are unrelated to performance.'   Working Party on Government Expenditures, Report and Recommendations of the Working Party (Nairobi, 1982) p.45.

Chapter Nine

MONOPOLY ELEMENTS

Public enterprises present elements of monopoly not
only in developing countries but in developed countries also. However, certain aspects relating to
the former merit special notice. We shall examine
them in this chapter and suggest policy measures
that are appropriate to deal with the situation.

(a) Small sizes

First, there is the problem of uneconomical
monopolies on grounds of size. In several countries the markets for certain products are so small
that no more than a single infra-optimal plant is
all that is necessary. It at once assumes a monopoly position - a fact that has, in fact, been a
positive reason for the emergence of many public
enterprises in countries like Zambia (1), Ghana,
(2) and Barbados (3).

The number of countries vulnerable to sub-
optimal monopoly formations is fairly large in the
developing world. Nine of the low-income countries,
twelve of the middle-income (lower) group and nine
of the middle-income (upper) group in the list contained in the World Bank's Report (cited earlier)
are small in terms of population (below five million). The first two groups have the additional
disadvantage of low purchasing power on the part
of the domestic consumers. The number is really
larger when we consider many of the countries
(island economies in particular) not covered by
that list - such as Cape Verde, San Tome and
Principe, Seychelles, Fiji, Bahamas, Samoa,
Solomon Islands, Barbados, Grenada, St. Lucia,
Surinam, Guyana, Oman, Bahrain, Qatar, Djibuti
and Comoros.

At this point some explanation of the concept of uneconomical size is helpful. It may refer to a minimum necessary size on technical grounds, which, however, remains under-utilised because of limited demand. The actual unit cost is uneconomic for this reason, but there is, by hypothesis, no way of producing the product at lower cost. Or, the size of the unit may be brought down to the level of demand by adopting a simpler production function or 'appropriate technology'; but whether the cost will be as low as in the former case is the question. Perhaps the right combination of machine, labour, raw material, fuel and maintenance inputs can be found so as to attain the cost level of the former size. This needs active experimentation. The public enterprise monopoly status can offer some advantage in such purposeful experimentation. It is equally possible, on the other hand, that the management may be complacent and follow the easy path of demanding protective duties on imports so as to offset its cost disadvantage. Further, it may encourage the government against the option of seeking the supply of the product by a multi-national at a lower price, though not through local manufacture.

One way in which the small-sized monopoly can hope to become economical is by developing an export market which permits it to produce to capacity, if not expand to a more economical capacity than the minimum technical unit necessary. This has been difficult except in a few cases like Singapore and Hong Kong.

There is one other possibility which merits active exploration. Inter-public enterprise arrangements among neighbouring countries may be evolved in such a way that, without duplicating infra-optimal capacities everywhere, large-sized plants may be established at one or a few places with advantages of economy for all concerned. While easy to appreciate, the prospect of such joint ventures is conditioned by five considerations in practice:

(i) technological problems in transporting certain outputs, e.g. electricity and gas;

(ii) inertia of governments which basically limit their public sector operations to the boundaries of their own countries;

(iii) political relationships among the
countries concerned (4);

(iv) subtle machinations of multi-nationals
disrupting the fruition of such ventures;
and

(v) difficulties in effecting radical changes
in certain existing conditions - e.g. a
national airline in every case (5).

The factor that sustains the longevity of such
joint ventures is not just the initial perception of
production economies but the eventual actuality concerning the division of benefits - in respect of
employment, output, net revenue and foreign exchange
- taking into account the direct as well as the allied or ancillary activities. Several attempts at
public-enterprise joint ventures have been made in
West Africa, in the Arab Middle East and in the
Caribbean. The progress so far achieved is no-
where near the need. One may venture the view that
this will be an area in which public enterprises of
small developing economies will soon have to initiate co-operative efforts in the interest of technical economy in production activity. Incidentally,
this may be one way of maximising their capability
in the export markets.

Another possibility, in the same direction, is
to seek a joint venture agreement with a foreign
private enterprise, including a multi-national, if
the coveted result of economical output expansion
can be realised on the sure basis of export markets.
Two substantive qualifications need attention: (i)
There is an open or disguised cost attached to the
foreigner's participation; and this should be lower
than the economy that the enterprise gains by expansion to optimality. (ii) There has to be a
reasonable assurance that the arrangement stands
in force for an adequate span of time during which
the enterprise can develop strategies of self-
reliance if and when deemed essential.

(b) Large enterprises

Let us turn next to the more general problem
of monopoly emergence - through the evolution of
large enterprises in the public sector - in developing countries, small and large. Their structure
can be heterogeneous, as shown in Figure 2.

101

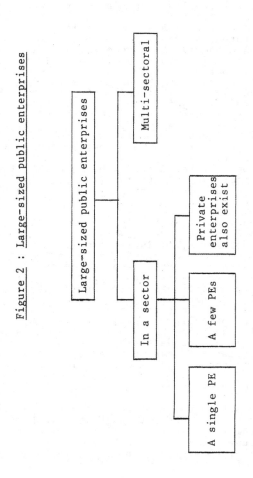

Figure 2 : Large-sized public enterprises

Monopoly elements are most obvious where, in a given sector, a single public enterprise operates — e.g. Bharat Heavy Electricals Ltd. in India. They can develop through concert where a few units exist in the public sector — as in steel or coal in India. Even where private enterprises also exist, the overall supply of a product may be short of the aggregate demand so much so that the industry as a whole comes within the impact of monopoly power. This phenomenon, illustrated by the fertiliser sector in India and Pakistan, can be quite common in many developing countries.

A large multi-sectoral public enterprise, illustrated by many holding company structures in developing countries (6), does not necessarily possess significant monopoly in individual sectors, unless some of its constituent enterprises come within the description of the preceding paragraph. However, it can have certain of the implications of a monopoly organisation. For example, it can facilitate inter-enterprise cross-subsidisations even on an inter-sectoral basis; and the inefficiencies of any of its enterprises get protected so that they manage to compete, unfairly, with outside enterprises in spite of their inherent weaknesses.

The organisational arrangements outlined in the previous chapter indicate a bias towards the emergence of monopoly. For instance, all the public sector fertiliser units in Pakistan are brought under the National Fertiliser Corporation; and the marketing function of each subsidiary is hived off into a distinctive subsidiary designated for marketing, viz., National Fertilizer Marketing Ltd. All coalfields in India are unified under Coal India Ltd., with the exception of Singareni Collieries Ltd., and all paper units in Tanzania under Tanzania Karatasi Associated Industries Corporation.

The extent of monopoly in the public enterprise sectors of developing countries is quite large, going beyond the public utility area where the situation is similar in developed countries too. The data for Pakistan and Nepal, cited below, illustrate the situation:

An analysis of the market structures in Pakistan made in 1975 show that 68.9 per cent of the outputs of public enterprises were in the nature of monopoly, 3.4 per

103

cent of duopoly and 15.9 per cent of
oligopoly; only 9.1 per cent faced
competition (7).

A study in Nepal estimated the monopoly
segment in public enterprise at 47 per
cent, in terms of value added, duopoly
at 23 per cent, oligopoly at 18 per cent,
'privileged market' conditions at 7 per
cent, and competition at 5 per cent (8).

And there can be little doubt about the existence of monopoly in the public enterprise sector
in those countries where nearly all national enterprises are in the public sector - e.g. Somalia,
Ethiopia, Egypt and Syria.

With so much of monopoly in their public enterprise systems, developing countries have established
very little effective monopoly control. Apart from
price controls (9) by the government as a matter of
general policy and public utility regulation (10),
specific efforts at a review of possible monopoly
practices or disadvantages of public enterprises
have been rare indeed.

The consequence, strangely, has not necessarily
been excessive profit-making. In fact, in spite of
being monopolies, many public enterprises are found
to be sustaining losses. Two factors have been responsible for this paradoxical situation. For one
thing, costs have been 'excessive' as a result of
development disadvantages, investment mistakes or
managerial inefficiency; and losses have resulted,
not because prices have been uneconomic, but because costs have been uneconomic. For another,
governments have, rigidly in many cases, frozen
prices at levels that did not make profits possible.
Yet the debates between the enterprises asking for
higher prices and the governments occasionally conceding small enhancements have not adequately
referred to the propriety or otherwise of the cost
structures. Governments seem to have proceeded
from social considerations, without, however, making
any convincing methodology underlying their decisions available to the public. It is possible
that in several cases the permitted price levels,
alleged by enterprise managements as uneconomic,
are broadly correct when allowance is made for
their cost inefficiencies. But the point is
generally missed, and the villain of the piece

seems to be the frozen prices.

(c) Policy measures

Let us look at helpful policy measures on the monopoly problem.   It would be unrealistic to expect governments to develop an interest in breaking monopolies on organisational grounds.   The weights attached to such factors as scarce managerial resources, need for co-ordination and desirability of close governmental involvement in managerial decision-making, continue to support the organisational basis of monopoly power in public enterprise. Three lines of approach are, however, possible:

(i)   Rigorous analysis may be initiated of the economies of scale in respect of the existing large enterprises, so that, even if the apex is allowed to remain, the constituent units are reorganised so as to prevent scale diseconomies through excessive largeness.   There can be no standard principle of size; the desideratum depends on a combination of circumstances on the supply and demand sides. What is important is that each unit, which may be called an operating unit, should be offered autonomy in operations so that expansions in output get concentrated in the more efficient units and pricing decisions are substantially influenced by the costs at the more efficient units.

(ii)   Even where the above step is not taken, the government may provide, or ensure the provision of, operating criteria that serve as an approximate proxy for market forces, so that public enterprises (and their constituent parts) cannot bask under the convenience and complacency of their monopoly powers. This step bears fruit if only the operating criteria are expertly drawn and effectively applied to the enterprises.

(iii) In any case, an effective system of monopoly control should be set up.   It helps the consumer by adjudicating the permissible cost basis of prices and by exposing price and supply practices that are exploitative or undesirable.   It helps the enterprise by establishing admissible levels of returns it can aim at.   It helps the government by pointing at areas that merit monitoring, control and legislation.   However, three factors stand in the way of governmental enthusiasm in introducing proper monopoly power.   First, there is the inaccurate

notion that public enterprises making low or no profits could not be suspected of monopoly consequences.
Second, there is the fear on the part of governments
that unfavourable findings of monopoly commissions
might constitute an indirect indictment of governmental involvement in enterprise affairs as well as
a reflection on their pro-public sector strategy of
development. Third, governments do not like monopoly control agencies raising questions on the social
implications of any input or pricing conditions traceable to governmental policies. But there is no
reason why the terms of the agencies cannot be so
formulated as to exclude their incursion into such
policy areas. Besides, governments can reiterate
their policy constraints despite the agencies' findings.

In conclusion, attempts to exorcise the consequences of monopoly power in public enterprise should
be considered a part of the strategy to improve international competitiveness of the developing countries. The need for such a strategy is ubiquitous
indeed.

There is another good result of effective monopoly control over public enterprises in a mixed economy. It will reveal their real merits as enterprises as distinct from their monopoly profits.

NOTES

1. Regarding Zambia: 'In our industrial
development we have no choice but to make use of
monopolies ... In relation to some products it simply
cannot sustain more than one factory.' K.R. Kaunda,
Zambia's Economic Revolution (Lusaka, 1968) pp.65
and 22. And, in 1972, monopoly enterprises were to
offer 51 per cent of shares to the public holding
company INDECO.
2. Regarding Ghana: 'It will generally be
the practice to seek some measure of government participation or adopt other methods of safeguarding
the interests of the community whenever an enterprise operates under monopoly conditions.' Second
Development Plan, Ghana (Accra), p.104.
3. Regarding Barbados: Barbados Marketing
Corporation is an interesting example. It 'has
been given a monopoly on imports of chicken parts
and other agricultural products. Given the small-
ness of the country, imports of goods and related

items are made by a few importers, in an oligopolistic market.   Therefore, given the country's balance of payments problems, the principle that a public enterprise should have a monopoly for certain food imports may be in the country's advantage'.   (Inter-American Economic and Social Council, Permanent Executive Committee,   Sub-Committee on Barbados. <u>Situation, Principal Problems and Prospects for the Economic and Social Development of Barbados</u> (1974).

4.   Referring to the East African Community (composed of Kenya, Uganda and Tanzania), Mwai Kibaki, Minister of Finance and Planning, Kenya, observed: 'For some time we have followed different   political philosophies than our neighbours and our economic policies have moved steadily further apart ... Community of interest and willingness to work together no longer exists.'   <u>Budget Speech</u> (Nairobi, 1977), p.5.

5.   Aussie Walker describes the impediments in the way of creating multi-national African airlines with advantages of size, in <u>Executive</u>, January 1983, pp.23-24 (Nairobi).

6.   For example, Uganda Development Corporation, National Development Corporation (in Tanzania) and GUYSTAC (in Guyana).

7.   Reza H. Seyed (Ed.) <u>Role and Performance of Public Enterprises in the Economic Growth of Pakistan</u>.

8.   H.M.G. Office of Corporation Co-ordination Council and Industrial Services Centre, <u>Performance of Public Enterprises in Nepal (Macro Study)</u>, (Kathmandu, 1977), p.155.

9.   For example, under the <u>Regulation of Prices Act, 1973</u>, in Tanzania, 'to determine reasonable price structures on a national basis'.

10.   For isntance, under the <u>Public Utilities Commission Act, 1966</u> in Trinidad and Tobago.

Chapter Ten

SECTORAL COVERAGE

This chapter reviews, first, the circumstances that
have led to the wide sectoral coverage of public
enterprise in developing countries and then examines the implications of it for public policy determinations. The question will also be considered
as to how far the sectoral coverage satisfies
'equity' considerations that most developing
countries uphold.

It is difficult to assert that no developed
country is marked by a comparable coverage. Despite the predominance of public utility and basic
categories in the generality of the public sectors
of developed countries, there are, for instance,
many cases in the UK where other industrial fields
have been touched through shareholding in company-
form enterprises; in France where the socialist
government has brought about a broad range of nationalisation measures; in Italy where IRI, originally
for salvage reasons, holds a diversified industrial
empire; and in Spain with the multi-sectoral INA.
Some differences exist, however, between the developed and the developing countries in this respect.
The latter have a rather large segment of light,
low-technology and small-scale industries in their
public sector, which, in several cases, occupy a
significant proportion of industrial activity in
the country; and most of them are the result of
governmental creation rather than of nationalisation.

The reasons why the governments of many developing countries have accumulated a highly diversified public sector may be summed up as follows:

(i)   The dearth of private entrepreneurship

applied even to medium-sized, light industry; (1) for example, even in pre-revolution Ethiopia government shareholding in industrial undertakings was quite considerable. The need to invite foreign technology and skills has almost obliged some governments to step in as partners in joint ventures, as evidenced by the large number of subsidiaries of the Industrial and Commercial Development Corporation in engineering, radio, batteries, pharmaceuticals, tyres, metal cans, textiles etc.

(ii)   Large-scale nationalisations such as those in Zambia, Tanzania and Guyana, touching both domestic and foreign capital, brought into the public sector both medium and small-sized activities in a variety of production and trade sectors - e.g. milling, retailing, and saw mills. Where the socialisation of the means of production was the declared policy of the country (2), there was no alternative for public enterprise but to cover almost all industrial and commercial activity in the country.

(iii)   The concept of comparative advantage in public, as against private, enterprise has been too generously interpreted in favour of the former in several countries, by intensifying the weights attached to the social content of the operations - such as model employment, low prices and reduction of regional disparities. This has led governments into sectors that might normally be considered as the preserve of private enterprise.

The difference between developed and developing countries, in the present context, is that in the former the coverage of public enterprise has depended on what governments (rather cautiously) decided to nationalise, whereas in the latter it has been influenced by what governments felt had been left untouched by private enterprise.

Data showing the sectoral spread of public enterprise in developing countries are provided in Appendix 3, for select countries - India, Pakistan, Kenya and Colombia. The purpose is to illustrate that it extends not only to transport, electricity, steel, oil and minerals but to chemicals, pharmaceuticals, engineering, consumer goods (such as textiles, sugar and paper),ceramics, cement, agro-based industries, trading, construction, consultancy services, tea factories, livestock, small scale industry, beverages, fishing, insurance, tourism and many

kinds of financial services. It is said of Kenya
that 'the commercial investments of Government have
taken it into almost every area of private sector
activity' (3).

We shall examine the implications of the highly
diversified sectoral coverage of public enterprise
in developing countries under three heads: (a) problems of organisation, management and supervision;
(b) the 'total viability' concept; and (c) 'equity'
considerations.

(a)   Problems of organisation, management and supervision

Basically what governments face is not the
problem of individual enterprises but that of a
substantial cross-section of the economy as a whole,
to which is applied some degree of deliberate substitution of governmental decision for market forces.
The fact that many enterprises have been created de
novo in the public sector, complicates the problem
of investment choice (4) and inter-industry inter-
actions.

The point may be illustrated by the fixing of
financial targets for individual public enterprises.
It has not been too easy to determine these meaning-
fully even in the UK (5), which has a relatively
small number of public enterprises; nor has the
parallel device of 'contrats de programme' been
formulated, even with limited success, in respect
of more than a few public enterprises in France (6).
The complications in arriving at agreed returns targets, which pre-suppose agreed governmental commitments as to investment funds and any necessary subsidies, are bound to be far more serious in developing countries. Small wonder that policy steps
have not been taken in this direction in these
countries (7). For, what will be required is a
strategy that not only quantifies the expected returns in each of the many sectors covered by public
enterprise which go far beyond public utilities or
basic industries but also maintains appropriate
inter-industry relativities. The alternative will
consist of random inter-industry subsidisation
through the operating results of the enterprises.
The strategy is no doubt difficult, but there is
no other choice.

The difficulties encountered in fixing finan-

cial targets are traceable substantially to lack of
clarity in the determination of the objectives of
the individual enterprises, both financial and
social. The determination implies also a balan-
cing of the two sets. To identify the social returns of a single enterprise and decide how far to
go in compromising its financial-returns aims is
not an easy task, as the limited experience of
developed countries shows. To formulate the most
appropriate decisions concerning enterprises in a
wide range of sectors is even more difficult; yet
the need to maintain appropriate relativities among
the enterprises belonging to different sectors is
crucial as well as complex. No wonder the majority of countries have been unable to cope with the
problem; and their public enterprises seem to operate with random and limited objectives, often gene-
rated by the managements themselves (8), or with no
publicly set objectives at all.

The further the enterprises are from the public utility and the basic industry sectors, the
greater the need for marketing skills. But in
these, most public enterprises in developing countries possess limited competence. Unsteady demand
(unlike in electricity or transport) and effective
import competition add to their difficulties; and
unforeseen consequences may occur such as demands
for excessive protectionism in the name of import
substitution.

Further, enterprises in light industry possess
a high degree of the foot-loose character, facilita-
ting errors of investment decision on non-viability
criteria, as regional and political pressures build
up in favour of the multiple, dispersed and sub-
optimal units.

To state that the foregoing problems accompany
a highly diversified sectoral spread of public enterprise is not to suggest contractions as a necessary
solution. The grounds on which the government went
into any given sector are the more important factor
to consider; the comparative advantage of an enterprise in the public sector should be the determining
consideration. (See chapter 14 for a full discussion
of this concept.) Subject to these two considera-
ions (which are the obverse of each other in ultimate analysis), the first step in policy measures on
the part of the government has to be conscious determination of the potentialities of the financial

and social returns and of the balance between the two in the case of each public enterprise. This has to be followed by effective communication, to the enterprise managements, of the objectives of performance and targets of returns expected of them. (The determinations may be easier sector-wise than enterprise-wise, though the case for the latter is distinctive. For example, an electricity enterprise in one region can have a different scale of social returns than one in another region.)

In the case of enterprises in light and small industry sectors the most fruitful approach will be to insist on operating criteria that constitute a close proxy to market forces. One of the impressive examples of this approach is provided by IRI of Italy, whose numerous subsidiaries work as if in the private sector; so does Renault in France with its multitude of subsidiaries.

Two other suggestions are relevant. The need for watchfulness as to the appropriateness of set objectives, targets and criteria, increases with time, the wider the sectoral coverage of public enterprise. In fact, the latter represents a mini version of central planning. In addition, governments in mixed economies have to keep a constant eye on shifts in comparative advantage on the part of individual public enterprises in a dynamic setting. These can be relatively common in the non-infrastructural and non-basic sectors.

(b)   The 'total' viability concept

Widely diversified public sector coverage develops in the minds of the government and the general public the vague concept of overall viability of public enterprises. This, critically speaking, has limited validity – in the arithmetic context of the finance minister being interested in budget balance in relation to the large government investments. From the same angle, an increase in the total net earning would be considered a satisfactory development. Whereas the real issue is how each enterprise, or each sector of enterprises, is faring. It is such individual viabilities that are paramount analytically. That some enterprises gain compensatorily from others, lacks validity on criteria of socio-financial viability that ought to apply to every individual public enterprise activity. It is possible that there are certain activities, which, in the government's view, need not be financially viable and which the government intends to subsidise. (That they are in the public sector is a secondary consideration. They could even be privately undertaken, with public subsidy thrown in).

Besides, the fact that some public enterprises make losses – probably through government policy – ought not to constitute an argument for extending the public enterprise sector to include gainful enterprises, so as to produce 'total viability'. Such a rationale for extension is illogical; for it is to depend essentially on grounds of comparative advantage. By the same token, if reasons exist for the denationalisation of an enterprise, the plea that it makes profits and is therefore helpful in compensating for the losses of certain other public enterprises is not, by itself, to be considered as substantial. For, inter-public enterprise subsidisations are a vehicle of disguised taxation and subsidisation. They have to be considered inferior to direct budgeting decisions touching the consumer groups concerned. An incidental merit of the latter is that, in the process, a rethinking may prompt itself on the eligibilities of the beneficiary groups; and some of the losing enterprises may be persuaded or directed to aim at a break-even, if not a profit. The 'total viability' concept blunts such desirable possibilities.

Thus, the utility of generalised comments to the effect that the government investments, on the whole, earned X per cent return, is limited to their indication of the cross-section of public enterprise performance. They can be emotive and often mask the basic anatomy of public enterprise performance. This matter is the more serious in developing countries where political conditions already subdue the tones of criticism.

(c)   'Equity' considerations

Let us examine how far wide sectoral diversifications of public enterprise in developing countries further the aims of distributional equity. Almost every development plan contains some distributional objectives; and the strategy of achieving them includes public sector initiative of one kind or another. Emphasis has recently been growing on tackling the problem of absolute poverty

114

('concentrated' among such low-income countries as
India, Bangladesh, and South Asian economies, China,
sub-Saharan Africa, and East Asia) (9). Most of
these are countries with large public enterprise
sectors. But are these so diversified as to include, adequately, activities that help in alleviating poverty - essentially in the rural areas? A
close glance at the sectoral coverage of public enterprises recorded, on a global scale, in the IMF's
Government Finance Statistics, Volume V, reveals
that, apart from small scale industry, not enough
yet falls within the field of public enterprises
as an anti-poverty instrumentality. Irrigation,
water, agricultural activity, fertiliser, village
industry, marketing, warehousing, credit, rural
electrification, seed, agricultural appliances,
dairy and poultry, are, in varying degrees, parts
of some public enterprises, no doubt; but their
efficacy is far from pronounced, according to
recent evidence collected by the World Bank (10).
Besides, these do not constitute a major segment of
public enterprise. Substantial extension of public enterprise into these areas can give rise to
several difficulties.

(1)   The unit costs of operation - in whatever terms - are bound to be high, because (i) the
average intake per customer is low, whether it be
credit or seed or electricity; (ii) the size of the
operating unit is small; (iii) the markets to be
served are scattered; (iv) risks of payments by
customers are great - e.g. in repaying loans (11);
(v) monitoring the use of the supplies made over
to the customers is difficult; and (vi) costs of
supervision of staff activities are high. Many
segments of the enterprise operations are likely
to belong to the financially non-viable category,
though their distributional validity may be quite
convincing to the government. For this to be
realised it will be helpful if the social costs
implied in the operations are quantified and made
over to the enterprises concerned through the appropriate ministry vote. Further clarification
is provided if the enterprises are broadly bifur-
cated into commercial and non-commercial segments
right below the apex level of the enterprise, and
offered a distinctive set of criteria of performance, attuned to 'equity' aims.

(2)   The problem is not simply high costs;
it has organisational aspects that force enterprises

into difficult experiments in administration. (i) In the nature of the activities, they call for almost continuous co-ordination between government budgets and enterprise operations. (ii) The end target of controlling rural poverty requires, for reasonable success, co-ordination among different departments of government even before government-enterprise co-ordination is sought. (iii) The activities are such that several layers of government have to act in satisfactory concert if the enterprises' operations in the field are to succeed. To illustrate from Indian experience, these include the central government which helps in rural electrification and agricultural finance, the state government which deals with irrigation, village industries, etc., and the local government which shoulders responsibilities of a local character. Such co-ordinations are not too easy to achieve - especially in still evolving and, in several cases, relatively over-centralised administrative systems.

(3) The problem goes beyond administrative streamlining; it gets complicated with politicking. For, the lower the hierarchic level of an activity, the greater the likelihood of local, if not petty, politics interfering with the criteria of operational excellence. In certain political systems (or circumstances) it may not be easy to exorcise such influences.

In conclusion, we may note that in the area of anti-poverty operations, the need to combine elements of private or co-operative enterprise for the sake of operational efficiency with public sector elements for the sake of overall finance and social-cost subventions, is prominent. The nature of the input and demand conditions met by many such enterprises requires emphasis on flexibility in operations and management; and several versions of joint ventures involving private, worker or consumer initiative are bound to be helpful. The character of governmental involvement may tend substantially towards public aids and budget actions, though passed through enterprises that have a nominal, constitutional public enterprise status. Governmental participation may offer organisational stability and financial strength; while private participation may offer operational flexibility. The basic aim should be to implement equity policies effectively rather than merely subserve the de jure status of the enterprises in the public sector.

NOTES

1.   As in Niger, where a UNIDO study found it 'worth mentioning' that there was 'not much interest on the part of the nationals in industrial development'.   The 'local preference' was for 'trading rather than industrial enterprise'.   (ID/WG.234/13, 1977), p.33.

2.   For instance, Julius K. Nyerere observed, with reference to Tanzania, "We have put a stop to any further large-scale exploitation of our workers and peasants through the private ownership of the means of production and exchange ... We rounded off a number of smaller measures ... by nationalising the banks, the insurance business, a number of large firms involved in the food industry, etc.'   Ujama, Essays on Socialism (Dar Es Salaam, 1968), p.163.
Somalia is another example where 'nearly all large sized industrial projects are in the public sector'.   (UNIDO, ID/WG.234/13, 1977), p.36.

3.   'Today Government owns shares, directly or indirectly, in textiles, shoes, sugar, tyres, alcohol, pharmaceuticals, canning, mining, salt, drilling paper, hotels, cement, batteries, vehicles, radios, fishing, engineering, beverages and food processing.'   Report and Recommendations of the Working Party on Government Expenditures (Nairobi, 1982), p.42.

4.   To illustrate from Kenya (covered by Appendix 3):   'Examples of unsound and poorly controlled investments can be readily be found in such areas of activity as fertiliser, sugar, textiles, and power alcohol.'   Working Party on Government Expenditures, op.cit., p.42.

5.   Describing the financial targets of nationalised industries in the UK as an 'essential governing device', Michael Posner comments, 'Alas, there has never been a time when there are agreed targets for all the industries; there are some times when there are no agreed targets for any of them; and almost at all times a good proportion of these financial targets which do exist are regarded as dead numbers by one or other side of the table.' Public Money, Vol.1, No. 2, September 1981, p.11.

6.   For the complexities of the 'contract' device in France, see Diana Green, 'Government and Industry in France: a contractual approach.' Public Money, Vol.2, No.2, September 1982.

7.   Reference may be made to one recent version of a rare policy enunciation. The Government of Syrian Arab Republic planned, in respect of its agricultural enterprises, during the fourth five-

year plan (1976-1980):   'To determine a level representing a minimum for the profit-earning capacity
of the public sector production establishments and
consider this level as a standard for all the various
efficiencies inside the establishment through which
the activity of the establishment will be assessed.'
The Fourth Five-Year Economic and Social Development
Plan in the Syrian Arab Republic 1976-1980, p.248.
        8.   Interesting illustrations are excerpted
(in Appendix 4) from the annual reports of some major
public enterprises of Thailand, indicating how un-
satisfactorily the concept of objectives manifests
itself in practice.
        9.   World Bank, World Development Report
1982, p.80.
        10.   'Instances of ineffective parastatal
organisations involved in the marketing of agricultural products and the supply of inputs abound.'
(p.50).
        There has been a 'dearth of trained and ex-
perienced manpower, which has largely drawn into other,
more buoyant sectors' in Nigeria (p.50).
        'Because of its political and economic sensi-
tivity', crop marketing - 'often the key to opening
up subsistence agriculture' - has often been a public monopoly ... Serious inefficiences have characterised the operation of many parastatal marketing
agencies ... State-owned agencies also frequently
monopolise the supply of inputs.   They often fail
to buy and distribute seed, fertiliser, and pesticides at the time farmers need them because funds
are not yet available from the national budget.'
        Regarding credit: 'small farmers find access'
to agricultural banks 'difficult and rely mostly on
informal credit sources'.
        World Bank, World Development Report 1982, pp.
74-76.
        11.   A recent illustration comes from Kenya's
Agricultural Finance Corporation's heavy bad debts
in the realm of rural financing; many borrowers are
not traceable; and the contingency of write-offs is
considerable.   Nairobi Times, 3 February 1983,
Editorial.

Chapter Eleven

THE FINANCIAL PERFORMANCE

This chapter contains a comment on the current state
of financial returns from public enterprises in developing countries and reviews the concept of financial and social returns combinations expected of
them.   We shall then refer to the growing emphasis
on improving the financial returns and consider options of policy on the acute problems of deficits.
The financial performance of public enterprises in
developing countries is, in general, poor.   Exceptions exist; but, by and large, the cross-section
comes within this description (1).   Close empirical
reviews suggest that this is not so much a function
of gestation (of the multitude of enterprises concerned) or of a temporary slump in their business
conditions as it is a consequence of such basic
handicaps as wrong investment decision (2), chronic under-utilisation (3),   low productivity (4),
managerial inefficiency compounded by governmental
interventions (5), and defective financial structures
applied to the enterprises, which have aggravated
their cash problems from time to time (6).

(a)   Financial and social returns

        Let us look at an important qualification to
our comment on the financial returns.   Admittedly,
public enterprises constitute an institutionalised
case of social returns being superior to private or
financial returns.   Hence, exclusive emphasis on
the latter is inappropriate.   (An interesting instance of deviation between the two rates is provided
for Egypt in a recent study of twenty public enterprises; in most cases the social rates of return are
found to be far larger than the financial rates.)(7)
Conceptually, different combinations of financial
returns and social returns are possible out of the

119

operations of an enterprise, as represented in the
following graph. Here the social returns are conceived of as an addition to, not inclusive of, finan
cial returns; and it is assumed that, with reference to the enterprise to which the curve applies,
increasing rates of financial return imply dimini-
shing social returns and vice versa. To think in
terms of such a curve is relevant to policy making
in the public enterprise sector, since its very
rationale in a pragmatic mixed economy stems from
the certain emergence of social returns varying -
generally inversely - with internal financial
returns.

Figure 3 : <u>Financial and social returns of</u>
<u>a public enterprise</u>

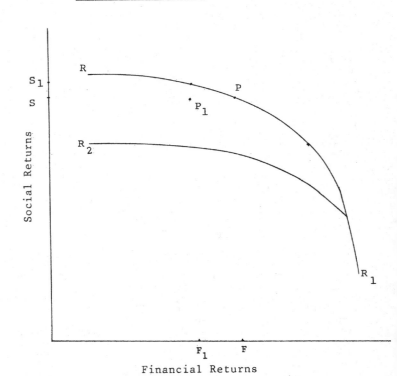

But we have problems. First, experience suggests that for the generality of public enterprises
no specific point on the curve is chosen by the policy makers and made known to the managements. The
managers, whose decisions do not consciously incorporate choices on the social returns scale, have a
residual effect on what social returns are possible
once they choose a fiancial-return target. That
they consciously choose the latter is not clear in
itself, empirically. Not knowing or being told
what net earnings to aim at - unlike, say, in the
UK, where financial targets, however imperfect,
exist - they aim at raising enough to service the
debt charges at least, or raise an indeterminate
monopoly surplus, or, as is most common, find themselves ending with some unplanned return. (The
mere fact that a formal budget is formulated at the
beginning of a year does not necessarily imply that
a conscious choice on the financial rate of return
has been made.)

The most representative situation in developing countries is that, as against F which, let us
assume, represents the break-even point, public
enterprises record a financial return of F_1. One
may assume that the social returns then jump to S_1
from S that corresponds to F. This is doubtful,
for the diminished financial returns may have arisen
from managerial inefficiences that have no automatic
yield of extra social returns. The actual co-ordi-
nates of financial and social returns may be represented by P_1, if the original assumption of S with
F is indeed correct. A typical instance is provided by Zambian public enterprises which, according
to a recent study, have 'huge accumulated losses';
and 'in social terms the picture is not different';
'in short, both the social and financial efficiency
of parastatals in Zambia is very low' (8). To cite
the example of Kenya, most public enterprises 'expected to be viable have not been profitable'; at the
same time some of them led to 'some de-Kenyanisation
of the economy, which was not the original intent'
- a case of social diseconomy (9).

Second, we do not come across many convincing
computations of social returns of individual public
enterprises that go with varying financial returns.
(Even the Egyptian calculations, cited earlier,
admittedly depend on value-judgement assumptions.)
Generalisations on the subject do little justice to
what happens to be the most relevant point, viz.,

that the combinations of social and financial returns illustrated in the preceding graph in fact
take quite diverse shapes among enterprises and
countries from time to time.   Further, they
depend on who determines the valuations concerned.

Figure 4 : <u>Financial and social returns:</u>
<u>different combinations</u>

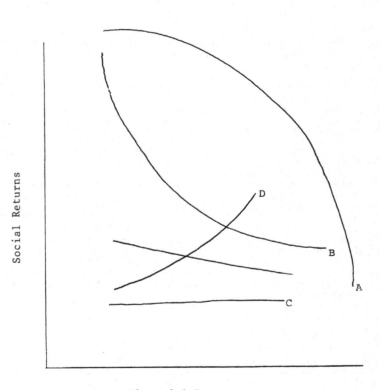

Social Returns

Financial Returns

Curve A signifies a rather low sacrifice in
social returns in the early stages of increase in
financial returns, as against a steep fall in the
former associated with small increases in financial
returns at the higher level.   Curve B signifies
just the reverse.   C implies constancy of social
returns, irrespective of the rate of financial returns; and D suggests a rise in social returns along
with a rise in financial returns - for example, where
the latter comes through price enhancements that curb
harmful or conspicuous consumption.   In fact, E may
represent the returns configuration of most public
enterprises in diverse sectors today, indicating
that the loss in social returns for an increase in
financial returns is rather small and that a gain
in the former by forgoing the latter is nominal.
So the real value of social returns as an extenua-
ting ground for low financial returns can only be
conceded if the precise configuration of the curve
relevant to a given enterprise is correctly conceived and low financial returns occur in acceptable
cases.   Unfortunately, these occur at random - in
mining, tourism, agriculture and industry in Zambia;
in sugar, meat, railways, cereals and agricultural
finance in Kenya; in heavy machines, lignite, textiles and road transport in India; in industry, development financing, and dairying in Uganda; and so
on.

Third, at this point we may introduce the time
element.   Though the curve RR_1 in the first graph
represented the original perception of social returns, the actual situation may be closer to R_2R_1 in
that the forgone financial returns of the enterprise
are not accompanied by perceptible social benefits.
This may be illustrated by electricity prices in
developing countries.   Low prices which might have
been justified at one time on grounds of assisting
agriculture or small industry may today be reaching
consumer groups that are established enough to bear
far higher prices.   In fact, the R_2R_1 type of returns combination may merit being considered anti-
social, in that it subsidises non-needy beneficiaries, while the enterprise forgoes financial returns (10).

Fourth, the time seems to have come when developing countries should sharpen their focus on the
financial returns of public enterprises, even assuming that a given perception of social returns is
valid.   There are several reasons.

123

(i)   Except in the few cases where a public
enterprise is a technically superior agency for the
realisation of the social returns, the government
can decide to implement the social policies concerned through budget measures.   It can insist on
sizeable financial returns at the enterprise level
and judiciously syphon a part of those to the public exchequer.

(ii)   The social returns an enterprise yields
by   forgoing its financial returns accrue to specific
groups limited to its own consumers and input sup-
pliers.   Whether, on macro grounds of equity, they
are the most deserving of the benefits, is important
for governments to consider.   In most countries,
they are now concerned about alleviating the lot of
the rural poor; whereas large groups of public enterprise beneficiaries are urban.   Governments' resources being relatively limited, there will be great
substance in adopting a policy of encouraging public enterprises to improve their financial returns
and increase their contributions to the public exchequer pool, from which the preferred public decisions on social-benefit conferments can be financed.
This is far from being an argument against social
returns as an aim; it implies an optimal strategy
of resource use in promoting social returns.

(iii)   The sheer constraints experienced by
the public exchequer in many developing countries,
partly on account of public enterprises themselves,
make it imperative to aim at far higher financial
returns from public enterprise operations than have
hitherto been realised.   Details of this argument
will be found in Chapter 13.

Fifth, experience has shown that the conceptual validity of social returns offsetting low financial returns has limits in practice.   Where the
national economy is constrained to effect compromises
with equity policies in favour of growth policies,
public enterprises should themselves be brought
within the impact of such compromises.   This makes
for compatability between budget policies and enterprise operations.   Today several developing countries are found to curtail expenditures on housing
as against productive factories, curb wage enhancements, marketise social services and withdraw subsidies to consumption.   Such policies should have
a lesson for public enterprises, viz.,that they
should lay stress on financial returns.

It is worth noting that in many developing countries governments have begun to be concerned with the problem of public enterprise losses or poor returns. The recent observations by the Working Party on Government Expenditures, followed by the President's pronouncements in Kenya, illustrate the shift of policies towards financial improvement in public enterprise performance (11). The present government of Sri Lanka nearly obliges public enterprises to make profits or face liquidation. Egypt has recently offered, through Open Door Policy, superior conditions of pricing autonomy to public enterprises. Algeria is 'greatly disturbed by the overall performance of public enterprises' and remedial measures are being designed (12). And indirect measures of de facto emphasis on financial returns are clearly traceable to the encouragement of joint ventures between public enterprises and others in countries like Ethiopia, where the admission of foreign capital up to 49 per cent has recently been announced.

(b) Policy options on deficits

To revert to the main point, public enterprises in developing countries, as a cross-section, are characterised by heavy accumulated deficits. In several cases there is a continuing prospect of deficits. It will be purposeful to examine the policy options open to governments in such a situation.

A. Accumulated deficits

First, as to the accumulated deficits. While conceiving of public policy measures, the anatomy of the deficit figures merits scrutiny.

To the extent of deficits that are a normal sequel to operations during gestation (i.e. within break-even or full utilisation - assuming that this will be possible in the foreseeable future), no public action is needed. The hope is that, as the enterprise nears full utilisation, it will have the opportunity of compensating itself for the past losses. This happens to be normal in business.

It is the rest of the deficits that call for specific public policy responses. An apparently simple option consists of inducing the enterprise to economise on costs and/or raise prices so as to earn a net revenue which, over a few years, will erase the accumulated deficits. This turns out to be quite complex in practice. For, the demand conditions may be such that at no point of higher price will large enough net revenues accrue. Or, the high levels of prices that can do the trick may not seem permissible to the government on its own macro criteria. Possible economies through changes in product-mix, such as pruning postal services in remote areas or curtailing rural electrification, may not appeal to the government on social grounds. A more fundamental question arises too: will it be legitimate to shift to the consumers the burden of the high costs that led to the deficits, irrespective of the causes of the high costs? The causes may have ranged over national gestation, wrong investment decision, and inefficient management. (The question will be pursued further when we come to continuing deficits.)

The accumulated deficits represent loss of capital and are quite substantial in several developing countries. Three instances may be cited. The oldest and largest of Uganda's public enterprises, the Uganda Development Corporation, had an accumulated deficit of 128 million Uganda shillings, as compared with its total share capital of 159 million shillings, by the end of 1977. (It was 90 per cent of the value of its fixed assets.) (13) Some data from India, presented in Table 4, indicate how high the accumulated deficits have been as a percentage of paid-up capital.

Similar data relating to Pakistan are presented in Table 5, to illustrate losses of capital in public enterprise.

Whatever the explanation, significant losses of capital have occurred in many public enterprises in developing countries. It will be not only fruitless but positively frustrating to the managements to have these carried over in the balance sheets from year to year. It will be commendable to write them off.

In doing so, the government may have to introduce cash where the deficit figure exceeds its capital outlay; or else the deficit has to be partially financed by creditors on a continuous basis. And the enterprise may be vulnerable to court action by creditors.

126

Table 4

Accumulated deficits of selected Indian public enterprises (1981-82)

Enterprise (1)	Deficit as % of equity (2)
Indian Firebricks & Insulation Co. Ltd.	279
Bharat Coking Coal	191
Heavy Engineering Corporation Ltd.	170
Jessop Co. Ltd.	211
Mining & Allied Machinery Corp. Ltd.	240
Triveni Structurals Ltd.	156
Biecco Lawrie Ltd.	627
National Instruments Ltd.	667
Central Inland Water Transport Corp. Ltd.	353
Garden Reach Shipbuilders & Engineers Ltd.	123
Scooters India Ltd.	604
Bharat Ophthalmic Glass Ltd.	259
Rehabilitation Industries Corp. Ltd.	627
Tannery & Footwear Corp. of India Ltd.	222
Banana & Fruit Development Corp. Ltd.	269
National Textile Corp. (Delhi etc.) Ltd.	173
NTC (Maharashtra North) Ltd.	116
NTC (Maharashtra South) Ltd.	120
NTC (UP) Ltd.	228
NTC (W.Bengal etc.) Ltd.	242
Elgin Mills Ltd.	317
Cotton Corp. of India Ltd.	269
Jute Corp. of India Ltd.	1297
Hindustan Prefab Ltd.	129
Hindustan Steel Works Construction Ltd.	251
Engineering Projects (I) Ltd.	719

Source: Bureau of Public Enterprises, Public Enterprise Survey 1981-82, Vol.3 (New Delhi, 1983).

Table 5

Accumulated deficits of selected public enterprises in Pakistan (1980-81)

Enterprise (1)	Deficit as % of equity (2)
Antibiotics Pr. Ltd.	363
Kurram Chemical Co. Ltd.	196
Pakdyes & Chemical Co. Ltd.	134
Pakistan PVC Ltd.	360
Ravi Rayon Ltd.	100
Ravi Engineering	495
National Fertilizer Marketing Ltd.	472
Bannu Sugar Mills	1067
Utility Stores Corp.	167
Printing Corp. of Pakistan	264

Source: Government Sponsored Corporations 1981-82 (Islamabad, 1982)

The story does not end there.   Several of the enterprises, caught up in this situation, lack working capital, without which, while the balance sheet looks clean, current production activities are bound to be constrained.   Frequent short-term borrowing at expensive rates of interest will become necessary. It is likely that funds will be available only in inadequate amounts, leading to curtailed operations and under-utilisation.   Once again, the forces making deficit will be in motion.

Finally, these enterprises may have no cash flow from depreciation for replacement of fixed assets. So they need a fresh injection of cash (capital) - not for additions to capacity, but to prevent the enterprise from being unable to produce on the original scale.

All this may look alarming, but there is no choice.   The only nominal option open to the government is that in respect of working capital it may try to induce the banking system to help.   It may turn out, however, that the (willing) banking sector is itself a public sector agency in ultimate analysis, and the government may be obliged to guarantee the loans.

The problem, as presented above, is beginning to be realised by governments today. However unpleasant, the write-offs and capital reconstructions are necessary, in spite of the following difficulties:

(i) The first reaction of governments can be that the write-off does not lift the debt off the public exchequer's shoulders and that the budget continues to carry the costs of debt-servicing.

(ii) Governments find their own cash position heavily constrained and their borrowing ability is ceiled by considerations of expensiveness or, at the extreme, by IMF advice or conditions which, in reality, reflect the government's own desire to achieve economic stabilisation.

(iii) It may be difficult for governments to go to Parliament with a measure that amounts to open admission of the failure of colossal investments in public enterprises.

These may serve as explanations for inaction, but do not justify it. What has been happening is that, in the absence of bold action on logical lines, the enterprises are put to the discomfiture of presenting continued red in the bottom line. Everyone knows it for a fiction that they have a heavy capitalisation to aim at remunerating. Governments know that they will be forced from time to time to make cash transfers under some designation – grant, loan, or open subsidy – in an ad hoc manner. There prevails no system among enterprises or even among different points of time with regard to a given enterprise, in dealing with the problem. Public enterprises constitute a continuous butt of political ridicule, overt or covert.

B. Continuing deficits

We shall next consider continuing deficits. On the assumption that the problem of accumulated deficits has been properly dealt with, continuing

129

deficits imply that, in spite of the relief that
capital write-off gives, the enterprise is unable
to operate with a net revenue.   In this situation
one must analyse the precise causes of the deficits
so that the right option of policy may be chosen.
To suit our analysis, these may be grouped under
four heads: (i) costs of national gestation (14),
which have an almost permanent impact on the cost
structure; (ii) costs of poor investment decision
from which flow consequences of excessive fixed
costs as well as revenue expenditures; (iii) inefficient management ranging over all areas of operations - production, marketing, finance, industrial relations, etc.; and (iv) uneconomic prices.
(High cost social obligations assigned to the
enterprise are covered under (iv), in that prices
are now allowed to be high enough to recover all
costs incurred.   In some cases there may be no
demand at the high prices needed.)

All options in dealing with the problem of
continuing deficits centre on a choice between the
consumers concerned and the   taxpayer in general
for financing the deficits.   The choice is not
easy.

(i)   <u>National gestation</u>: Take the case of
the costs of national gestation.   It is helpful to
distinguish between costs specific to an industry
and costs that are in the nature of overheads in
respect of a wider spectrum of industry.   There is
some justification in the former being passed on to
the consumers concerned, whereas the latter, assuming
that they can be distinguished and identified, may
be passed on to the government budget.   The consumers will be relieved of them in their contributions
towards the costs of outputs taken by them from a
given enterprise.   Where industry A carries costs of
national gestation the like of which industry B does
not, just because it comes later on the established
heels of A, it is doubtful if the consumers of A
should be exclusively obliged to bear the burden of
these costs.   These, in a sense, are overheads in
the development of industry far beyond A.   So a
mechanism has to be designed for transferring part
of these costs to the government budget.

We may refer to specific (and common) instances
of national development costs incurred through the
medium of public enterprise, viz., technology development and indigenisation of imported technology, re-

search and development of a basic character, and technological training on a large scale. It may be estimated as economical for the country to implement these through a given enterprise, though the extent and scale of the activities are clearly beyond the input needs of that enterprise. The solution in this case may take one of two forms. The government may make a payment to the enterprise that roughly equals the costs incurred by it, implicitly, for purposes and benefits that lie beyond its own domain (15). This can be treated as a contractual function undertaken at government instance. The problem remains, of course, of satisfactory computation of the payment. Alternatively, the function concerned may be disintegrated, if technically feasible, and entrusted to a separate organisation which can implement it on its own merits of scale and feasibility. In this case the enterprise makes a payment for that part of the organisation's output that it (the enterprise) takes.

An arrangement on the lines of activity disintegration was considered, though not implemented, in India in respect of the townships that several public enterprises have been building and maintaining. (Not many private enterprises undertake such activity.) The idea was to establish a separate organisation to take charge of the townships, relieving individual enterprises of the task and costs of maintaining them. Whatever subsidy was necessary on grounds of public enterprises being 'model employers' could then be implemented through that single organisation.

(ii) Investment decision: The costs of poor investment decision are somewhat different in cause from the costs of national gestation. These are costs that could have been avoided but were sustained either at government instance or through inefficiency at the board level. Experience suggests that the former has been the more common reason, for almost all original decisions on capital investment in public enterprises have been taken by governments in developing countries. Even subsequent expansion decisions have been largely under government influence, even if non-political. (The inevitable nature of diseconomy in such decisions has been discussed earlier.) The policy option in this case is fairly simple: the consumers should be spared the burden of costs of wrong investment — e.g. excess capacities, inefficient technology, uneconomical location and inappropriate product mix. Of each one of these we

have examples in the history of public enterprises
in developing countries. If a public enterprise
operates under conditions of competition, its rivals,
free from these 'excessive' costs, force it to operate at prices below the level of cost-recovery.
Where it enjoys monopoly – and this is quite a usual
case – the temptation to oblige the consumers to pay
towards such costs gains currency, the more casually
the less efficient the system of monopoly control.
The right policy measure consists of transferring
these costs to the government budget (16).

(iii) <u>Managerial inefficiency</u>: The policy options on managerial inefficiency as a cause of high
costs may be simply presented: improve the management; supersede the managers; or, as a last resort,
liquidate the enterprise or privatise it. The last
option sounds drastic but not too unrealistic of
late, as current thinking in countries like Sri Lanka,
Kenya and Pakistan illustrates. Besides, a great
deal of privatisation has crept into the public sector through the mechanism of joint ventures in many
countries. In any case, it would be ironical if
unrectified managerial inefficiencies should continuously oblige the consumers to pay high prices or
necessitate budgetary subventions to wipe off the
deficits. Unfortunately, both these tendencies
are too common today. Many public enterprise managements remain either technically inadequate or vulnerable to external forces that inhibit managerial
efficiency. Even where, rightly, the costs of inefficiency are not totally passed on to the consumers
(17), the unrequited costs stay in the books as a
deficit; what ought to happen, rather, is a manga-
gerial rationalisation.

(iv) <u>Pricing</u>: We now turn to the toughest
area of policy decision, viz., pricing. Here we come
across not only conflicting pressures but invalid
assumptions as well. An instance of the latter
is where a public enterprise makes a plea for equity
capital rather than loans from the government on
the assumption that, as no interest payments are
obligatory on equity, the costs to be recovered
prove lighter and the bottom line may not look
red. The fact is that, when all costs of capital
are considered, there may be a deficit. Equity
may be set aside as a fictitious option, though
it undeniably offers an oft-needed convenience in
cash-flow.

The more important forces are the substantive ones. On the one hand most public enterprises contend that their prices are frozen at uneconomic levels; and even monopolies like electricity may be making deficits. Given their way, they can raise surpluses by appropriately proportioning price enhancements to the target of surplus. Several expert reviews and international agencies' findings broadly confirm that uneconomic prices are a major cause of public enterprise's continuing deficits in many countries.

While conceding this to be basically true, one has to start with a major qualification to the policy option of raising prices (18). This derives from the preceding argument. Not all deficit-causing prices are uneconomic. Raising them, unexceptionally, so as to wipe out deficits does not necessarily represent a sound policy. In respect of costs that the consumers ought not to be required to shoulder, price rises are intrinsically objectionable. How to separate these costs is a difficult technical problem, but the principle and direction of policy should be clear.

It is difficult to generalise on what proportion of deficit-making public enterprises can benefit through price enhancements after full weight is given to this qualification. In theory, if the right options of policy suggested above are adopted in respect of the cost excesses under different heads, the residual cause of continuing deficits is then the price level. But at this point of the argument, the policy decisions of governments are clouded by the concept of social returns, which tend to be forfeited variously at different levels of surplus-raising prices. The concept is incontrovertible, but the caveats enunciated earlier in this chapter should be recalled, so that (a) the social returns are real; (b) price suppression below the economic levels is consciously undertaken, and (c) the financial consequences are borne by the government budget. Such a compensation device is all too familiar today and even finds a place in certain statutes (19); but it is neither put to expert computation nor adequately, if at all, acted upon by governments. One reason why they let deficits remain in the books of the enterprise without being duly met by subsidies is that they have no money to offer. Ultimately, however, the enterprise will accumulate a deficit big enough to warrant a capital write-off.   Truly, governments are losing bits of capital all the time.

At this point reference may be made to the World Bank's presentation of an inverse relationship between price distortions and growth rates in 31 developing countries in the 1970s (20).   The data found in Table 6.1 of the Report are shown graphically in Appendix 6.   The simple group averages of price distortion indices and annual GDP growth rates (per cent) are 1.95 and 6.8 respectively for the ten 'low' distortion countries, 1.95 and 5.7 for the nine 'medium' distortion countries, and 2.44 and 3.1 for the twelve 'high' distortion countries.   The spread of data as well as the line connecting the group averages in the graph illustrates the association between high price distortions and low growth rates and vice versa.   True, other factors than price distortions were also at work.

This empirical finding has relevance to our discussion on two grounds.   First, though price distortions characterise the economy as a whole, the share of public enterprises in causing or implementing them is relatively high in developing countries, since they offer themselves as ready instruments of government interference with the price mechanism.   Second, public enterprises have been the recipients of relatively large proportions of capital expenditures in transport and communications, mining, manufacturing, energy and finance in recent years.   Thus, price policies concerning public enterprises tend to have a fundamental effect on growth through the price-distortion route.

Jamaica, Bangladesh, Ghana, Ethiopia and India, which illustrate the association of relatively high price distortion indices with relatively low growth rates, are all heavily public-enterprise oriented economies.

We may conclude this chapter by observing that the price option, however difficult politically, is overdue in most developing-country public enterprises.

To recapitulate: first, establish the costs recoverable through prices; second, establish the prices intended to bear elements of subsidy to be derived from the government; and third, raise the other prices to 'economic' levels, given publicly accepted targets of net revenue or savings.   Not to

adopt this kind of approach will only aggravate losses of capital and provoke – not the pleasantest –
IMF or World Bank strictures or conditions.   It is
surely the latter that have proved persuasive in
several cases (21), though these are strictly implicit, in most cases, in the national instruments
governing the operations of the enterprises concerned.

NOTES

1.   The following excerpts from recent stu-
dies relating to different countries support the
inference:
From the International Workshop on Financial
Profitability and Losses in Public Enterprises,
ICPE, Ljubljana, 1981:

> Bangladesh: 'The overall financial picture
> of the public enterprises... shows substan-
> tial negative returns.' (p.23)

> Somalia: 'The production enterprises run at
> a heavy loss.' (p.24)

> Tanzania: 'The majority of the public enter-
> prises are being run at heavy losses.' (p.24)

> Algeria: 'The general picture of the finan-
> cial situation of the Algerian public enter-
> prises was one of losses.' (p.24)

> Sri Lanka: 'A majority of public enterprises
> were making heavy financial losses.' (p.25)

> Thailand: Though 'on an aggregate basis' pub-
> lic enterprises make profits, 'the size of
> the profit has been decreasing for the last
> few years.' (p.25)

> Tunisia: 'In certain sectors such as mining,
> textiles and transportation, the enterprises
> are suffering financial losses.' (p.26)

> Jamaica: 'By and large the public enterprises
> are being run at substantial losses.' (p.26)

Zia V. Ahmed (Ed.) <u>Financial Profitability and Losses
in Public Enterprises of Developing Countries</u>,
(Ljubljana, 1982)

Indonesia: Subsidies to public enterprises rose from Rp. 1.368 billion in 1978 to Rp. 4.553 billion in 1981 (M. Siswohardjono, 'Government policy to overcome losses in public enterprises' – the same Workshop).

Zambia: Parastatal performance was negative in terms of net profit in mining, tourism, agriculture and miscellaneous industry, and also, on the whole, in 1978. (Third National Development Plan, Lusaka) p.416.

Sudan: 'The financial performance of the public sector enterprises registered deterioration' (over 1970/75). 'The past record of financial performance of public enterprises clearly indicates that their net contribution to domestic capital formation has been minimal.' The Six Year Plan of Economic and Social Development 1977/78-1982/83, Vol. 1 (Khartoum, 1977) pp.13 and 68.

Mexico: Public enterprises, excluding State Petroleum Company, showed a net loss of 1.2 per cent of GDP in 1980.

Senegal: Public enterprises recorded a deficit in 1977-78 and again in 1979-80.

In a sample of 27 developing countries in 1976-79, current subsidy and other transfers from government to nonfinancial public enterprises represented 1.4 per cent of GDP.

World Development Report 1983 (Washington, 1983), p.74.

2. For example, in Pakistan. T.Z. Farooqi, 'Financial Profitability and Losses in Public Enterprises: Pakistani Experience', op.cit. pp.136-139.
3. For example, in Tanzania, op.cit. p.24.
4. For example, in Somalia, op.cit. p.24.
5. One of the most revealing accounts of public enterprise problems comes from a recent 'high level Seminar' held under the Chairmanship of Chairman Mengistu Hailemariam of Ethiopia in 1979. This is shown in Appendix 5.
6. For instance, the capital structure of Algerian public enterprises has been almost exclusively loan-oriented, entailing heavy debt-servicing costs. Financial Profitability and Losses in

Public Enterprises, op.cit. p.25.

7.   Heba Ahmad Handoussa, 'The impact of economic liberalisation on the performance of Egypt's public sector industry', Second BAPEG Conference on 'Public Enterprise of Mixed Economy LDCs', Boston, 1980, p.21.

8.   The Zambia National Report on the Role of the Public Sector in Developing Countries, ICPE, Ljubljana, 1982, pp.40, 42.

9.   Working Party on Government Expenditures, Report and Recommendations of the Working Party (Nairobi, 1982) pp.40-41.

A similar message is implied in the comment made by Chairman Mengistu Hailemariam of Ethiopia that, 'following the government take-over the farms seemed to have turned into a consumption of available assets instead of producing income'. Ethiopian Herald, 18 March 1979, Addis Ababa. As cited in J. Kinfu, in his paper at the Workshop on the Role of Public Enterprises in Development in Eastern Africa, Nairobi, 1980.

10.   For instance, energy and food subsidies in Egypt in 1979 reached 'the relatively more affluent urban areas and 62 per cent of these went to the richer half of the urban population'. World Development Report 1983 (Washington, 1983) p.76.

11.   Working Party on Government Expenditures (Nairobi, 1982), Chapter V. President Daniel T.arap Moi, Kenyatta Day: Message to the Nation (Nairobi, 1982) 'I am ... convinced that a number of these public enterprises could be made more productive and more profitable in the hands of private Kenyans as owners and managers.' (p.20)

12.   Financial Profitability and Losses in Public Enterprises in Developing Countries, op.cit. p.25.

13.   The Role of Public Enterprise in Development in Eastern Africa, op.cit. (Nairobi, 1980), p.111.

14.   As described in Chapter 7.

15.   One recent version of governmental financing of technology development is available from Japanese experience. Companies working on a new technology can get a 50 per cent subsidy from the government, under certain conditions (Time, 21 April 1980, p.52).

16.   An interesting and recent instance may be cited from the working of the British Steel Corporation. The non-closure of the integrated plant at Ravenscraig has been an 'extremely costly political' decision whose costs, the Industry and Trade Committee recommended, 'should be borne directly by the

Government'.   Second Report from the Industry and
Trade Committee (Session 1982-83) <u>The British Steel
Corporation's Prospects</u> (London, HMSO, 1983), p.xvii.
        17.   An example may be cited of cement pricing
in Sudan on the basis, not of actual capacity used,
but of a larger norm, though not equal to total
capacity.   'Price Policy in Public Enterprises in
Sudan', by Babiken El Fadil Hasan, Workshop on
Pricing Policies in Public Enterprises, ICPE,
Ljubljana, 1980.
        18.   For example, under conditions of heavy
costs of national gestation, investment mistakes
and managerial inefficiency.
        19.   Two examples may be cited from Kenya.
Section 11(3) of the Agricultural Development Corporation Act, 1965, reads as follows: 'If the Minister after consultation with the Minister for the
time being responsible for finance, instructs the
Corporation to initiate, assist or expand any undertaking which it considers economically or otherwise
unsound, the Corporation shall not be required to
proceed with such initiation, assistance or expansion until the Government has undertaken to reim-
burse the Corporation with any losses incurred
thereby.'
        Section 8 of the Kenya Tourist Development
Corporation Act provides: 'The Minister may ...
give directions ... in relation to matters which
appear to him to affect the public interest, and
the Corporation shall give effect to any such
directions:
        Provided that the Corporation shall not be
required to give effect to any direction of the Minister which, if given effect to, would oblige the
Corporation to engage in any activity or undertaking
which the Corporation considers to be unsound,
whether economically or otherwise, unless that direction states that the Government has undertaken to
pay the amount of any loss incurred by the Corporation by reason of giving effect to that direction.'
        20.   <u>World Development Report 1983</u> (Washington,
1983), pp.60-61.
        21.   A recent observation by Maurice Garner
on Thailand illustrates the point: 'Not having itself set the enterprises objectives, the Government
sometimes finds that it is called upon to accept
for the enterprise objectives set by others, notably
by the World Bank and other overseas financial institutions.'   These 'may also serve to protect the
enterprises from governmental pressures for uneco-
mic prices or other unbusinesslike practices.'

Financial Performance

'Public Enterprise in Thailand', a paper presented at the Semianr on Public Enterprise and the Developing World, London Business School, 10 March 1983.

Chapter Twelve

THE REAL COSTS OF PUBLIC ENTERPRISE

Let us pick up for purposeful annotation a major
point of the previous chapter, namely, that the
current state of financial performance of the
cross-section of public enterprises in developing
countries is poor.   The position is, in fact,
worse than what it appears to be from their annual
accounts.   The real costs are far higher than the
costs found in their books of account - a point
that merits notice in a dispassionate appraisal of
the socio-economic comparative advantage of public
enterprises.

        The reasons for this suggestion may be pre-
sented under two heads (a) economics of accounting;
and (b) shadow pricing.   (The implications for
the public exchequer will be considered in chapter
13.)

(a)   Economics of accounting

        The circumstances of capital procurement by
public enterprises - mainly from government sources
- and the accounting practices adopted by them tend
to understate the real costs of capital below the
full, opportunity costs of the resources employed.
It is useful to establish the latter at least in
notional terms so that proper decisions may be
reached on investment, pricing and subsidies and
so that meaningful evaluations of comparative
advantage of a given enterprise may be made.   The
major sources of the problem are outlined below.

        (i)   Some public enterprises receive 'grants'
from the government, without obligation to pay interest on the amounts or to repay the principal in due
course.   There is a place for grants, no doubt,

provided the decision to offer funds under that head corresponds to a governmental determination that the operations or outputs facilitated by them are subsidisable (to a corresponding extent) and that funds from any other – interest-seeking – source are not available within the constraint of prices that the government imposes on the relevant outputs.   Two points need notice, however.   First, even under this logic it is undeniable that there exists a real cost, though it does not rank as a recoverable cost in the accounts.   Second, it is far from certain that in every case the grants accurately reflect conscious quantification of the subsidisability of the concerned outputs.   Further, it is doubtful that the elements of the subsidisability remain constant over time; yet the cost suppression, owing to the grants device, does.

(ii)   The cross-section of public enterprises has derived loans from governments (or under government guarantee) at rates of interest far lower than the market rates; quite often there is a moratorium on interest payment and, in some cases, the loans are interest free.   The costs of loan capital appearing in accounts are bound to be lower than the real costs in all these cases.   Even where substantive justification exists for relatively low prices in the case of certain outputs, it is doubtful if the loan-interest device is an appropriate policy. It seems to have been applied so indiscriminately to all kinds of public enterprises that one can suspect that the most obvious reason for the practice is simply that the government is the source of funds.   (A healthy movement of interest rates on government loans towards the market rates is visible today in some countries.)

(iii) Interest accrued but not paid may be shown as a creditor item in the accounts – assuming that it is provided for; however, provisions may not be made in subsequent years for the interest that accumulates on the credit-obligation.   (The accounting treatment would be different if interest accrued were capitalised.)

(iv) A substantial segment of the equity component of the capitalisation of public enterprises has functioned as if it were a costless resource. For it has not been rewarded with dividends in most cases.   Not that the cost of such capital has been earned by the enterprises, though they have not passed on the earnings as dividends; in numerous cases of non-payment of dividend the enterprises have usually not been earning enough to meet the cost of equity. In fact, the managements have, on occasions, put forward claims for equity or for conversion of loans into equity so as to be free from the obligation to earn enough to service the capital. The equity device is not without a case in public enterprise, but it should not simply constitute a channel of cost suppression over long periods of time (1).

(v) The deficits of public enterprise covered by subsidies from the government leave no trace as a past cost in the accounts. True, past deficits are not to be treated as an element of current costs, except for items which ought to have been treated as deferred revenue expenditures whose utility is currently realised. But in an appraisal of what a public enterprise has cost the nation up to date, account has to be taken of the deficits already written off. This calls for research into past accounts.

(vi) There is no legal obligation to compute the cost of internal resources (such as reserves) used in business; and this may get overlooked as a recoverable cost in enterprises whose viability is of a poor order.

(vii) Practices in respect of depreciation vary widely among enterprises - even in developed countries (2); and the cost impacts tend to be suppressed when depreciation provisions are not based on replacement costs (3).

(viii) It is possible that the accounts do not reflect the full weight of obsolescence, the more so in enterprises which are deficit-making and have technologies that are subject to rapid change.

(ix) Special mention may be made of the provisions for bad debts in the case of enterprises engaged in financial rural credit and small industry. The real size of non-recoveries may be far higher than the book figure.

Besides, there may be cases where a government department may be rendering services for an enterprise without recovering from it the full costs in-

143

volved (4). (Governmental expenditures - e.g.on travel - in connection with arrangements of foreign collaboration or buying major equipment such as aircraft for public enterprises are a common example.)

(b)   Shadow pricing

In most developing countries the cost one has to attach, conceptually, to the use of capital is higher than is represented by the interest rates entering the enterprise accounts. Public enterprises call for particular attention for various reasons.

(i)   By and large their capital intensities have been high.

(ii)   Their draft on foreign capital has been relatively substantial (5).

(iii)   Mistakes in capital expenditure strategy have been so numerous that the actual capital employed per unit of output has been 'excessive'.

(iv)   The ease of getting funds has diluted caution in investment planning.

This is how, in general, the cross-section of public enterprises has been marked by relatively high real costs of capital which, however, are not reflected in their accounts. Prices based on the apparent costs tend to be artificially low. They illustrate the price distortions prevalent in developing countries - a point raised in the previous chapter.

To sum up. Proper measures of policy in dealing with the problem ought to commence with an accurate quantification of the full costs involved in the operations of individual public enterprises. This is not easy in many developing countries. For, the required techniques of establishing the costs with reasonable reliability are not readily or adequately available. More importantly, the will to let such computations take place is doubtful. It is the politicians and governments that have to take the decisions to encourage the task; but they tend to be over-defensive in their attitudes to public enterprise matters and may even consider such quantifications as an avoidable means of self-exposure.

The Real Costs of Public Enterprise

The real costs of capital are a major factor in the cost problems of public enterprises in developing countries. Hence, no amount of attention to conservation in the use of capital will ever be too much. While care can be taken as regards future investments, the existing ones can be economised through meticulous attempts at output expansions faster than capital additions, substitution of less scarce factors for capital and physical retrenchments, wherever possible, in equipment.

The basic question is whether governments are keen on finding out if a given public enterprise possesses a comparative advantage over any other form of organisation at a given point of time. If they are not, measures aimed at establishing and minimising real costs are unlikely to go deep enough.

NOTES

1. For a full discussion and empirical evidence, see V.V. Ramanadham, Capital Structures of Public Enterprises, The Fifth Shoaib Memorial Lecture, Pakistan, November 1983.

2. Vide the accounting practices in nationalised industries in the UK prior to the recent adoption of the current cost accounting guidelines of the Nationalised Industries Chairmen's Group. Even the financial targets fixed by the Government rest on CCA assets in some cases and on historic cost assets in others. Also see Andrew Likierman, 'Nationalised Industries: accounting for inflation' Public Money, December 1981.

3. It is true that, if a revaluation of assets is carried out, the enterprise ends up with a capital profit or reserve. But this has an implication for the new cost base for pricing. It goes up as well in order that the current costs of the increased capitalisation are met.

4. For example, the Ministry of Livestock Development in Kenya incurs certain expenses in buying cattle for the Kenya Meat Commission but does not pass these on to the enterprise.

5. For instance, nonfinancial public enterprises accounted for 28 per cent of all Eurocurrency borrowed by developing countries in 1980, according to World Development Report 1983 (Washington, 1983), p.74.

Chapter Thirteen

THE IMPACT ON THE PUBLIC EXCHEQUER

The view has been gradually gaining ground in developing countries that the financial circumstances of public enterprises constitute a part of the total problem of public finance, rather than being mere problems of individual enterprises. Both the size of deficits and their wide spread over the cross-section of enterprises seem to have added momentum to this somewhat overdue viewpoint; and governments are eager to insist on changes in their operating criteria such that the impacts on the public exchequer may be lightened.

In this chapter we shall analyse the way in which the poor financial performance of public enterprises have consequences for the public exchequer. We shall note, with some statistical evidence, that the bias towards public investments is extensive in developing countries and that we encounter a paradoxical situation in which the need for gainful performance of public enterprises is as acute as it is low.

(a)   Effects on taxation

Continuing deficits of public enterprises have the almost automatic consequence of making unavailable to the government the expected interest and dividend receipts. The government will have to devise ways of bridging the budget gap – through taxation, primarily. What the consumers of given enterprises do not pay is thus transferred to the shoulders of the general taxpayer.

The following is a graphic presentation of the situation.

Figure 5 : Impact of public enterprise on taxation

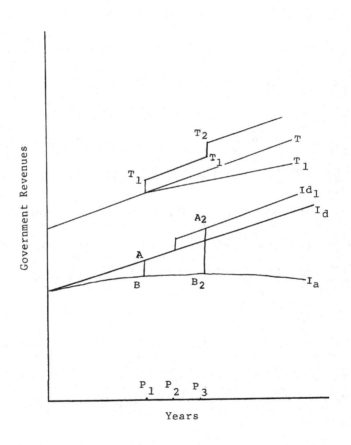

Impact on Public Exchequer

Assume that the interest and dividend incomes expected of public enterprises are represented by Id. The upward slope of the curve is a function of two factors: increased investments over time and profit expectations at increasing rates. Assume also that the government has a strategy of general taxation as represented by the curve T, so as to achieve budgetary balance or control a budget deficit, given the Id returns from public enterprises.

As the actual receipts from the enterprises fall short of Id and run along Ia, the government may have to raise tax revenues so as to maintain its budget strategy – from T to T_1 at some point in time, say P_1. This is how it tries to make up for the shortfall in public enterprise payments as represented by BA. If the deficits continue on a larger scale as investments expand over time, and/or if the government treats any of its cash transfers (to meet enterprise deficits) as advances involving additional interest obligations, the Id curve rises to Id_1, say, from time P_2. Assume that Ia remains constant. The gap in public enterprise payments to the public exchequer widens to B_2A_2; and the need for raising taxes arises all over again, say, at time P_3 from T_1 to T_2. And this chain of events continues.

Another version of the tax consequences of underpayments by public enterprises to the public exchequer may be presented as follows. Assume that, corresponding to the profit expectations implicit in curve Id, the government plans on a level of taxation at a slightly declining rate as time goes on, as represented by curve Tr from, say, time P_1. That cannot be implemented. In other words, the prospects of relief to taxpayers are impeded. This can have unfavourable repercussions on the growth of the economy.

Another impact is probable if the government adopts the write-off option commended in the preceding chapter. This unfolds itself in three stages. First, the curve Id has to be re-written, reduced for the returns no longer possible from the capital written off, though the government continues to bear the burden of the debt-servicing charge. Second, new borrowings may be raised by the government in providing cash to wipe out heavy deficits. Third, new borrowings again will be necessary for providing new working capital or, in quick steps, replacement capital. While the second and third factors may raise Id somewhat, the first is almost certain to compel the government to look to an improvement, not in Id, but in curve T. That is, general taxation has to rise, since the enterprises do not pay towards the interest charges on capital written off.

At this point some empiricism may be introduced to suggest that most governments of developing countries cannot afford to let budget deficits continuously widen (1), nor do they find it easy to raise tax revenues.

IMF data on budget deficits (or surpluses) as per cent of total central government expenditure and lending minus repayments during the recent years (1980 or earlier in some cases) indicate that, of the low-income countries and the middle-income (lower) countries, half or more have budget deficits exceeding 15 per cent; whereas the middle-income (upper) countries and the high-income countries have at least half of them coming within the 15 per cent and 10 per cent ranges respectively. Seven out of the ten most seriously placed countries belong to the low-income and middle-income (lower) categories.

It is interesting to find in the above-30 per cent group many countries with large public enterprise sectors, e.g. Somalia, India, Sri Lanka, Ghana, Zambia, Jamaica, Lesotho and Zaire. The 20-30 per cent group also includes many such: e.g. Nepal, Tanzania, Sudan, Kenya, Bolivia, Egypt, Nigeria, Dominican Republic, Morocco, Malawi, Haiti and Liberia.

The intention here is not to convey that the budgetary deficits of governments are the product alone of public enterprise deficits, nor that an improvement in public enterprise finances will ipso factor reverse the budgetary position. The emphasis is on the aggravating impact of public enterprise deficits on budgetary deficits and on the relief that public enterprise surpluses can give to the budgetary problem.

Impact on Public Exchequer

Table 6

Overall deficit/surplus of central government

(as per cent of total expenditure and lending minus repayments)

GNP per capita $ (1)	Surplus (2)	0-10 (3)	10-15 (4)	15-20 (5)	20-30 (6)	30 and above (7)	Total (8)
Low: 0-420	2	3	6	2	5	4	22
Middle 1: 420-1,300	2	7	2	3	8	3	25
Middle 2: 1,300-4,500	4	6	3	3	5	2	23
High: 4,500 and above	2	8	5	3	1	1	20
	10	24	16	11	19	10	90

Source : International Monetary Fund Government Finance Statistics Year Book, 1981, Vol.V.

The other area of relevant data is that of tax revenues. Most of the developing countries have their central government revenues composed predominantly of indirect taxes – domestic taxes on goods and services, and taxes on international trade; and the limits of direct taxes seem to have been approached in many cases. The following data reveal a clear pattern, viz., that the indirect taxes are the most important in a relatively large number of low-income and middle-income (lower) countries, but are not in the middle-income (upper) and high-income countries.

Table 7

Total of domestic and international taxes on goods and services

(as per cent of total revenue of central government)

% (1)	Low-income countries (2)	Middle-income (lower) countries (3)	Middle-income (upper) countries (4)	High-income countries (5)
60 and above	15	11	2	
50 – 60	2	7	4	1
25 – 50	5	5	11	7
Below 25	–	2	5	9
	22	25	22	17

Source : International Monetary Fund, Government Finance Statistics Year Book, 1981, Vol.V.

If budget deficits caused by public enterprises begin to be filled by tax revenues, it may be
the regressive taxes that will increase rather than
the direct taxes in many countries.

Several possibilities of subsequent detail
exist.   Some of the indirect taxes may touch public enterprise outputs that originally escaped economic price fixation.   If this is resisted, for
any reason, increases in general taxation follow,
resulting in random cross-subsidisations among consumer groups.

It may prove far simpler to deal with the
deficits of public enterprises on their own merits
and effect the necessary price enhancements, where-
ever justified, as discussed in a previous chapter.
This has a special justification today.   In several
developing countries a substantial amount of capital
has been lost in public enterprise.   In order to
cushion this sustained risk a general increase in
the public enterprise price levels, rather than in
taxtion, may prove preferable, as a practical strategy.   (Individual expectations are always possible if demonstrated as defensible.)   Or else, the
task of the budgeting authority will continue to be
unenviable, tossed between ad hoc resorts to taxation, borrowings and unmethodical price enhancements.

(b)   Heavy public enterprise investments

Many developing countries present a paradox
in the context of their public enterprise finances.
They are in need of mobilising savings as far as
possible in the interest of their development programmes.   A major part of their development expenditures has gone as public enterprise investments
whose role in the savings effort should, therefore,
be high.   Unfortunately, they contribute too little
to the national pool of savings.

Data, extracted from IMF statistics give us a
clear indication of the relative importance of both
capital expenditures and expenditures on economic
services on the part of the governments of developing countries.   The following two tables provide
the gist of the data.

In more than a third of the low-income countries 30 per cent or more of central government expenditures were on economic services; three-fourths of

Table 8

Expenditure on economic services

(as per cent of total expenditure of central government)

GNP per capita $ (1)		0-15 (2)	15-20 (3)	20-30 (4)	30-40 (5)	40 and above (6)	Total (7)
0-420	L	2	2	8	6	1	19
420-1,300	M_1	3	6	10	2	2	23
1,300-4,500	M_2	5	4	9	1	3	22
Above 4,500	H	10	5	2			17
		20	17	29	9	6	81

Source : International Monetary Fund, Government Finance Statistics
Year Book, 1981, Vol.V.

Table 9

Capital expenditure

(as per cent of total expenditure of central government)

GNP per capita $ (1)	0-10 (2)	10-15 (3)	15-20 (4)	20-30 (5)	30-40 (6)	40 and above (7)	Total (8)
L 0-420	2	7	4	2	3	1	19
M_1 420-1,300	1	2	5	10	2	2	22
M_2 1,300-4,500	3	6	4	4	4		21
H above 4,500	18	1		1			20
	24	16	13	17	9	3	82

Source : International Monetary Fund, Government Finance Statistics
Year Book, 1981, Vol.V.

them and two-thirds of the middle-income (lower) group spent 20 per cent or more in this direction. Most of the high-income countries spent no more than 20 per cent in this direction; in fact, more than half of them spent less than 15 per cent only.

A similar picture is presented by the data on capital expenditures. Such investments are most conspicuous in the case of the middle-income (lower) countries as a group. Most of the high-income countries occur in the below-10 per cent category - 18 out of 20.

It is interesting to note that the highest relative figures of capital expenditure are, in many cases, in countries with significant public enterprise sectors: e.g. Sri Lanka, Tanzania, Madagascar, Sudan, Yemen Arab Republic, Indonesia, Cameroon, Nicaragua, Peru, Nigeria, Jamaica and Dominican Republic.

A word of qualification as regards the figures of capital expenditures. They relate to the central government only. They do not represent investments in public enterprises only. But it is probable that a very large proportion belongs to that category in developing countries. This can be illustrated with the reasonably detailed data we have for Sri Lanka. Appendix 7 shows the capital expenditures of the government by ministry on public enterprises and the total for the government for 1982 (2). The former account for 74 per cent of the total capital expenditures.

Let us go back to the IMF data on expenditures on economic services and on capital expenditures. These are plotted in the graphs below, each point referring to a country on the income scale (on X-axis). Two points come out distinctly: that the high-income countries are concentrated in the lowest expenditure ranges (below 20 per cent in the case of economic services and below 10 per cent in the case of capital expenditures), and that, while the middle-income countries are fairly scattered, the lower group among them is mostly in the above-15 per cent range of capital expenditure figures, while a few more - in absolute as well as relative terms - of the upper group among them do occur in the below-15 per cent range.

Figure 6 : Central government: capital expenditure as per cent of total expenditure

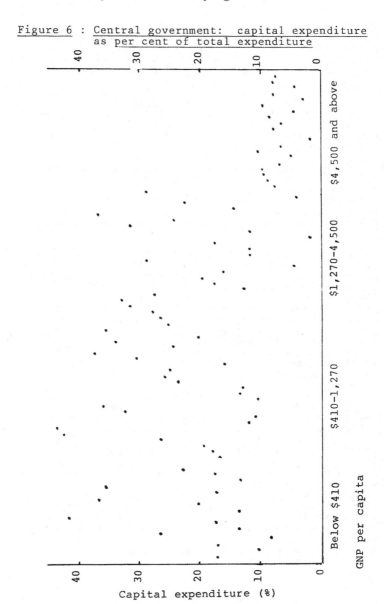

Figure 7 : Central government: expenditure on economic services as per cent of total expenditure

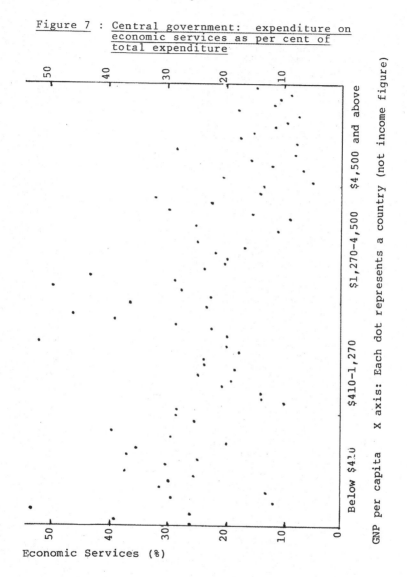

GNP per capita   X axis: Each dot represents a country (not income figure)

The broad differences among regions in respect of the two expenditure figures are shown by the following graphs on the basis of the data of regional totals provided in the IMF volume, for the period 1974-1980. The industrialised countries come out the lowest; and insofar as capital expenditures are concerned, the African countries came out the highest, barring the oil countries; then come Latin America and Asia. One may deduce that the impacts of public enterprise finances on the government budgets, as analysed in this section, are likely to be at the maximum in the African region. If actually their public finances are also the most precarious, the severity of the impact is obvious.

A better impression of the relative importance of public investments in developing countries can be derived from detailed data on public and private investments. To the extent available, referring to the early 1970s, figures on the planned share of public authorities in total gross investment are expressed in percentage terms in Appendix 8 for some developing countries for which the data have been readily available. In fact in nine countries - Togo, Iraq, Nepal, Syria, Cameroon, Mauritius, Nigeria, Zambia and Iran, half or more than half of the total investment originated in the public sector.

Likewise some data on investments in manufacturing are presented in Appendix 9, indicating the public sector's share. (The data refer to more recent years than the earlier figures.) Half or more of the investments were in the public sector in Egypt, Somalia, Tunisia, Yemen, Turkey, India, Iraq, Pakistan, Sri Lanka and Venezuela.

According to the World Development Report, 1983, public enterprises in most developing countries 'account for at least a quarter of total capital formation'. In some countries it is significantly higher - e.g. Algeria, Burma, Zambia, Pakistan, Ivory Coast, Ethiopia, Venezuela, India and Bangladesh.

In one sense, all these data simply confirm the theory that developing countries have been in need of government investments. The argument we build up is, simply that the time has been reached when the high proportion of public investments ought not to be unmindful of its savings responsi-

Impact on Public Exchequer

<u>Figure 8</u> : <u>Central government: capital expenditure</u>
          <u>(as per cent of total expenditure)</u>
          <u>(regional figures)</u>

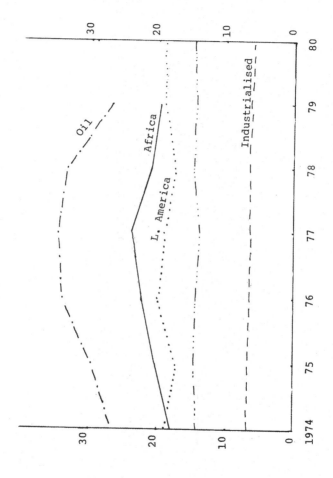

Figure 9 : <u>Central government: expenditure on
economic services (as per cent of total
expenditure) (regional figures)</u>

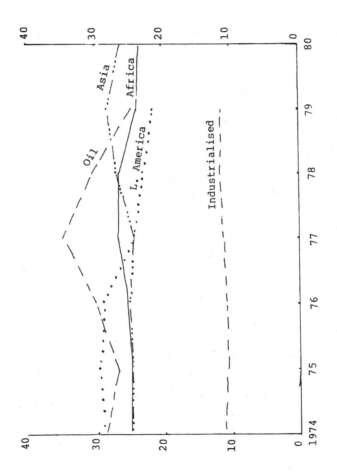

bilities.   To the extent that these are neglected,
a disproportionate extent of the nation's savings
has to be derived from the private sector.   How
easy this can be is one question; and the other
concerns the distributional implications of encouraging the private sector to be the source of savings so exclusively.   If savings are sufficiently
raised from the public sector, their ownership as
well as the recurring returns (by way of interest
and profits) on them would correspondingly belong
to the public sector.   The longer and deeper public enterprises continue to be deficit-making, the
more serious the loss of this distributional benefit.

(c)   Public debt and public enterprise investments

A brief comment may be made, in conclusion, on
the relationship between the size of public debt and
the size of public enterprise investments and its
implications for the public exchequer in developing
countries.   No doubt, the reasons for public debt
extend beyond the needs of public enterprise investment;   there are other capital expenditures and possibly needs of financing budget deficits.   Likewise
not all public enterprise investments occasion public debt; some may have been derived from budget
surpluses or foreign grants.   Nevertheless, public enterprise investments constitute a substantial
cause of public debt in developing countries.

Subject to these qualifications, let us illustrate the point from Sri Lanka and Kenya.

In Sri Lanka, the total public debt by the end
of 1981 was Rs.64,999 million.   Investments in public enterprises (equity plus loans) amounted to
Rs.47,696 million.   This figure was equal to 73 per
cent of the figure of public debt.   They earned Rs.
1,852 million (before tax and interest) - i.e. 3.7
per cent of the outlay.   This compared poorly with
the interest charges on public debt - Rs.3,716 million, which worked out at the rate of 5.7 per cent.
The nature of impact on general taxation and/or
budget deficit financing, implicit in this situation,
should be obvious (3).

In Kenya, public debt amounted to K£1,320 million by the end of 1982; and government investments
in public enterprises were about K£900 million.   The
latter worked out at 70 per cent of the figure of
public debt.   No overall figures of net revenues

are available, though their utter lowness can be inferred from a number of published reports. Their shortfall below the interest charges on public debt, which rose 'faster than the size of the debt itself', must have had consequences for general taxation or the overall budgetary position which progressively deteriorated in recent years (4).

NOTES

1.   The impacts of under-earnings by public enterprises on government budget balance may be illustrated from Sri Lanka.   The difference between revenues and recurrent expenditure of the government was Rs.2,304 (provisional) in 1982.   Current transfers from the government to public corporations amounted to Rs.1,750 million (provisional) in that year. It may be noted that 'public corporations' do not represent the entire public enterprise sector.   For example, the posts and telecommunications and the heavily losing railways are departmental enterprises; and current transfers of government funds to them are outside the above figure of Rs.1,750 million. (Central Bank of Ceylon, Annual Report for the Year 1982, Colombo, 1983, Tables 27 and 33.
2.   Performance 1982 (Ministry of Plan Implementation, Colombo, 1983).
3.   Data on public debt are from Central Bank of Ceylon, Annual Report for the Year 1982, Colombo 1983, pp.114-115.   Data on public enterprise investments and returns are from the Report of the International Team on Government and Public Enterprises in Sri Lanka: A Study in Relationships, Colombo, 1983.
4.   Economic Survey 1983, Nairobi, 1983, pp.43 and 85; and Report of the Working Party on Government Expenditures, Nairobi, 1982, p.114-115.

Chapter Fourteen

THE CONCEPT OF COMPARATIVE ADVANTAGE

Considering that many developing countries have a
sizeable public enterprise sector, let us examine
the question of its relative extent in the national
economy.   Two categories may at once be distinguished: countries in which public enterprise is an
ideological decision and countries which claim to
adopt it on pragmatic criteria.   Whether the decision is explicit or otherwise, several countries
come under the former description.   Here, the
question whether a public enterprise has a comparative advantage in its institutional form is of
limited practical value.   However, in countries
where it is 'chosen' on non-ideological grounds,
the assumption is that an activity gets organised
as a public enterprise since, in terms of social
cost-benefit analysis, there is an advantage for
the national economy from its operation as a public enterprise rather than as a private enterprise.
(At the minimum it should be at no comparative disadvantage.)   This is the concept of comparative
advantage emphasised in this study (1).

      The purpose of this chapter is to elucidate
the concept, indicate the circumstances in which
changes in comparative advantage can occur and
mention the problems encountered in identifying
the changes and in introducing policy responses.
The chapter does not exclusively emphasise privatisation.   Reference will be made to cases of
private enterprise losing comparative advantage
and thereby deserving nationalisation.

      Whether comparative advantage is in favour
of a public enterprise in a given case (i.e.
industry or activity) may be determined by evaluating the following criteria:

165

Table 10

Criteria of comparative advantage

	Criterion	Pro-public enterprise (2)	Pro-private enterprise (3)
(i)	Degree of monopoly:	High	Low
	Amenability to effective control:	Low	High
	Desirability of monopoly (for revenue purposes or for consumption control)	High	Low
(ii)	Viability	Low due to long gestation	High
		Low due to policy pricing constraints	
		Low due to absence of demand at economic price	
(iii)	Technology and skills	Importable	Local
(iv)	Capital investment	Importable	Local
(v)	Deconcentration goal	Strong	Casual
(vi)	Social policy preference	Strong Surplus-adverse	Nominal Surplus-neutral
(vii)	Costs of public sector organisation	Low	High
(viii)	Political 'gains'	High	Low

The list may not look exhaustive. But several popular lines of justification sought for public enterprise choice can be accommodated in it. For example, investment strategy in favour of capital goods industries fits in the viability criterion; desired price subsidisations also are covered by it; labour intensity, ancillaries, export promotion, regional development, employee townships, and model employment come under social policy preferences; and so on.

A simple explanation of the chart may be presented in the following terms. The comparative advantage of a public enterprise is positive

(i)   where the activity is prone to be a monopoly or has to be maintained as a monopoly for some governmentally approved reason, and control over it, if in the private sector, is unlikely to be effective;

(ii)   where viability is (or is kept) low for any reason that the enterprise management cannot surmount;

(iii)   where technology is only importable and prompts governmental intervention of a regulatory or control nature so as to avoid or minimise foreign managerial control over the enterprise;

(iv)   where capital resources are only importable and the government seeks to avoid or minimise managerial control over the enterprise by the foreign supplier of funds;

(v)   where the potentiality of the enterprise to add to the concentration of wealth and income in the community is high and therefore prompts policy intervention by the government;

(vi)   where the government's social policy preferences so touch the enterprise as to affect its surplus position adversely; and

(vii)   where the organisation of the enterprise in the public sector does not expose it

167

to any costs additional to those it would sustain by being organised in the private sector.

As regards (viii), the argument is not too simple. Strictly, the comparative advantage in organising an activity as a public enterprise is to be deemed as high when it can be free from introducing elements of political exploitation with impunity. But, in practice, sectarian interests of politicians may prompt them to attach weight to a decision in favour of establishing a public enterprise.

The concept of comparative advantage of a public enterprise is a useful guide to decision, though computing it is not easy. It encounters two obvious difficulties, which it shares with cost-benefit analyses in general. The units in which the advantage may be measured under the different heads are heterogeneous; and the weights assigned to the different heads may be arbitrary. One can produce the desired answer, in an extreme case. Items (vii) and (viii) on the chart present special problems. It would not be easy to compute, convincingly, the not-too-apparent costs of governmental decisions, interventions and control regulations, or the costs of politicking, even if these were established.

Assume, however, that the government, in principle, rests its entrepreneurial decision on the concept of advantage (2), however imprecisely it may be quantified. The point suggested here is that one has to be constantly watchful to find out if any significant changes have occurred in the circumstances that originally supported the creation of a public enterprise. These may be noticed under five heads.

(i) Markets may have become less imperfect over time (3). The influence of market forces may have become stronger in mobilising resource flows, in linking prices to related costs, in promoting effective consumer choice in several sectors, in creating a supply of the needed inputs of skills, technology and equipment and, in general, in breaking the barriers to investment on the part of potential investors. The extent to which such changes diminish the original comparative advantage of a public enterprise depends on the development status of the country. In some countries such as the least developed, the need for the influx of foreign capital may be indispensable for a long time; and the policy of the government may be biased towards attracting it in partnership with local, i.e. government, investments. In fact, several cases of foreign investors preferring such joint ventures are on record, with one consequence, among others, of the government being held hostage for the benefit of the foreigner's involvement as supplier of funds, technology, skills and management.

(ii)   Changes may have occurred in social preferences in such a way that deviations from market-oriented policies in respect of inputs and outputs of the enterprise, which were once deemed necessary, do not appear to be important any longer – for example, subsidised prices, surplus staff, and uneconomical plants.   The benefits of a promotional policy on the part of a public enterprise, especially of the infrastructural category, are relatively high in the early stages of development of a beneficiary activity or region.   The elasticity of response from the latter to a low-price policy of the enterprise can be significant.   But as time passes and the beneficiary's economic status improves, the utility of the low price diminishes and so does the case for its continued application.

(iii) The efficiency of a public enterprise may have turned out to be low, whatever the reasons, and beyond prompt redress.

(iv)   Public enterprises may have developed an unsuspected degree of unaccountability, the crucial responsibility for it resting with the managers, the government departments or politicians.

(v)   Financial constraints experienced by the public exchequer may bring about a change in the approach of the budgeting authorities so as to prune relatively non-viable investments, expansions and pricing policies.

Some of these changes are of an overall nature, applicable to public enterprises in general, though the precise impact may vary from one enterprise to another.   So adjustments in entrepreneurial structure have to be initiated on a case-to-case basis.

The central problem in this area concerns the very identification of the loss in comparative ad-

169

vantage. This may be relatively easy where a public enterprise operates in competition with a private enterprise. Here inter-firm comparisons, though in need of qualifications, can be of help. Where a public enterprise operates in a monopoly area – and this is a common case, the review is far from simple, not only on technical grounds, but on institutional grounds as well.

Two aspects of the latter may be mentioned. It has to be recognised all round that the loss of comparative advantage on the part of a public enterprise is not synonymous with its inefficiency and does not necessarily have the force of a stigma for the management. As argued above, the reasons may have stemmed from certain macro changes in the national economic circumstances and from changes in the scales of social preferences.

Further, the evaluation of changes in comparative advantage has to be entrusted to a machinery that can work independently of any pressures of brief for the government. Though it is not aimed to be an inquisition, some of the grounds for a loss of comparative advantage may be established as originating in governmental involvement in decision-making and interventions in management, and political pressures of an overt or covert nature. The more serious these circumstances, the more certain the loss of comparative advantage; and, unfortunately, the less inclined the government towards setting up a rigorous evaluation. The short-run objective of saving face probably tempts it not to unearth any basic changes in comparative advantage of given public enterprises.

It is possible that, in some of the least developed countries and countries with permanent handicaps of small markets and poor natural resources, severe losses in comparative advantage of public enterprise, in general, may occur far less commonly than in better-placed countries. Nevertheless, it would be desirable to review the position from time to time.

The major hurdle to promoting the needed evaluation derives from the fact that it turns out to be bad politics for most parties in power to make an issue of public entrepreneurship.

However, we can discover the beginnings of a

rethinking on the entrepreneurial question in some
countries like Kenya, Sudan, Sri Lanka (4), Bangladesh, Brazil, Jamaica, Korea, Pakistan, Peru, Philippines, and Zaire, though it is bound to be unrealistic to expect any large-scale reversals in ownership
structures in the immediate future. The aim of our
analysis is to rationalise the need and content of
such rethinking, not necessarily to recommend any
reversals as an end in themselves. In fact, hasty
denationalisations can produce harm, in different
ways in different countries.

An interesting version of recognition to the
concept of comparative advantage of public enterprise is found in the terms of reference set for
the Task Force on Divestiture of Government Investment recently constituted in Kenya. The Government
plans some divestment from the public enterprise
sector, but on a discriminating basis. The Task
Force is required 'to carry out a careful review
of the parastatal sector and come out with two distinct groups of parastatals, namely, those which
are public oriented and which provide public goods
and services, and those which are private oriented'.
(5). The idea implicit in the 'public goods and
services' is that public enterprise has comparative
advantage in respect of them, while 'private-oriented
goods' represent activities in which private enterprise has comparative advantage. A demarcation of
this nature cannot have universal application in
respect of several sectors of activity. Its relevance is within a given spatial and temporal context.
It follows, therefore, that lines of comparative
advantage need to be redrawn as the spatial and
temporal context changes.

The major circumstance that has activated
certain governments to rethink is that of chronic
deficits of public enterprises. (We leave aside
reversals into private entrepreneurship consequent
on assumption of power by rightist groups.)
Strictly it is not the mere fact of a financial
deficit but a decline in comparative advantage
that should set the government athinking on the
desirability of any entrepreneurial change. For,
deficits in certain cases are intended (6); and
the activities concerned are undertaken in the
public sector with the object of being subsidised
from the government budget. It is where the losses
accrue in the absence of such a planned objective
that the appropriateness of reforms right up to

171

entrepreneurial changes may be explored. To start
with, the problem may take the shape of how to avert
the losses. But it may lead to the finding that
public entrepreneurship has lost its elements of
comparative advantage in a given case and that the
economy would be better served if the enterprise
moved outside of the public sector.

Despite the plausibility of this argument in
theory, there can be several hurdles to policy decisions in practice. The most obvious is the political complexity that constrains such a decision.
Even with an openness of mind, most governments
find it far from easy to give up public ownership,
unless the technical or financial case is overwhelm-
ing as well as widely recognised. Among the non-
political hurdles, problems arise as regards the
sale of the enterprise - both the price and the
purchaser (7). Unless care is taken, the situation
can degenerate into a sale under buyer-pressure.
For one thing, the price may be a give-away price,
the more so the less ethical the negotiations, and,
for another, the ownership of the enterprise may be
so relocated as to aggravate the concentration of
wealth and income in the country (8). Where people
begin to suspect this as a motive underlying the
transfer of public enterprises to the private sector,
social tensions begin to ferment, to the disadvantage of the country far beyond the context of public private sector ownership.

Another major problem stems from the fear that,
once an enterprise has been denationalised, it may
escape government control almost totally. This may
appear an unappealing prospect to certain parties;
and arguments will be raised perhaps so strongly as
to thwart the very denationalising measure.

It is possible to introduce as a helpful way
out the policy of converting a public enterprise
that has lost its comparative advantage into a
joint venture with some private holding. (This
happens anyway when a needed resource - mainly
technological - has to come from a (foreign)
private source or from a source that demands, or
is best offered, an ownership interest.)

The transformation may be brought about through
the transfer of some shares in the enterprise from
the government to a private party, or through the
expansion of the enterprise with private financial

172

contributions, or through the conversion of any non-government loans into equity capital, or through the creation of a subsidy that is majority-owned by private interests.

The climate for changes in governmental entre-preneurship of enterprises somewhat improves, when the government has a policy of rotation of public funds among sectors and activities in such a way that funds are withdrawn, by design, from an enter-prise where the need has declined, for whatever reason, and invested in another where the need is relatively pressing (9). Such has been the pious wish of many developmental agencies - e.g. those engaged in agricultural finance or small industry promotion. But the first investments are so inex-tricably stuck that the funds hardly become available for any other purpose. The promotional and cataly-tic nature of the government's entrepreneurship proves ineffective in practice. Where well planned divestments are possible with opportunities of re-investment elsewhere, the entrepreneurial changes implicit in such actions are likely to attract less hostile criticism than they would otherwise.

Another propitious circumstance for divestments from public enterprises presents itself when there is need for large-scale expenditures by the govern-ment in areas of agriculture and rural welfare, for which strong political support exists, and when the only practical way of finding the resources neces-sary lies in a release of government funds that are locked up in directions without advantage any longer. Many countries come within this descrip-tion.

Let us turn to the case of a public enterprise that has suffered in its comparative advantage and yet makes a profit because of its monopoly power. Trading monopolies in the public sector occasionally illustrate this situation. A change in the entre-preneurial structure may have the benefits, by hypo-thesis, of reduced costs of operation, improved marketing skills, and either increased profit or reduced prices, according as the price-fixing level is inclined towards one or the other objective. However, the change may prove difficult to intro-duce, for motives will be read into it on the ap-parently confusing ground that the government plans to give up a source of revenue. Besides, ministries of finance are unlikely to be enthused into such a policy decision, except under ideological pressures of a political nature.

On close analysis the issue that deserves attention in this case is not that the enterprise makes a profit but that it has lost its comparative advantage as a public enterprise; that is, its financial-cum-social returns are smaller than they could be. If profit (at a given level) were permissible in the markets concerned, there is no reason why it should be deliberately made over to private enterprise. If there is a way of preserving it for the public sector without the enterprise being handicapped by a material loss in its comparative advantage, it will be desirable to do so. One of the ways in which this can be achieved is by privatising the operating criteria of the enterprise so significantly that, even while continuing to work within public ownership, it is managed with the autonomy and profit motivation of a private enterprise. It will be a helpful step to make the operating units optimally small and confer on them adequate managerial autonomy. The enterprise can be private in ability to raise profit but public insofar as profit accrual is concerned. This will not be too easy a process in many cases; but wherever such an option exists a full reversal of entrepreneurial structures can be kept at bay as far as necessary, without forgoing any substantive advantages.

It may be seen that the emphasis of this section has been, not on entrepreneurial changes as an end in themselves, but on changes where certain public enterprises have lost their comparative advantage. Developing countries, being in acute need of conserving resources and maximising the returns from investments, are likely to gain from such openness in policies in the long run, subject to political feasibility.

The fundamental theme of the chapter is that in a mixed economy an enterprise is justified in retaining its public sector status on grounds of comparative advantage. So far we have discussed the case of a public enterprise having lost its comparative advantage. There can equally be cases of a private enterprise losing its comparative advantage; or, to put it in different terms, comparative advantage begins to accumulate on the side of a public enterprise in respect of the activity concerned. A growing mixed economy is generally likely to witness

an improvement of market forces and corresponding
additions to the comparative advantage of private
enterprises.   Yet an individual private enterprise
may be estimated to have lost it in situations such
as the following:

(i)   where the management becomes inefficient or
        fraudulent, to the disadvantage of the con-
        sumer, and the government cannot effectively
        control it:

(ii)   where the enterprise becomes exploitative
        (of the consumer and labour) and the govern-
        ment cannot effectively control it;

(iii)   where the enterprise places its short-run or
        narrow financial advantage ahead of a basic
        public interest such as conservation of a
        resource or investment in efficient tech-
        nology, and the government cannot effectively
        control it; and

(iv)   where a substantial need arises for replac-
        ing the market criteria by social criteria
        in the context of the input and output poli-
        cies of an enterprise, and this cannot be
        effectively achieved through a system of
        controls and subsidies.

        In such circumstances the comparative advantage
criterion   certifies to the conversion of a private
enterprise into a public enterprise.

        In conclusion, we may refer to a difficult
situation in which to implement the comparative advantage criterion dispassionately and rigorously,
viz., where both public and private enterprises operate in a given field.   To the extent that substi-
tutability among their outputs is real, competition
may be expected to settle the issue.   But two problems can arise.   First, the competition may, in
fact, be imperfect, in the sense that the public
enterprise probably has certain disguised advantages in respect of costs of capital, input licences
etc., so much so that its competitiveness in the
market is less real than it appears to be.   And it
carries on, despite any real qualifications to its
record of comparative advantage.

        The second problem is that, even where its
comparative advantage is recognisably low or shrin-

king, the government may search for excuses whereby to constrain the operations of the competing private enterprise. Some kind of market sub-divisions may be promoted so as to restrict the competitive area of operations; or at the end of the scale there can be an extension of nationalisation so as to bring the whole or most part of the industry within the public sector. This, in theory, ought not to be the implication of entrepreneurial decision-making in a mixed economy; but, in practice, it might be on occasions.

Reference may be made to an interesting aspect of the process of perceiving a loss in comparative advantage on the part of a public enterprise. At least three levels of perceivers can be distinguished; the government, the top managers of the enterprise and the middle and lower levels of managers. The last group is the first to come to grips with the problems of shrinking advantage at the operating levels; the top managers can draw lessons in the total performance context; and the government has views on the extra-enterprise aspects of the enterprise's operations. The perceptions of these three levels need to be synthesised; of course, the expert has a role in doing this and in evaluating the circumstances of shrinking advantage. But, basically, the management structure of the enterprise should be such as to make possible effective communication from the third level to the second and from the second to the government. Though apparently simple, this cannot be taken for granted in many public enterprise structures in developing countries. Large, monolithic and holding company organisations complicate the problem as between the third and the second levels; and dominant government presence in enterprise direction and management can inhibit the right flow of perception from the enterprise level to the government.

Apart from the above complexity, identification of changing comparative advantage is a part of the general problem of evaluation of public enterprise, into which we do not go in the present study. The question of who should do it is also kept out.

This chapter should be of policy interest to mixed economies among developing countries, in that it emphasises the concept of comparative advantage on which the choice of public entrepreneurship should depend, suggests that this might change over time

and that corresponding changes in the nature of entrepreneurship would be in the national interest, and
refers to certain practical aspects of effecting the
desirable entrepreneurial changes. What is important is that at least major shifts in the comparative
advantage of a public enterprise should prompt a
policy response from the government, if the objective were national well-being rather than an entrepreneurial form.

NOTES

1.   It represents the comparative advantage
of a public enterprise over a private enterprise
within the national economy, and has no reference to
the element of comparative advantage in international trade.

2.   A recent clear instance of loss of comparative advantage on the part of a public enterprise
is provided by the ten power loom projects of the
government of Sri Lanka sold to the private sector.
'Under private sector management these have shown
significant improvement in the levels of production.
As against previous productivity levels of about
40 per cent, some of these units have been able to
achieve productivity levels of 90 per cent of their
rated capacities.' Performance 1982 (Ministry of
Plan Implementation, Colombo, 1982), p.67.

Some other examples of changes in comparative
advantage in favour of private enterprise are available in the field of road transport in Buenos Aires,
Chiengmai (in Northern Thailand) and Calcutta.   In
Calcutta the State Transport Corporation 'requires
subsidies of $1 million a month', while private
buses operating without subsidies account for two-
thirds of all bus trips'. World Development Report
1983 (Washington, 1983) p.52.

3.   Evidence is available from Sri Lanka on
how, since the introduction of open market policies
in 1977, there has been a lessening of 'market imperfections created by rigid exchange and import controls, raw material quotas, state monopolies ...
uncertainties of capital flows and threat of possible
state take-over'. Public Investment 1981-85,
Ministry of Finance and Planning, Colombo, 1983,
p.41.

4.   For instance, 'the rapid growth of private omnibus services' in 1982 was 'the immediate
result of the new policy pursued by the Ministry
in providing flexible services and allowing the
sector to develop with few or none of the restraints

that hindered development earlier'.   Performance
1982 (Ministry of Plan Implementation, Colombo, 1982)
p.116.
        Many rice, flour and cotton mills have recently
been denationalised in Pakistan, and a large number
of jute and textile mills in Bangladesh were re-
turned to the private sector.   Jamaica sold three
enterprises.
        'Hungary legislated in 1982 to allow the for-
mation of private companies employing up to 150
people.'   World Development Report 1983 (Washington
1983) p.51.
        5.   Presidential Order setting up the Task
Force on Divestiture of Government Investment, Nairobi,
June 1983.
        6.   For a discussion on this question, see
V.V. Ramanadham, 'Public Enterprise Losses and Public Policy Options',   in Financial Profitability and
Losses in Enterprises in Developing Countries (ICPE,
Ljubljana, 1982) pp.112-115.
        7.   To cite an instance, though from a de-
veloped country: The Iron and Steel Trades Confedera-
tion urged the Industry and Trade Committee (UK) to
'probe' privatisation transactions concerning British Steel Corporation 'with a view to establishing
whether public assets are being sold below their
price'.   (Second Report from the Industry and
Trade Committee (Session 1982-83) The British Steel
Corporation's Prospects (London, HMSO, 1983), p.33.
        8.   The problem may be complicated, additio-
nally, by the racial factor, as in Kenya and Malaysia.
        9.   For instance, in Sudan the government
would 'consider phased disinvestment in public sector enterprises on a selective basis.   This would
provide capital for the public sector's pioneering
role in planned directions where private investment
is lagging'.   The Six Year Plan of Economic and
Social Development 1977/78 - 1982/83, Vol.1,
(Khartoum, 1977), p.48.

Chapter Fifteen

CLASSIFICATION OF DEVELOPING COUNTRIES

The preceding chapters have indicated that the working of public enterprises in developing countries
is under the impact of certain basic features of
the national economy. Differences exist among
the countries in point of development. Correspondingly, there exist structural reasons for heterogeneity in their public enterprise experience.

There are serious limits to establishing statistical relationships among the indices of development (or combinations of them) on the one side and
the performance of public enterprise on the other,
for the simple reason that we lack the necessary
data on performance – even in terms of investments
and returns. The analysis may, therefore, be limited to appropriate grouping of countries with a view
to drawing qualitative inferences.

Possibly this chapter smacks of a little di-
gression at certain points and may appear to be concerned with developing countries as such rather
than, directly, with their public enterprises. But
it serves, with emphatic empiricism, the purpose of
suggesting that there can be significant variations
among groups of developing countries in problems of
public enterprise.

The first step in the analysis consists of a
classification of the developing countries on the
following criteria:

1.   Average annual growth rate (%) during
     1960-89.

2.   Size of population (mid-1980).

3. Manufacturing as per cent of GDP (1980).

4. Percentage of labour force in agriculture (1980).

5. Average annual growth of labour force (%) estimated for 1980-2000.

6. Urban population as per cent of total population (1980).

7. Enrolment in higher education as per cent of population aged 20-24 (1978).

8. Energy consumption per capita (Kg of coal equivalent) (1979).

9. External public debt as per cent of GNP (1980).

The data are taken from the World Development Report 1982 (World Bank).

The countries are divided into five categories (A, B, C, D and E) under each criterion; A representing the least 'favourable' value and E the most 'favourable'. The term 'favourable' is already tendentious: the connotation is that an A value has the significance of a problem or disadvantage in the context of economic development and, in many cases, represents a situation in which the government may be seeking an improvement. Conversely, the nearer to an E value, the more conveniently placed the country in a given respect. The details of the classification (along with the class intervals) in all the nine cases are tabulated in Table 11.

The broad connection between a country's status in respect of each of these indices and its development prospects, including public enterprise performance, may be noted at this stage.

The average annual growth rate which is the result of interaction of all development forces, reflects the weight of handicaps that a country experienced during the recent two decades. Those in the lower classes (e.g. A and B) were more vulnerable to difficulties in growth and, by implication, in the working of public enterprises than the others.

Classification of Developing Countries

The size of population has some impact on development in that the smaller the size the smaller the domestic markets and perhaps the smaller the (skilled) labour available. Exceptions do exist, but the market limits can impose severe diseconomies in production structures.

Lower indices of manufacturing as per cent of GNP suggest the lack of a base of technological and managerial expertise helpful in modern economic development.

Indices of labour force in agricultural constitute, in a sense, the obverse of those on manufacturing and have a purport from the standpoint of terms of trade, income distribution, and diversification in the production system.

The estimates of average annual growth rates in labour force during 1980-2000 reveal the nature of impacts they are likely to have on decisions on investment allocation, technology and productivity. The higher the rates, the more probable compromises with productivity and economy in production costs, and the higher the 'social' content in investment decisions.

The density of urban population can have some meaning through its influence on the organisation of the production units and on distribution costs - for example, in electricity supply. The lower the urbanisation, the greater the likelihood of small-sized units or regional unifications, with unfavourable cost effects.

Enrolment in higher education is an index of value in showing up the problems of technology and skills in industrial development. The lower the index, either the more expensive the industrialisation, or the more imminent expatriate employment (or both). This can have a somewhat direct effect on public enterprise: viz., costly dependence on foreign project-formulation and technology and on joint ventures or management agreements with foreigners.

Energy consumption is, broadly, a corroborative index with the same significance as the manufacturing index. It is possible that a low index suggests, in several cases, low technology and high energy costs. The latter can stem from uneconomical

Table 11

Development indices: classification

Symbol of index (1)	Average annual growth (%) 1960-80 (2)	Population (million) mid-1980 (3)	Manufac- turing as % of GDP 1980 (4)	Percentage of labour force in agriculture 1980 (5)
A	Below 1.0	Below 3	Below 10	70 and above
B	1.0-2.0	3 - 5	10 - 15	50 - 70
C	2.0-3.0	5 - 10	15 - 20	30 - 50
D	3.0-4.0	10 - 30	20 - 25	15 - 30
E	4.0 and above	30 and above	25 and above	Below 15

Source of all data : World Development Report 1982 (World Bank)

Classification of Developing Countries

Table 11 (cont'd)

Development indices: classification

Average annual growth of labour force (%) 1980-2000	Urban population as % of total population 1980	Enrolment in higher education as % of population aged 20-24 1978	Energy consumption per capita (kg of coal equivalent) 1979	External public debt as % of GNP 1980
(6)	(7)	(8)	(9)	(10)
2.5 and above	Below 20	1 or less	Below 100	50 and above
2.0-2.5	20 - 30	2 - 5	100 - 250	30 - 50
1.5-2.0	30 - 40	5 - 10	250 - 500	15 - 30
1.0-1.5	40 - 60	10 - 20	500 - 1000	1 - 15
Below 1.0	60 and above	20 and above	1000 and above	0

scales of electricity generation and distribution.

External public debt, relative to GNP, reflects the costs of development efforts in a sense. The higher this figure, the greater the debt servicing charges - in hard currency, and the greater the needs of raising savings from the enterprises.

The purport of each index has to be understood with caution. No moral judgement is involved in such cases as urban density or agricultural labour. It is not to be understood that unlimited movements of an index in the direction of E are necessarily the most desirable: for example, in urban density or size of population. The indices, however, have some value in reflecting problems in development. Appendix 10 contains the classification in full.

Now we have a problem: how do we get an integrated idea of the development status of each country on the basis of the nine indices? There is no easy way of weighting them. A simple procedure is, therefore, preferred, of classifying the countries according to the number of A-and-B indices that each has. None has all nine As and/or Bs; some have eight; and, at the other end, a few have none. Table 12 shows the scatter of the countries over the A-B scale; besides, they are also classified by income. (The high-income countries are excluded from the table. They all come in the 'nil' column.)

It is clear from the tabulation that distinct differences exist among countries in terms of the development indices. For instance, fifteen have 7 or 8 A-and-Bs, 30 have 6 or 5, 22 have 4 or 3, 18 have 2 or 1, and 5 have no A or B. The former groups are likely to possess conditions of relatively high costs of development, simpler technologies, weaker managerial skills and poorer savings potential with reference to their public enterprises than the latter groups do. This has to be taken as a broad generalisation; exceptions are always possible.

An interesting 'regional' inference emerges from the spread of the data. In the least favourably placed group of 15 - columns (2) and (3) - 11 are African countries; in the next group of 30 - columns (4) and (5) - 20 are African; whereas most of the Latin American countries occur in the

relatively well placed groups. The Asian countries
are spread over all ranges, though to a rather limited
extent in the 7 or 8 range.

Let us superimpose on this a classification by
income (per capita) - shown in the first column of
the table. As if in partial support of the generalisation suggested above, the relative association of poor incomes with a large number of A-Bs
and of higher incomes with a low number appears
clearly. Almost all countries with an income
below $410 have five or more A-Bs; in fact, 25 out
of the 30 in this low income range have six or more
A-Bs. In the middle income group, practically
none in the lower half has more than six A-Bs,
while none in the upper half - above $1,300 - has
more than four. The shift of numbers from six
of A-Bs to nil is quite clear in so far as the
middle-income countries are concerned.

The following graph gives us a corroboratory
impression of the scatter relationship between income and development indices. (A-Bs as well as
E-Ds associated with each country are shown in it.
Each dot on the X-axis represents a country.)

For all the low-income countries and most of
the middle-income (lower) group the frequencies of
A-B exceed those of E-D; and for almost all the
middle-income (upper) group and the high-income
group the E-D frequencies exceed the A-B frequencies, the more conspicuously the higher the income.

Table 12 : Unfavourable indices (A and B)

Income per capita	8	7	6	5
(1)	(2)	(3)	(4)	(5)
Below $220	Chad Mali 2	Bangladesh Nepal Somalia Burma Burundi 5	Ethiopia Upper Volta 2	Afghanistan(6) Vietnam (6) 3
$220 to 410	Sierra Leone Sudan Togo 3	Haiti Guinea Uganda Benin 4	Zaire Malawi Mozambique (7) Sri Lanka Tanzania Central African Republic Pakistan Niger Madagascar 9	India 1
$420 to 630	Mauritania 1		Kenya Lesotho Yemen Arab Republic Liberia Honduras 5	Yemen Indonesia Senegal Angola (7) Zambia 5
$660 to 1,270			Congo, People's Republic Nigeria Ivory Coast 3	Cameroon Papua New Guinea 2
$1,300 to 2,090				
$2,150 to 4,500				
	6	9	19	11

Classification of Developing Countries
of low and middle income countries

4 (6)	3 (7)	2 (8)	1 (9)	Nil	Total
					12
	China (6)				
	1				18
Ghana	Egypt				
Bolivia	Zimbabwe				
2	2				15
Nicaragua	El Salvdaor		Philippines		
Morocco	Thailand		Dominican		
Jamaica	Peru		Republic		
	Guatemala		Colombia		
3	Ecuador 5		3		16
Malaysia	Paraguay	Lebanon	Korea Dem.		
Panama	Tunisia	Turkey	Republic		
Algeria	Jordan		Syrian Arab		
			Republic		
			Cuba		
			Korea, Rep.		
			Brazil		
3	4	2	Mexico 6		15
Trinidad	Israel	Chile	S. Africa	Rumania	
& Tobago		Uruguay	Venezuela	Portugal	
		Iran	Singapore	Argentina	
		Iraq		Hong Kong	
1	1	4	3	Greece 5	14
9	13	6	12	5	90
			(10)		(11)

187

Figure 10 : Development indices of countries

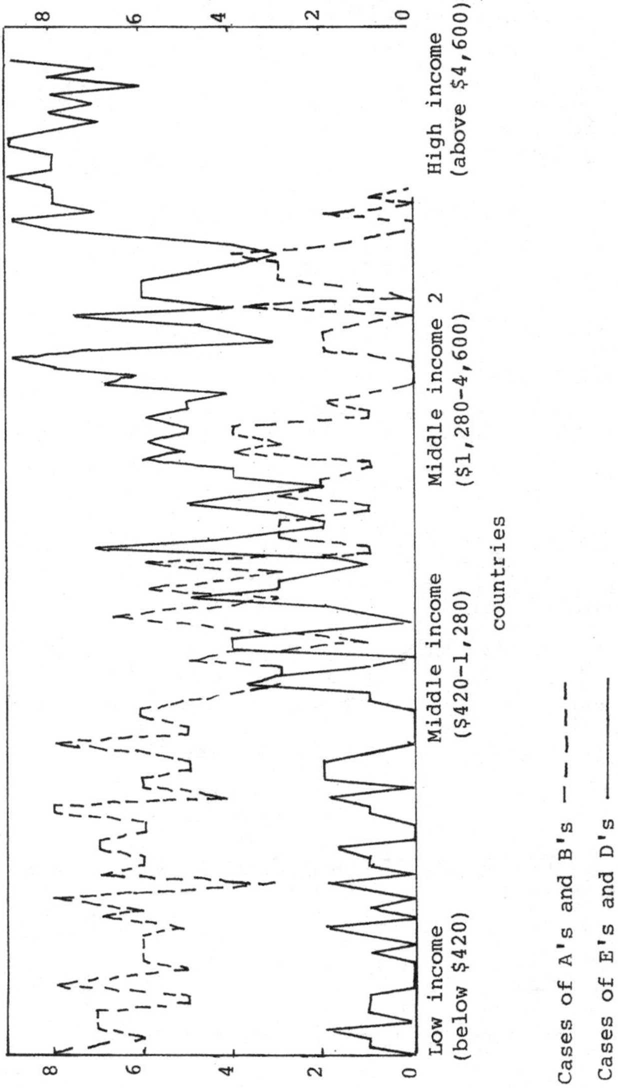

Cases of A's and B's — — — —

Cases of E's and D's ————

Classification of Developing Countries

To recapitulate: the tabulation and the graph suggest that certain groups of developing countries are distinctly unfavourably placed vis-à-vis development and have relatively low incomes as well. These are countries that are most likely to attract public enterprise; and its performance is bound to be under the unfavourable impacts of their development indices.

Unfortunately, we do not have data on total investments in the public and private sectors in all the countries covered by the previous table. Some use may, again, be made of data (uniformly) available for all countries on capital expenditures by governments (expressed as percentages of total government expenditures and lending minus repayments) from IMF sources. The qualifications to the use of these data mentioned in chapter 13 may be recalled.

Subject to these, we mark out the countries in Table 12 that are characterised by a figure of 30 per cent or more of capital expenditures out of all government expenditures. These are underlined. Nine of the fifteen such countries are in the ranges of 5 or more A-Bs; none is found in the 2-or-less A-B ranges. Included in the nine are countries which have significant public enterprise sectors - Sudan, Sri Lanka, Tanzania, Yemen Arab Republic, Nigeria, Indonesia and Malawi.

Part III

DECENTRALISATION OF PUBLIC ENTERPRISE CONTROL

Chapter Sixteen

THE THEME

The present study does not seek to cover the whole
problem of control of public enterprises; nor does
it directly go into questions of what controls are
necessary or what merits individual control instruments have (1).   The focus is on the role of non-
government agencies in the control system with a
view to making it substantively efficient.   The
government's own role comes out at many points in
the discussion and is summed up in chapter 12. The
review keeps out of its purview procedural controls,
e.g. the submission of a report or accounts within
a specified period, honesty controls (meant to keep
the managers from dishonesty, nepotism, corruption
and laziness) and penal controls.   The theme relates
to such substantive elements of control as pricing,
investment, cross-subsidisations, costs, productivity, monopoly power, performance indicators, surplus generation, wages, employment, research and
development, and technology.

A word on the term 'control' as employed here.
Broadly, it connotes the entire area of control or
regulatory relationships between a public enterprise
and external agencies.   There are at least three
segments:

(a)   Control instruments themselves: for example,
        that the enterprise shall not borrow or in-
        vest more than a specified sum of money in
        expansions in a given period, or that it can
        raise its prices by no more than a set per-
        centage figure at a given time.   The term
        control instrument is used here to signify
        a decree, directive or stipulation from
        the government (generally (2), or from any
        other agency empowered to issue it).

(b)   Public appraisals that are substantively
        requisite for the control instruments: for
        example, reviews of investment options and
        feasibility, given one or several possible
        figures of resource available, or the impli-
        cations -   for the enterprise, the consu-
        mers and the tax payer - of price enhance-
        ments by different percentages.

(c)   Extra-enterprise concerns or impacts that
        do not necessarily lead to any control in-
        struments but probably serve as satisfac-
        tory substitutes for control instruments:
        for example, consumer scrutinies and pres-
        sures as regards the quality of output (3),
        and the exposure of a public enterprise to
        market discipline vis-à-vis rates of inter-
        est on borrowings.

These three areas of public involvement in public enterprise matters comprise the control relationships that this study refers to.

The main theme of the study is simply that public 'control' of public enterprises, as understood in
the above terms, can be more effective or efficient
if it is appropriately decentralised to some extent
than if the government departments keep exclusive
hold of it.   The important aspects of the proposition are: what is the nature of 'appropriate' decentralisation and 'to what extent' is the decentralisation to go?   These will be covered in the course
of the study.

At the outset a few basic points in support of
the theme of decentralisation in the control system
may be set out.

First, many prevailing systems of control over
public enterprise represent bare control instruments
(4) rather than the entire fabric of control relationships as visualised here.   For instance, there may
be a mere control against price enhancements, without
being preceded by a macro-economic analysis of the
implications for the consumer, for anti-inflation
policies and for the tax payer, of any consequential
compensations, and of the possible options on permissible price levels.   Or, there can be a control
against capital expenditure when the enterprise has to
look to the government for funds, while it is left
relatively free to undertake the expenditure if it is

financed from its own reserves. Or, there may be
a blunt restriction against foreign travel by public enterprise managers, without a full review of
the overall balance-of-payments results of the travel.
Under these conditions, no wonder the control functions are heavily, if not exclusively, concentrated
in the ministries. But, as an efficient system of
control replaces the mere bundle of control instruments, the benefits of decentralisation will begin
to reveal themselves. At the minimum it places
some control functions and powers in the hands of
institutions that can wield them more expertly than
the parent ministry or the Treasury. It reduces
the ministries' burdens of the control function without damaging the efficiency of the control system.
And it helps conserve the ministries' energies in
favour of strategic concern - for example, in favour
of the prerogative of notice, approval or adjudication
of the control exercise undertaken at the decentralised levels.

Second, the rationale of government (or public)
control over a public enterprise cannot be abridged
into 'ownership control'. It transcends the interest of ownership which, by itself, can be expressed
in terms of a given (or high) net revenue. If this
is all that is implied, a simple control instrument
by the government - at the instance of the Treasury
- will do. But there is more to public enterprise
than this. The case for control rests on considerations of macro economic and social goals, synthesised with the narrow interest of raising a (high)
net revenue. Though vaguely recognised, this theme
is not adequately translated into a process leading
to the enunciation of appropriate net revenue targets. (In fact financial targeting is itself want-
ing, except in the UK in the main.) As such an
approach becomes popular, some degree of decentralisation in the control system will be of help not only
in emphasising the substantive elements basic to the
control instruments but in scrutinising the conditions that may have to accompany a control instrument. For instance, a financial target is meaningful only when certain specified conditions regarding
prices and outputs are satisfied.

Third, there is a conceptual virtue in decentralising the control system. It makes necessary a
rigorous determination of the criteria by which the
decentralised agencies are expected to work. While
preserving for the government, under parliamentary

checks, the right to determine the broad goals that
the controls seek to achieve, this lends clarity to
the way in which these goals are formulated.   What
society gains is not simply that the enterprises
adhere to the letter of a control instrument – 'do
or don't' – but that they are controlled in terms
of the 'socially' best, among available, options
of behaviour and decision.   To illustrate, the
entrustment of the price controlling function to
a decentralised level presupposes that the government sets out the broad guidelines of what the
prices in the case of a given enterprise are expected to achieve; for example, are they to benefit
any specific groups or consumers?   Where the control
function is wholly a ministerial preserve, governmental interest in enunciating the criteria underlying
a control instrument is weakened, as in the case of
the external financial limits imposed on the British
nationalised industries without 'clear guidance on
investment criteria ' (5).   Here the control instrument is a blunt one; and the criteria applicable
to an imposed limit are not explicit.

The non-government agencies through which decentralisation in the control system can be implemented will be discussed in the following chapters
under four heads:

(a)   independent commissions or expert
tribunals, boards or authorities
set up under specific legislation;

(b)   institutional devices in respect of
public enterprise organisation
itself;

(c)   consumer councils, enjoying legal
recognition; and

(d)   the market.

NOTES

1.   For a comprehensive treatment of the subject, see V.V. Ramanadham, Control of Public Enterprises in India (New York, 1964).
2.   For illustrations see Government Policy
for the Management of Public Enterprises,   Volumes
I and II, which codify many control instruments that
emanated from the Government of India (SCOPE, New
Delhi, 1979).

3.   If these lead to formal controls, they
go under category (b).
4.   Of relevance in illustration is H. Boneo's
observation that 'The Latin American system of public enterprises is not characterised by the tendency
to issue directives and to specify the results, but
by its tendency to control specific behaviours of
public enterprises.' (Underlining mine) Final Report
of the Seminar on the Management of Public Enterprises
in Latin America and   Italy (Rome, 1978) p.62.
5.   For example, the Monopolies and Mergers
Commission refers to 'the confusion between commercial and social objectives' of the British Railways
Board and concludes that, 'clear guidelines on investment should be given to the Board by the Government'.
The Monopolies and Mergers Commission, British Railways Board: London and South East Commuter Services,
8046 (London 1980) p.166.

Chapter Seventeen

INDEPENDENT COMMISSIONS

Whatever their name - committee, commission, tribunal, board, authority, agency, etc. and whatever
the epithet - expert, advisory, regulatory, etc.,
the two characteristics of these bodies most relevant in the present context are that they enjoy a
material degree of independence from the executive
branch of government and substantial access to
expertise on the subjects of remit to them. While
not yet numerous in the area of public enterprises,
they have been in use in several countries as helpful agencies in the exercise of public control in
economic matters.

The relative merits of independent commissions
are familiar in the literature on economic administration (1). Steering clear of repetition on the
subject, let us concentrate on certain areas in
which such agencies can play a commendable role
with reference to public enterprise.

(i) A basic complexity in the control of public enterprise arises from the fact that they are expected to fulfil their own financial objectives as
well as certain extra-enterprise or social objectives. Governments have been conscious of this.
Yet too little has yet been done by way of enunciating either the former or the latter objectives in
clear terms. (For instance, the Administrative
Reforms Commission, in India, recommended in 1969
that the government should 'make a comprehensive
and clear statement on the objectives and obligations of public undertakings' (2). The government
accepted the recommendations. But, to this day,
nothing approximating to its fulfilment has been
done.) Besides, in the exercise of governmental

powers of control in many countries, there has been a neglect of the financial criteria of public enterprise operations, or untested notions of social gains. There is ample evidence of underpricing in public enterprise (3).

Independent commissions entrusted with price regulation functions can have good effects – not by concentrating on financial returns to the neglect of social returns, but by proceeding to examine precisely what social returns are realised from a given pricing system and whether, without prejudicing them, the prices can be so regulated as to serve the direct enterprise objectives also. This can assure the consumers that the prices are the best possible in the circumstances and that they do not involve objectionable cross-subsidisations. No one loses in this scenario – neither the enterprise, nor the consumers, nor the government.

(ii) Independent commissions processing final or semi-final powers as regards prices, investments, costs and efficiency, can insulate the enterprises and their consumers from serious exposure to the political interests of the party in power (4). Broad aims such as assisting the rural poor or limiting the foreign share in investment within a certain proportion, can be realised by means of appropriate guidelines. But less defensible interests which represent 'politicking' can be kept aside once an independent commission takes charge of a control function.

It would be interesting to refer, at this point, to a recent study on Ghana (5) in which something like a theory was developed to the effect that the public corporation has a novel raison d'être in developing countries, namely, that it is conceived of as a vehicle that confers special benefits on political personages. Tempting as this inference may be, the point is rather that the control system has been so centralised in the government that the minister easily wields the control instruments to his narrow advantage. If independent commissions functioned, this might not have occurred.

(iii) If independent commissions are given a role in the control system, the prospect of stability in the control instruments over time can improve. For two reasons. First, the control instruments would be derived from set criteria on which the commissions steadily work. Second, business acumen, logicality and expert analysis as inputs in the control process become weightier than when the control power is centralised in the government.

Further, there ensues a qualitative improvement in the control system in that it is substantially relieved of the disadvantage of un-coordination among different departments of government and of the resulting ad hocism in the formulation of the control instruments. For example, an order might be issued to stop a coal mine from closing on employment grounds, at the same time as manpower reductions are insisted upon in steel or on railways on productivity grounds. The basic issue common to both controls really concerns the national policy on employment and productivity. But it loses force, for the government 'lacks a single corporate presence' (6), to use John B. Heath's words in a like context. It will not be out of place to venture a view at this point: the less effective co-ordination within government towards the control instruments, the more purposeful the use of independent commissions.

(iv) In several countries - both developed (7) and developing (8) - the involvement of the government in public enterprise management verging on details and day-to-day operations has been substantial, though not always established in clear terms. In some countries there is a sizeable proportion of officials on the boards of directors. In these circumstances, the government develops an indifference, if not unwillingness, to delve into the substantive basics requisite to the issuance of the final control instrument - for example, into investigations covering costs, productivity, manpower utilisation, quality of output, internal organisation, and the decisional process. For, at some point, the role of the government (or of official directors) may come out in unfavourable shades. An independent commission entrusted with, or partaking in, the control function can have no reason to keep away from such exercises. Without any interest in blaming anyone, it can bring out the right factual basis for any control instrument proposed or contemplated (9). In other words, the antecedents of a managerial circumstance do not pre-empt the formulation of the right control instrument.

There are two other situations in the context of government relations with public enterprises, in

201

which independent commissions can be purposeful.
First, where Parliament plays a limited role in the
control of public enterprises and in the control of
the government's part in their working, as in many
countries in Latin America (10), independent commissions can have an immense role to play by filling
in the gaps in the control system in the interest
of ensuring proper accountability of the enterprise
to society.   Second, where the government or a
minister fights shy of retracting from a control
instrument even though the interests of the enterprise as well as of society certify to such a step,
independent commissions which, by definition, are
free from political constraints, can recommend new
approaches and measures.   The minister or the government can revise the control instrument as if in
studied response to an independent recommendation.
In this way, they can be a source of welcome assistance to the minister.

We shall proceed to discuss four issues of
policy concerning the creation of independent commissions:

(a)   Can a commission be set up commonly for
       public and private enterprises?

(b)   Can there be one commission for many or
       almost all subjects of control or is it
       preferable to have different commissions
       for different subjects?

(c)   Are the conclusions of the commission to
       be mandatory or recommendatory?

(d)   What are the appropriate composition and
       coverage of the commission?

(a)   A bi-sectoral commission

As we look round there are but few independent
commissions set up exclusively for public enterprises.
The most prominent ones, relating to price control,
have been established in many countries to help in
governmental exercise of general price controls,
irrespective of whether the outputs concerned come
from the public or the private sector.   The Price
Commission in the UK illustrates the point.   Set
up in 1973 to administer the Price Code, it applied
to 'the prices of all goods and services supplied to
the United Kingdom home market' (11), unless speci-

fically exempted. (Similar was the nature of the
Pay Board in the UK.) There are also instances of
bi-sectoral commissions which originally started
with jurisdiction limited to the private sector.
The Monopolies and Mergers Commission (MMC) in the
UK, which, along with its earlier versions – the
Monopolies and Restrictive Practices Commission and
the Monopolies Commission – had long been restricted
to the private sector, derived powers of enquiry into
public enterprises as recently as 1980, on 'questions
relating to (a) the efficiency and costs of, (b) the
service provided by, or (c) possible abuse of a monopoly situation' (12).

A bi-sectoral commission can be a useful device
in three ways:

(i) It establishes the principle of unifor-
mity in governmental approach to both private and
public enterprises, with reference to a given aspect
of business behaviour – a healthy principle in a
mixed economy. From this angle it is unfortunate
that certain agencies like the Monopolies and Restrictive Practices Commission in India are restricted
to the monopoly and restrictive practices of private
enterprises only (13).

(ii) A bi-sectoral commission has advantages
in a situation of public enterprises operating com-
petitively with private enterprises in a given sector.

(iii) Where the number of public enterprises
or their relative role in the economy is small, a
bi-sectoral commission may be adequate on grounds
of work load.

The major limitation of a bi-sectoral commission is that it may do inadequate justice to the
special obligations that public enterprises face
and to the special problems of performance that
they present. This may be illustrated with reference to the MMC of the UK, which is excluded, in
its investigations, from 'any question relating to
the appropriateness of any financial obligations or
guidance as to financial objectives (however expressed) imposed by a Minister' (14). The MMC
could, therefore, no more than make such observations as the following in its reports:

Although British Railways Boards are set
several specific financial targets, there

are no specific formal targets or constraints on the quality of service
expected of them. (15)

Financial constraints arising from Government policy have become much stricter
in recent years. In accordance with
Section II(8) of the Competition Act, we
have not considered the appropriateness
of these constraints. (16)

With reference to several governmental constraints on the procurement policies of the Central
Electricity Board,

It is not for us to express any view
about the justification of the policies.
(17)

The level of the EFL conflicted with the
level of investment planned by the Board
and authorised by the Government. (18)

It is possible to draft special provisions to
apply to public enterprise in the legislation or regulatory codes governing the functioning of the independent commissions (19). But, in countries where
public enterprises constitute a sizeable bulk of the
national economy, their socio-economic role tends to
be so distinctive that an exclusive agency for public enterprises may be desirable to deal with them.
At least a distinctive sub-agency with its own elaborate codes of functioning has to be set up within a
given bi-sectoral commission. Or else, the control
framework applicable to public enterprises does not
get the full review that it deserves. Nor does the
precise nature of synthesis attempted as between
social and financial objectives attract the required
attention at the hands of the commission.

Let us illustrate this with reference to some
of the distinctive problems that public enterprises
present to the independent control commissions in
the context of pricing and monopoly power.

Many public enterprises derive government
capital at relatively low rates of interest. Do
these represent all the capital costs to be recovered? How are the capital costs to be computed in
situations of a public enterprise competing with a
private enterprise in certain sections of the market?

Some public enterprises are so set up as to possess extensive elements of excess capacity. Are the total costs of capacity to be recovered through prices?

Some of them undertake large volumes of social expenditures – e.g. on housing for employees on a scale larger than in private enterprise. Are these to be considered as costs wholly recoverable from prices? Besides, what are the limits of social expenditure that they may be permitted to incur?

The answers in such cases cannot be cut and dried. They bristle with enterprise concerns, consumer interests, taxpayers' equity and the government's thinking on related issues of national development. It will be too difficult for a bi-sectoral commission to deal with them as if a footnote to its main techniques of functioning.

(b) One commission

Should there be one independent commission for all delegated control aspects, or should different commissions be set up for different control aspects? This depends, partly, on the extent of the control tasks to be performed at the commission level. Where the size of the public enterprise sector is large, a single commission may find itself overburdened if entrusted with all aspects of control.

More importantly, the answer depends on the degree of technical homogeneity of the control aspects. Broadly one can think of financial targets, prices, investments, external financial limits, costs and efficiency as constituting a related area. So are procurement questions. Employee questions such as recruitment, promotion, training, dismissal, pensions and wages may be considered as one group. Perhaps wages may be taken out and considered as an important major issue of incomes policy and placed under a distinctive commission – e.g. the Pay Board in the UK set up under the Counter-Inflation Act of 1973. Likewise monopoly may be treated as a subject in itself though it is closely allied to several of the other issues mentioned above.

It is doubtful if adequate thought has been given by governments on this subject. For there are yet too few independent commissions that have control functions concerning public enterprise.

In the area of finance, price control agencies of one
kind or another (bi-sectoral in many cases) have been
fairly common, but none else.   So have questions of
monopoly been entrusted in a few cases to independent
commissions.   Some bodies exist in the area of personnel - e.g. the Statutory Authorities' Service
Commission in Trinidad and Tobago, the Standing Committee on Parastatal Organisations in Tanzania, the
Statutory Corporations Service Commission in Nigeria,
and the (short-lived) Parastatal Service Commission
in Zambia; and in the area of procurement - e.g. the
Corporations Standing Tenders Board in Nigeria.
Some of these bodies generally apply to both the
government departments and certain - not necessarily
all - public enterprises.

The obvious caution necessary while setting up
multiple commissions is that their functions do not
overlap in such a way as to result either in duplica-
tion of control efforts or, what is worse, in conflicting conclusions on control instruments.

Perhaps it is worth referring here to the idea
of a Public Enterprise Commission (PEC) for which I
have argued since the early sixties (20).   The case
for such an independent commission (21) may be re-
formulated in the following terms in the present
context.

(i)   While a Price Commission or a Monopolies
Commission covers a single issue or individual enterprises or industries, a PEC can look at an issue with
reference to all public enterprises - e.g. cross-
subsidisations or public compensations for social
obligations - or at an enterprise (or industry) with
reference to all interrelated issues - e.g. pricing,
pricing structure, cost efficiency, investments and
growth, financial management and subsidies.   The
larger and the more diversified the public enterprise
sector in the national economy, the more necessary
such a horizontal or cross-sectional (pre-) control
machinery.

(ii)   A task which sectional agencies such as
a Price Commission may not be fitted to do is the
review of the impact that national goals or objectives ought to have on public enterprises.   Nor
would it be their function to formulate a control
framework conducive to the realisation of the goals.
On the other hand, a PEC can be charged to do this.
A few examples may clarify the point.   If invest-

ment controls are a national need, what role do 'external financial limits' have as a control measure? If fighting inflation is the national goal what place does price-freezing, followed by compensations, have in governmental control relationships with public enterprises? If the government has an incomes policy, how precisely do social expenditures or salary structures in public enterprises agree with it and what control instruments seem to be helpful?

(iii) A PEC can be of specific use, in view of its expertise, in resolving inter-public enterprise pricing problems. Such an arrangement will be of particular significance when these issues do not come within the direct purview of a Price Commission or a Monopolies Commission. Besides, it will keep decisions from being taken as a family affair, on ad hoc grounds and at government instance. (For example, 'keep coal prices down, or else the railways' costs will go up' !)

Reference may be made to the arrangement in India for 'pricing problems as between Government Departments and public sector enterprises or between different public enterprises, which cannot be settled through mutual discussions', being referred to the Finance Ministry and the Bureau of Public Enterprises 'for examination by ad hoc Pricing Committees. Such Pricing Committees are normally chaired by the Director General of the Bureau of Public Enterprises' (22). While this arrangement has some merits, to remit such issues to a PEC would turn out to be a superior technique that ensures expert determinations but under governmental guidelines.

(iv) A PEC can have the effect of forcing the government to develop, in a parallel manner, a 'corporate' nucleus of policy formulation within the government, which can respond to or adjudicate the PEC's determinations or recommendations.

A PEC need not be considered as duplicatory of existing agencies, for few, if any, exist yet in many countries. Nor does it make unnecessary, or trespass the terrain of, a Price Commission. Its purpose, approach and focus are all distinctive. And perhaps its findings can be given a recommendatory status — a question covered in the following section.

207

There is an interesting resemblance between the PEC idea and the recently created public corporation, CONADE, in Peru in the course of a total reorganisation of the public enterprise sector. CONADE is intended to direct and co-ordinate all entrepreneurial activities of the public enterprises. All proposed investments, except those in the financial system, are to be presented by CONADE to the Interministerial Commission for Economic and Financial Affairs for approval. CONADE is to ensure that each enterprise has adequate capital resources for its functions and that investment plans do not exceed the available funds; further, it is to verify cross-subsidisations. CONADE is to evaluate the operations and current state of the enterprises and establish the level of managerial efficiency and the degree to which the enterprises have met their objectives. Equally importantly, CONADE is to provide the Interministerial Commission with an annaul evaluation of the entrepreneurial activities of the government and propose any changes deemed necessary in the law governing public enterprise. Further, CONADE will serve as the technical secretariat to the Interministerial Commission which will have overall co-ordinatory and evaluating charge of public enterprises at the government level (23).

(c)   Mandatory or recommendatory commissions

A basic question concerning an independent commission is whether it should have mandatory powers as regards its conclusions or it should only have powers of recommending to the government well-processed courses (or options) of action. There are instances of both kinds. In the UK the Price Commission – abolished in 1980 – was to exercise its powers in such ways as appeared to it appropriate for the purpose of ensuring that the provisions of the price code prepared by the Treasury were implemented. In so doing it could 'restrict' any price (24). On the other hand, the Monopolies and Mergers Commission in the same country has only recommendatory powers. It has to make a report to the Secretary of State stating, 'with reasons, the conclusions of the Commission'. Where the Commission concludes that a course of conduct against the public interest exists, the report may include 'recommendations as to what action (if any) should be taken for the purpose of remedying or preventing what the Commission consider are the adverse effects of that course of conduct' (25).

An example of a mandatory commission in the
developing world is provided by Trinidad and Tobago
which set up a Public Utilities Commission 'to determine the rates for public utilities'. It can
'determine' complaints relating to rates, a public
utility's claims for an increase in rates, and dis-
putes between public utilities. (Unlike the British Monopolies and Mergers Commission, it can act
'of its own motion' and not only 'at the instance
of the Minister'.) Its awards cannot be 'chal-
lenged, appealed against, reviewed, questioned, or
called into question in any court on any account whatever' - except for an appeal 'on a point of law'
(26).

Two examples may be cited from Tanzania. One
is the National Price Commission empowered 'to determine reasonable price structures on a national
basis' (27), and the other is the Permanent Labour
Tribunal whose powers include the registration of
negotiated agreements and voluntary agreements between employers and employees of an enterprise and
'determining' related matters (28). It has the
power to determine if the wage and incentive emolu-
ments implied in an agreement comply with the national policy guidelines on the subject. And the Tribunal's awards and decisions are 'final'.

It is difficult to assert that a mandatory
commission invariably constitutes a superior technique. The answer depends on the circumstances
outlined below.

(i) How clear are the parameters laid down
for the functioning of the commission? The clearer
or more precise the bases on which it is expected
to act, the greater the case for its mandatory status. A good example can be derived from the Price
Code provided to the Prices Commission in the UK, in
which the major determinants of action were elaborately spelt out; e.g. the definitions of total
costs, allowable cost increases, depreciation,
profit margins, allocations of costs to controlled
prices, and multi-product enterprises. Besides,
definite criteria such as the following were set:
'prices ... may not be increased unless there is an
increase in total costs per unit of output'; and
'prices should be reduced ... where there is a net
reduction in allowable costs per unit of output'
(29).

On the other hand, where it is difficult to
render the criteria of control in conclusively precise terms, there should be a preference for giving
the commission recommendatory powers: for example,
where the issue relates to foreign collaboration,
technology and finance.

(ii) How free are the commission's functions
from value judgements? If, for example, questions
of price enhancements involve considerations of dis-
tributive justice, or enterprise expansions raise
questions of policy on concentration, ancillary industries and location of economic activity, a merely
expert commission may not be able to inject fully
into its findings the social-policy considerations
that the government wishes to consider before a
control instrument is issued (30). What it can
do and must, is to examine expertly the various
options available in giving effect to a given social
policy, establish the costs and benefits of each option and provide sufficient knowledge to the government and the public to enable them to arrive at the
best choice possible. This is where the case for
an independent commission is strong, even if it is
entrusted with recommendatory powers only.

(iii) How closely does the government intend
to use public enterprises as instruments of social
policy? Where the government decides to have unqualified freedom to intervene in the operations of
public enterprises, it does not suit it to give mandatory powers to the commissions — the more so when
it is inclined to avail of the enterprises as an opportunity for political gratification of one kind or
another. If, on the other hand, the government
wishes the enterprises to operate relatively freely
and as commercial enterprises, the case for the commission's powers being mandatory improves. The more
the government's wish to expose the enterprises to
market disciplines, subject to its strategic controls,
the greater the case for a mandatory, as against a
recommendatory, commission. For instance, the government may wish to offer a railway enterprise a specified (public service obligation) subsidy; but subject to this the commission can be given a mandatory
role in respect of control over the price structures.

(iv) The more mandatory the commissions'
powers, the less directly accountable the executive
branch of government for the control instruments.
Parliament may feel somewhat constrained in its

role of public enterprise control through control of executive actions (31).

(v) Finally, there is a point of strategy. Governments may be more willing to consider establishing independent commissions if they are to be endowed with recommendatory powers, for, the final powers of formulating the control instruments will remain with the government itself.

(d) Composition and coverage

(1) Composition: The basic characteristics of the commissions, viz., expertise and independence, have the best chance of being preserved when they are non-official in composition. Where officials dominate them, three limitations are likely:

(i) The claims of independence and expertise on the part of the commission cannot be sustained.

(ii) Clear criteria of action may not be set for the commissions, in the notion that it consists of officials who 'know it all'.

(iii) The officials are likely to bring random, if not disparate, briefs from the different ministries or departments they come from.

A few examples of official dominated commissions may be cited here. The Central Tenders Board of Trinidad and Tobago, which covers some public enterprises, has an official bias in its composition. Similar is the case of the Capital Issues Committee in that country. Without the Governor of the Central Bank as Chairman, it has representatives from the Ministries of Finance, Planning and Development, Industry and Commerce, Prime Minister's office, Inland Revenue Division, and the Industrial Development Corporation. The Public Enterprises Selection Board set up in 1974 in India 'to advise Government on appointments within its prerogative' 'of appointment of the Chairman, both part-time and full-time, and the Members of the Board of Directors' (32), consisted of a Planning Commission official as Chairman, a private sector executive, a public sector executive, and the Secretary of the Ministry of Heavy Industry; and the Bureau of Public Enterprises serves as the Secretariat of the Board. Two control agencies in Kenya, viz., the Inspectorate for Statutory Boards

and the Parastatal Advisory Committee, with significant control-related functions, are within the government and official in composition.

Official-biased boards such as the above perhaps bring some order in the control function, but
do not have the full advantages of commissions with
non-officials or a non-official majority. (Here, by
an official member of a commission,is meant one who
is on it while simultaneously holding his main post
in the government, or who holds the membership in
an ex-officio capacity.)

(2) Coverage: Several of the commissions we
know of cover subjects, not with major financial,
pricing, investment and monopoly implications, but
of management, which are rather the prerogative of
the enterprises themselves. While the chief merit
of an independent commission is that it somewhat de-
concentrates the public control function, commissions
dealing with the management-orientated functions tend
to lift certain essentially management functions away
from the enterprise levels.

A few examples clarify the point. The Corporations Standing Tenders Board in Nigeria takes over
and supervises the award of contracts in relation to
any project with which a corporation (to which the
Decree relates) is concerned, and enters into agreements or arrangements pertaining to any project in
which any such corporation is interested (33). The
Decree transfers to the Board 'all the powers of the
subject statutory corporations 'as to supervision of
award of contracts' (34). The Statutory Corporations Service Commission in Nigeria has the 'power
to appoint persons to hold or act in offices in a
statutory corporation' to which the Decree applies
and 'to dismiss and exercise disciplinary control
over persons holding or acting in such offices'.
It can also 'appoint official representatives of
the corporation as agents for commercial operations
of the corporation' (35).

Similarly, the Statutory Authorities' Service
Commission in Trinidad and Tobago has 'power to appoint persons to be or act as officers and to transfer, promote, remove and exercise disciplinary control over persons so appointed' (36).

Such boards have been set up in some cases as
a sequel to scandals found in public enterprises

(e.g. in Nigeria); and, in general, the aim has been
to prevent dishonesty or unfairness in recruitment
and procurement policies. However, such control
techniques can make the enterprise managers resent-
ful (37): who knows, new centres of power and patronage may build up.

Of a somewhat different nature is the Standing
Committee of Parastatal Organisation (SCOPO), set up
in Tanzania in 1976. Though covering personnel matters in the main, SCOPO has policy-level matters
within its purview and not matters of actual appointment
etc. Its functions are as follows (38):

(i) To review and approve existing and new
organisational structures for parastatal organisations with a view to ensuring maximum efficiency, effectiveness
and economy.

(ii) To review and approve salaries and
fringe benefits of employees in parastatal organisations in order to ensure
that they are consistent with the salaries and benefits payable to employees
in the Civil Service requiring the same
skills and qualifications.

(iii) To review and approve the conditions
under which officers in the Civil
Service are seconded to parastatal
organisations after such secondment
has been agreed upon by the Government
in order to ensure that their terms of
service remain consistent with those
of other officers in the same grade or
with the same skills.

(iv) To co-ordinate and approve terms of
transfers and secondments of staff
between the Civil Service and the
parastatal organisations after such
transfers have been agreed upon by
the Government.

(v) To advise parastatatal organisations
on the movement of middle and senior
level personnel within the parastatal
sector to ensure proper utilisation of
manpower.

(vi)   To monitor and co-ordinate training programmes for employees in the parastatal organisations.

(vii)   To review the localisation arrangements within parastatal organisations to ensure conformity with Government policy that all posts should be manned by trained and competent citizens as early as possible.

(viii)To issue instructions and/or regulations to parastatal organisations on matters stipulated under the provisions of this Notice as may be necessary and to ensure implementation of the same.

On the whole, SCOPO represents a well-intended decentralisation within the control system in the personnel and management development area. However, it keeps to itself certain powers that the managers need to possess in the interest of enterprise efficiency.

Further, it is official-biased in composition, consisting of a Chairman (an official part-timer), the Principal Secretaries of the Ministry of Manpower, Ministry of Labour and Social Welfare, and Prime Minister's Office, the Director, Public Investments in the Ministry of Finance and Planning, the Chairman and Managing Director of the National Development Corporation, the Director-General of Tanzania Audit Corporation, and Head of the Political Education Department.

In concluding this chapter, we may note two important caveats in the use of independent commissions.

First, they should not be so designed as to be unaccountable for their actions or to be able effectively to deflect final control prerogatives from the governmental levels. Necessary constitutional safeguards have to be created.

Second, their reports should be published, so that the nature of their actions or decisions or controls is adequately clear to everyone.

NOTES

1.   One recent reference in this connection
is the Report of the Post Office Review Committee
(Chairman, C.F. Carter) (London, HMSO, 1977).   Criticising 'the present arrangements for the Board and
for the ministerial control', the Committee concluded
that 'these vast and valuable, but potentially dan-
gerous, monopolies need to be scrutinised by a special and continuing body, commanding adequate resources for the serious study of the issues' and
recommended the establishment of an independent
Council on Post Office and Telecommunications Affairs.   The functions suggested for this body
range over many substantive areas relevant to the
issuance of control instruments on prices, investments, quality of service and expansions (pp.60-63).
    Also Murdock Taylor's recent observations on
the 'quangos' in New Zealand: 'they mitigate the
effects of centralised government'.   ('Accountability
in the Public Sector: Pressures and Problems' Public Sector, Vol.3, No.3, 1980, p.5).
2.   Administrative Reforms Commission,
Report on Public Sector Undertakings (New Delhi,
1969).
3.   A recent World Bank Study on Nepal, for
instance, mentioned that the non-financial public
enterprises 'have made only minimal contributions'
to the public exchequer and observed that 'with
improved performance' they could 'generate net returns sufficient to cover the financing required'
'to balance the budget, amounting to Rs.258 million
or 1.0% of GDP by 1983/84'.   A World Bank Country
Study, Nepal: Development Performance and Prospects
(New York, 1979).
4.   See Michael Corby, The Postal Business
1969-79: 'Governments took a penny-wise and pound-
foolish approach, and service cuts and price rises
were allowed or blocked according to the perceived
political needs of the moment rather than the needs
of customers.' (p.242).
    Also, see Robert C. Pozen's interesting obser-
vations in his Legal Choices for State Enterprises
in the Third World (New York, 1976):   'The Minister
imposed substantial losses on Tema Development Corporation to court favour with the Tema electorate.'
(p.120).
5.   Robert C. Pozen: 'The maintenance of
TDC as a corporation rather than a department gave
the current regime an additional source of patronage
not bound by the well-developed rules for the civil

service.' (op.cit., p.127) 'The legal form played some functions for important interest groups.' (p.131).

6. John B. Heath, Management in Nationalised Industries, Nationalised Industries' Chairmen's Group, Occasional Papers, No.2 (London, 1980), p.23.

7. The Industry and Trade Committee of the British Parliament observed with reference to the Post Office: 'We are left with the impression that since the separation of the Post Office and British Telecommunications there has been a return to a form of financial and managerial control in the Post Office similar to that exercised when the Corporation was a Government Department.' 'Our view is that the scrutiny by the Department of Industry of the Post Office's activities is too detailed and too intrusive for a body which is supposed to be a commercial enterprise.' Fifth Report from the Industry and Trade Committee (Session 1981-82) The Post Office (London, 1982), p.ix.

8. For example, the World Bank Country Report on Nepal referred to 'erratic government involvement in day-to-day operations' which has led to 'poor management decisions as well as frequent over-staffing'. Also cited are the 'inconsistent government pricing policies' which 'created marketing problems'. (New York, 1979), p.25.

9. For instance, the National Board for Prices and Incomes (in the UK) presented several 'unpalatable alternatives' of policy in the context of fare changes in London. London Transport Fares (Cmnd.4540, HMSO, London, 1970).

10. See H. Boneo's observations at the Seminar in Rome (op.cit) implying that in Latin America 'the role of Parliament is diminished'. (p.59).

11. Price Commission. A Guide to the Price Controls in Stage 4 (London, HMSO, 1975), p.3.

12. Competition Act 1980, Section II (London, HMSO, 1980).

13. The Monopolies and Restrictive Trade Practices Act 1969 (India) does not apply to any undertaking owned or controlled by a government company or by the government or by a corporation established under any Central, Provincial or State Act. (Section 3) The Report of the High Powered Expert Committee on Companies and Monopolies and Restrictive Practices Act criticised this exemption. (New Delhi, 1978).

14. Competition Act 1980, Section II(8) (London, HMSO, 1980).

15. The Monopolies and Mergers Commission, British Railways Board: London and South East Com-

muter Services (London, HMSO, 1980), p.32.
      16.   Op.cit., p.166.
      17.   The Monopolies and Mergers Commission, Central Electricity Generating Board (London, HMSO, 1981), p.292.
      18.   Op.cit., p.15.
      19.   For instance, the Counter-Inflation (Price Code) Order, 1976, says: 'A nationalised industry may, in addition to any increase' in accordance with the general provisions of the Code 'increase prices ... by such further amount necessary to provide sufficient revenue in the accounting year ... to ensure a surplus in that year of 2% calculated on turnover ... or, at the option of the industry, a return of 10% on net assets employed'. (Section 120 (2)).
      20.   V.V. Ramanadham, The Finances of Public Enterprises (Lectures delivered at the Indian Institute of Public Administration in 1961) (Bombay, 1963) p.51: V.V. Ramanadham, The Control of Public Enterprises in India (New York, 1964) Chapter IX: and V.V. Ramanadham (Ed.) Pricing and Investment in Public Enterprise (paper on 'The Concept of a Public Enterprise Commission' presented at a Seminar at New Delhi in January 1970) (New Delhi, 1974) pp.46-50.
      21.   The recent decision of the British Government to use the Monopolies and Mergers Commission 'in its strengthened form' as 'the main instrument for the external scrutiny' of the nationalised industries, illustrates certain elements of the PEC idea pursued here, though there are many material differences, of which the basic one is that the MMC is conceived of as an investigatory agency. (See Hansard, 30 November 1981, Nicholas Ridley, Financial Secretary to the Treasury, Columns 48-49).
      22.   Bureau of Public Enterprises, Government of India, Annual Report on the Working of Industrial and Commercial Undertakings of the Central Government, 1975-76 (New Delhi), p.155.
      23.   This account is closely based on 'Public Enterprises in Peru: The Perspectives for Reform' by Brian Branch (Institute of Latin American Studies) Austin, 1982.
      24.   Counter-Inflation Act 1973, Section 6 (London, HMSO, 1973).
      25.   Competition Act 1980, Section 10 (London, HMSO, 1980).
      26.   The Public Utilities Commission Act 1966, Sections 17 and 18.
      27.   The Regulation of Prices Act 1973, Section 6 (Dar Es Salaam, 1973).

217

28.   The Permanent Labour Tribunal Act, 1967
Section 16 (Dar Es Salaam, 1967).
29.   The Counter-Inflation (Price Code) Order,
1976.
30.   This can be illustrated with reference
to the Price Commission of Tanzania.   In determining the price structures it has to have regard,
among other things, to 'the commodities and services
essential to the community: ... the need to prevent
the income of peasants and workers in the United Republic from being affected adversely by unnecessary
and unjustified price increases; the need to maintain
fair relationships among the incomes of different
sectors of the community; the need to ensure the
continued ability of the Government to finance development programmes and recurrent expenditures:...
the need to provide circumstances conducive to a
healthy and orderly development of trade and commerce in rural as well as urban areas'.   The Regulation of Prices Act, 1973, Section 12(1).   These
are criteria that merit the government's determinations.
Also see R. Rice 'Tanzanian Price Control
System', in Papers on the Political Economy of Tanzania (Ed. K.S. Kim, R.B. Mabele and M.J. Schulteis)
(Dar Es Salaam, 1979), for the conflicts among the
criteria in practice.
31.   See Neil Johnson, 'Editorial: Quangos
and the Structure of British Government' Public
Administration (Winter 1979, Vol.57) p.389.
32.   The Gazette of India: Extraordinary,
Part I, Section I, 30 August 1974.
33.   The Corporation Standing Tenders Board
Decree 1968, Section 3 (Lagos, 1968).
34.   Op.cit., Section 1.
35.   The Statutory Corporations Service Commission Decree 1968, Section 4 (Lagos, 1968).
36.   The Statutory Authorities Act 1966,
Section 5 (Port of Spain, 1966).
37.   'Managements often view the Statutory
Authorities Service Commission as usurpers of their
rightful powers and as an obstacle that slows down
the decision making process.'   Vishun Ramlogan,
Organisation and Control of Public Enterprises in
Trinidad and Tobago (Mimeographed paper).
38.   The Official Gazette, 24 September, 1976,
General Notice No.1286 EBC.6/45/089 (Dar Es Salaam,
1976).

Chapter Eighteen

CONSUMER COUNCILS

This chapter has the limited task of reviewing the
role that consumer councils may be expected to play
in the context of public control of public enterprises.   The rationale of the proposition rests
on three grounds.

First, if the consumer were to be the 'king',
what would be more ideal than to let him assure himself that the enterprise behaves to his satisfaction?
Under perfect competition he need not undertake any
deliberate action.   But, under conditions of less
than perfect markets, he needs to organise himself
so as to wield his influence on the enterprise that
supplies the output.

Second, experience has shown it to be a common
shortcoming of public enterprise operations that,
even in the few cases where limited financial-targeting
has been practised, governments have not exercised
the control muscle as regards the enterprise's <u>duties</u>
or quality of output of service (1).   For example,
though given some financial targets, the British
Railways Board is provided with 'no specific formal
targets or constraints on the quality of service
expected of them' (2).   While the Board has begun
to use 'internally derived standards', the many components of the 'quality' consideration - such as
safety, punctuality, cancellations, cleanliness,
information, frequency of service, load factor, jour-
ney time, quality of rolling stock, and fares - need
a rigorous review, particularly because there exist
inter-relationships - sometimes inverse - among some
of them.   What is important is the price-quality
equation, whose relevance for scrutiny is the higher,
the greater the monopoly power of the public enterprise (3).   Here formal help from the consumers

can be of value to the government in the control exercise. A recent study on consumer councils in the UK in fact suggested that they should set 'targets for their industries – consumer objectives as standards against which the performance of nationalised industries could properly be measured' (4). Whether these councils should 'set' or merely recommend the standards can be a question for debate; however, that they have a role in the task is not.

Third, consumer agencies can be made to occupy a purposeful place in a control system designed to ensure the most appropriate proximity between what and how the enterprise supplies, and what and how the consumers want. But there is a major caveat. The broader the concept of the proximity – for example, when it covers the price level, rates of growth in output and the regional aspects of output expansions – the nearer the subject to national goals and preferences. Here other agencies, including the planning commission, the government departments concerned and Parliament have a material say in the context of a planned economy or a public expenditure planning economy. Besides, where the consumers are nearly the entire community, as in the case of electricity and transport, the broad subjects illustrated above legitimately end up in the lap of the government.

The relative merit of a consumer agency is at a maximum in the context of controls over second-order matters, such as conditions of supply and attention to quality criteria (even here there can be an overlap with first-order considerations), and in a situation where its representational coverage is far short of society as a whole, e.g. consumers of heavy machinery or consumers in a given locality.

There are not many countries in which consumer councils have been established for public enterprises. The UK is one that has adopted this institutional technique by and large (5). The Railway Users Consultative Committee is one of the very few such bodies in existence in India which has a large public enterprise sector.

The regime of consumer agencies is, on the whole, still in the future; and it is worth recognising, at this point, their limitations in concept (and in practice) as an instrument of decentralisation in the control system of public enterprise (6).

(i)   Unless their concerns are, more or less, limited to matters of detail (in helping the managements with knowledge of consumer preference from among a set of potential options open to them), the consumer agencies can impinge on, and conflict with, the concept of managerial responsibility in public enterprise.   Their contribution to the control structure will then be infructuous, neither the government nor the managements being ready to act on their verdict.   (No wonder, a recent study in the UK established that specific individual complaints constituted the major part of the consumer council's work; and no more than a tenth of it concerned independent monitoring of the industry's 'consumer performance'.) (7)   An interesting illustration of the distinction between first-order and second-order matters can be cited from the Monopolies and Mergers Commission's study of the Severn-Trent Water Authority in the UK (8).   To the former category being the relative merits of a straightforward RV-related charge and a two-part tariff, universal   versus selective compulsory metering, and interregional equalisation of charges; and to the latter, views on matters like optional metering, and checks and balances on management strategies.

(ii)   On a major matter of interest to consumers, namely pricing, there is a basic constraint on a consumer council's control status.   It is likely that in several public enterprises extra-enterprise criteria assume far greater significance than simple cost-price equations.   The government may mark out a given enterprise for raising a rather high surplus over cost, while it may decide to control another so as to institute prices that do not cover all costs. Or, the government may determine that national interests demand that a public enterprise pursue certain input policies which are expensive by enterprise criteria, but commendable by macro economic criteria; e.g. the use of domestic inputs as against cheaper imports.   In such cases the costs are so inflated as to prompt the consumers to protest at prices based on costs.   In other words, public enterprises bristle with extra-enterprise obligations that severely conflict with the consumers' focus on the lowest cost of supply of outputs and on cost-based prices.

(iii) The point may be stretched so as to cover aspects of overall strategy of a public enterprise, covering, for example, the size of output (is it to be increased or is there any resource constraint that stands in the way), the timing of expansions (do the investment priorities of the nation dictate or affect the commissioning of an electricity plant in the next five years or seven years ...), and the location of expansion activity (is this to be determined in terms of cost efficiency or of national requirements of regional development). In all such cases the interests of the consumers may vary from those of society at large; and the former have to be judiciously subordinated to the latter. But in doing so the consumer councils have some role.

At this point, it will be of interest to refer to a recent development in India concerning the vindication of the consumer interest. While consumer councils, as in Britain, do not exist, the Consumer Research Centre, an autonomous body, has been pursuing the route of available legal challenges against prices and quality of service of several public enterprises, e.g. electricity, road transport and air transport. The challenges are so formulated as to emphasise the point that, in the absence of an independent commission adjudging prices, quality, costs and efficiency, the interest of the consumers is endangered if the government simply permits, encourages or orders price increases or a deterioration in service. For instance, the Centre's arguments against a Road Transport Corporation are developed in terms of its statutory duty to provide 'an efficient, adequate, economical and properly co-ordinated system of road transport services ' (9). Use is made of statistical and other techniques in criticising the prevailing state of efficiency, adequacy and economy of the Corporation's services. Similarly, it bases its case, vis-à-vis the State Electricity Boards, on their statutory obligations for 'the co-ordinated development of the generation, supply and distribution of electricity within the state in the most efficient and economical manner' (10).

In concluding this chapter, we may note that consumer councils are yet an untried institution in most countries; the more so in their role as a decentralised means of public enterprise control. The conditions for their success in this regard may be outlined as follows:

First, their powers and coverage have to be delineated in adequate precision, so that they neither tread on the management's toes nor indulge in directions that predestine governmental indifference to their findings. On the government's side, there ought to be a genuine appreciation of their capacity to fill in the gaps in public control geared to the performance of duties by a public enterprise consistent with any set extra-enterprise parameters (11).

Second, a national or enterprise-wise consumer body possesses the qualities of strength in study as well as in presentation; but, paradoxically, it has to be kept from wasteful exercises touching on issues that happen to be the prerogative of the government, Parliament or the enterprise board itself. It is of equal importance to ensure the desirable degree of co-ordination between its activities and those of any other major independent commission dealing with prices, investments, monopoly power and overall efficiency.

Third, the status of the consumer councils has to be raised to that of public-funded agencies analagous to, say, price commissions and monopoly commissions, instead of making them dependent on the finances and other help from the enterprises concerned. The latter arrangement may be adequate as long as the goal is consumer-producer dialogue, but not when the goal is to make these agencies a part of the control system.

Fourth, clear thought has to be given to the question of how any sharp differences on major issues with policy implications between the consumer councils and the enterprise management get resolved. Do they reach the Minister or Parliament and what happens next? Will this device work so that issues that are not expected, under the governing Act, to concern the Minister or Parliament, begin to float up to that level?

Last, how widely are the consumer councils known and how do we prevent their being pockets of influence for the smarter sections of the consumers? Will there be separate sub-agencies for the more important sub-markets - e.g. industrial and domestic consumers? These questions are of value in connection with cost-price relationships, cross-subsidisations, and output rationing when the need arises; and agencies meant for streamlining public control ought not to end up as sectional pockets of influence and patronage.

NOTES

1.   On the importance of stipulating 'purpose and duty' of public enterprises and of defining them, see Alec Nove, Efficiency Criteria for Nationalised Industries, Chapter 6 (London, 1973).

2.   Monopolies and Mergers Commission, British Railways Board: London and South East Commuter Services, Cmnd.8046 (London, 1980) p.32

3.   For instance, the National Economic Development Office (in the UK) observed that 'many sponsor departments do not seem to have given prominence to the problem of relating prices to standards of service which customers require'. (A Study of UK Nationalised Industries: Their Role in the Economy and Control in the Future) (London, HMSO, 1976).

4.   Consumer Councils, Consumer Consultative Machinery in the Nationalised Industries (London, HMSO, 1968).

5.   Some exceptions exist, however.   The Iron and Steel Consumers' Council set up under the Iron and Steel Act 1967 was abolished on the UK joining the Common Market in 1973; for the Council's role in reaching the Minister on prices was considered incompatible with the Common Market principles. Today there is a non-statutory British Iron and Steel Consumers' Council.   Similar is the history of the Consumers' Council in the Coal Industry too.

6.   The potential utility of a consumer council in the control context may be illustrated with reference to the Post Office Users' National Council (in the UK) which is statutorily empowered to consider any aspect of Post Office policy and advise the Minister on any action to be taken. (Post Office Act 1969, Section 14(8)(a) (London, HMSO, 1969).

7.   National Consumer Council, Report No.1, Consumers and the Nationalised Industries (London, HMSO, 1976) p.54.

8.   The Monopolies and Mergers Commission, Severn-Trent Water Authority East Worcestershire Waterworks Company and the South Staffordshire Waterworks Company (London, HMSO, 1981).

9.   The Road Transport Corporations Act, 1950, Section 18 (New Delhi, 1950).

10.   Electricity (Supply) Act of 1948, Section 18 (New Delhi, 1948).

11.   It is relevant to cite here the recommendations of the Industry and Trade Committee (Session 1981-82) (UK) concerning the Post Office, that 'HMG review the constitution of POUNC with a view to making

it a potent and effective body.'   The Post Office
Users' National Council (POUNC) claimed its 'primary
duty' to be 'to ensure that the Post Office is
managed in the interests of its customers'. (Fifth
Report from the Industry and Trade Committee, Session 1981-82, The Post Office, HMSO 343:241-i-iv
(London, 1982).

Chapter Nineteen

TECHNIQUES OF ENTERPRISE ORGANISATION

There is an asymmetry between this chapter and the
preceding ones. The latter dealt with agencies
set up outside the enterprises and entrusted with
functions of control, direct or indirect. Here
we shall consider some techniques of enterprise
organisation which, though apparently internal,
have the effect of decentralising certain control
functions from the level of the government.

(a)   The holding company system

There are a large number of holding companies
in the public sector - both in developed and in developing countries. Italy, among the former, has the
famous IRI and ENI; Spain, the INA; France, the
Renault (with about 300 subsidiaries in 1979); and
the UK, the National Enterprise Board with 22 subsidiaries and 38 associated companies (in 1981). Far
more instances are available in the developing countries: particularly in Africa - e.g. the National
Development Corporation in Tanzania, INDECO, MINDECO,
FINDECO, RUDECO etc., in Zambia, the Industrial Development Corporation in Uganda, the sectoral corporations in the Sudan and Egypt, and GIHOC (though not
technically a holding company today) in Ghana.
Examples of holding company structures elsewhere are
Guyana State Corporation in Guyana, Pernas in Malaysia, the National Textile Corporation in India and
Indu Peru in Peru.

That a holding company can be utilised, to some
extent, as a vehicle in the control system can be
inferred from such legislative provisions as the
following, describing the Guyana State Corporation's
functions and powers:

'to exercise supervision and control' over
the public enterprises; to issue 'general
or specific directions' (a) for securing
co-ordination of the functions of some or
all of the public enterprises; and (b)
'in respect of matters relating to the
personnel, including conditions of service,
finance, management and organisation of
any such public enterprise' (1).

Even more elaborately control-oriented are
some of the functions defined for the National
Energy Corporation of Trinidad and Tobago, one of
the six holding company entities recently identified as desirable for the country:

1.　　'Approval of the awards of contracts
　　　above a certain sum;

2.　　approval for submission to the capital
　　　sole of any new negotiated loan;

3.　　approval for submission to the capital
　　　sole of all major plans for expansion;

4.　　approval of any major increases in cost;

5.　　liaison with all public undertakings and
　　　other government organisations.' (2)

Trinidad and Tobago provides a clear example
of the trend of thought in favour of holding companies constituting a limb in the hierarchy of the
control system - strangely, it may look, in a relatively small country where the quantitative handicaps
of a control system centralised in the government
may not be too serious.　A recent working group on
public enterprises recommended the following powers
for a holding company.　(Some of these constitute
control functions.)

To translate national economic objectives
and policies of the government into strategic sectoral objectives and programmes of
action;

to frame sectoral policy guidelines for
assisting the development of the objectives and plans of its subsidiary companies;

228

to consolidate and rationalise the operating lines and programmes of subsidiary
companies;

to study the annual reports of subsidiary
companies;

to report to the corporate sole on the
activities of the subsidiaries; and

to develop a general policy for industrial practices.

And these recommendations were 'totally accepted'
by the government (3).

Reference may also be made to the price controlling powers of ZIMCO (Zambia Industrial and Mining Corporation Ltd.) vis-à-vis its innumerable subsidiaries, though formally subject to the statutory
authority of the Price Controller and the requirement
of prior approval by the government of price increases
in respect of several essential commodities.

The possibility of the holding company representing an 'intermediation' between the government
and the operating enterprises is illustrated by IRI
in Italy. This ente di gestione has 'the task of
guiding and controlling' the enterprises it is responsible for; only this ente di gestione is under
government control and not the operating companies;
the latter come under its control (4). GIHOC of
Ghana provides another instance of the holding
corporation acting 'as an effective shield against
government supervision of corporation subsidiaries'.
(5). The government of Kenya accords a special
status to the development and financial holding
companies in the context of investment control
over the operating companies, as per the recent
guidelines on the approval of investment projects
in the public sector (6).

A plea was advanced before the Select Committee
on Nationalised Industries in the UK in favour of
setting up a large state holding company rather like
those that operate in Italy. A major purpose seemed
to border on minimising the political element in public control: 'to place the industries at one stage
further removed from political influence' (7).

The instrumentality of the holding company

229

technique in the control system of public enterprise may be summed up in the following terms:

(i) The holding company can be a helpful tool in translating public control goals into meaningful directives to the operating managements, more expertly than the government departments can do in many substantive areas.

(ii) It can provide the government with a well-processed frame of data on a contemplated social policy for implementation through the public enterprises concerned, on the basis of its reasonable nearness to the operating companies, combined with reasonable aloofness from them. And the government can decide on the best option to adopt.

(iii) It can offer itself as a first step in devising the most appropriate indicators of performance suited to each of its subsidiaries and in the monitoring of their performance. The need to link these with, or adjust them to, indicators of social performance emerging from some independent commission and government guidelines, still exists.

These represent the potential of a holding company from the angle of public control over public enterprises. Yet there is need for caution on several grounds.

First, there is the conceptual problem that the holding company represents an overlap and conflict between its responsibility for the performance of the enterprises constituting its subsidiaries and its responsibility for controlling their activities. The more its involvement in the operations of its subsidiaries, the less its suitability to the function of public control over them. Achieving the right balance will be a delicate task, and a board constitution such that the chief executives of the subsidiaries dominate the holding apex makes this all the more difficult (8).

Second, it will not be easy to resolve the power distribution between the sectoral ministries and the holding company board. The latter can become highly powerful - what with its room for discretion and patronage in such fields as appointments, contracts, distribution arrangements, construction work, foreign negotiations, and employee compensations. There can be a constant tug of war

230

between the ministries and the board, unless the former reconcile themselves to an attitude of aloofness or the latter is exorcised through control instruments that materially defeat its control instrumentality (9).

Perhaps it will be of interest to make a passing observation on the oft-quoted example of success - IRI of Italy. Here the impact of social policy is reduced, more or less, to the investment directives in favour of Southern Italy and the 'endowment fund' takes care of it. Subject to these, the IRI enterprises operate as if under market discipline. No wonder, IRI can function as an efficacious control agency intermediately between the government and the operating enterprises.

Third, large and powerful holding companies tend to attract as board members senior government officials, if not ministers (at least as chairmen). (The Zambia Industrial and Mineral Company (ZIMCO), with the President of the country as its chairman, illustrates this.) And they are likely to lose the merit of being a non-government control agency, though their controls are wielded <u>formally</u> from outside the government offices. Equally unfortunate will be the fact that, being heavily governmental in composition, they may not attract serious public attention to the consequences of the controls they exercise over the enterprises.

Fourth, the control potential of a holding company is qualified by the coverage of the apex unit. If it is confined to a single sector, its claims of substantive competence in arriving at meaningful control instruments in a given field of operations may be significant. If its composition is sectorally quite diversified its approach towards control tends to be of a non-specialist kind, and it may end up as 'another tier of control over the operating units' (10). There is another side to the situation of a sectoral holding company, viz., that it may be tempted to develop 'line' relationships. (The earlier point of overlap between performance-involvement and control may be recalled.)

The virtues of its control potential may be offset by the damage its interferences cause with the management of the operating units.

(b)   Policy Councils

These represent another organisational technique relevant to control decentralisation. A major
proposal recently made by the National Economic
Development Office (NEDO) in the UK at the end of
an elaborate study of the government-public enterprise problems, favoured the establishment of a
two-tier board system for each nationalised industry,
consisting of a Policy Council and the usual board
(of directors).   The Policy Council is 'to carry
out the functions of agreeing corporate aims and
objectives, agreeing strategic policies needed to
achieve these aims and objectives, establishing
performance criteria, endorsing corporate plans,
including annual budgets and related pricing and
cost assumptions, and monitoring performance, at
appropriate intervals, against pre-determined
policies and criteria' (11).   And the corporation
board will act 'as the executive authority' and
'manage the corporation within a framework of
jointly agreed policies, plans and performance
criteria' (12).

Though NEDO did not categorically propose
Policy Councils as a step in the control hierarchy,
the whole context in which the idea was advanced
calls for comment from the angle of how far such
an agency, if set up, can offer itself as a step
in control decentralisation – the theme of the
present discussion.

From the chorus of unfavourable comments
voiced by most of the British nationalised industries (13), it appears that a Policy Council substantially duplicates the board (14).   To the extent that it is meant to be different it can raise
the following problems.

First, its status as a step in control decentralisation will be marred by two possibilities:
viz., that the government is unlikely to delegate its
control functions (5) to the Council, composed as
suggested; and that the Council, on the other hand,
is likely to attract to itself certain board functions (16).   The net outcome may be an over-centralisation of management-cum-internal control, without   the compensation of a decentralisation of the
government's control prerogatives.

Second, the suggested composition is more

232

likely to nurse representational interests (17), constitute merely a forum for discussion (18) and be a source of 'discord and animosity' (19), rather than operate as an agency capable of expert control.

Third, it disrupts the idea that a good control system has to help promote good management. For, it can hinder it by delaying decision (20), by acquiring power without responsibility (21) and by becoming an additional layer in the enterprise organisation (22). Further, it can imbibe some of the dubious characteristics of a holding company apex cited in the preceding section if it has a whole sector or a large number of operating units under it. If, on the other hand, there are several public enterprises in a given sector and each one were to have a Policy Council, the role of the multiple Councils in control over matters of a given sector would be complicated.

Last, Policy Councils for individual enterprises, whatever their merits, do not provide the control system with economies of scale in expertise which such agencies as Price Commissions, Monopoly Commissions, Pay Boards, Investment Boards and Management Audit Boards do. Hence cross sectional problems of public enterprise continue to need other mechanisms suited to them.

This review of Policy Councils applies to any other version of similarly motivated bodies, of which the 'planning committees' recently set up for many statutory authorities - though not for government companies - in Papua New Guinea are an example. Composed of government officials and enterprise executives, these committees have certain functions of co-ordinating the technical, economic and social aspects of investments and of reviewing (prior to meetings) the plan implications of board papers. In this way they can be expected to be a step in decentralising control from government levels.

(c) Enterprise boards

Some explanation is necessary as we think of enterprise boards as a tool in control decentralisation. They go a step further than the holding apex in not being external to what is sought to be controlled. Their impact as a control agency is with reference to the operations below the board level; and their control function effectively pertains to

233

what goes under the name of internal controls.

Nevertheless, there are three reasons why the role of enterprise boards merits specific reference in our discussion.

First, one of the major problems presented by public enterprise concerns the disaggregation of overall control instruments into sectional bits that apply to the different parts of the enterprise. Let us look at financial targets for an illustration. The way in which an overall target is realised through the contributions of the various parts into which the enterprise can be sub-divided for this purpose, is of significance not only in the context of making the aggregate realisation possible, but in ensuring that the parts are controlled by appropriate sub-targets. The appropriateness of the sub-targets is partly a function of the commercial strategy of the enterprise and partly a matter of public concern, as in the case of the price structures of railways, electricity and posts and telegraphs. The best approach would be for the government or a public agency to issue guidelines on the basis of which the board should be left to work out the details of transmitting the overall target control to the various segments of operations within the enterprise. It would not be proper for agencies outside the enterprise to attract details of this task into their jurisdiction. At the same time they should assure themselves that the details are appropriately worked out within the enterprise. Thus, the board not only assumes a role in the control process, but has to satisfy the government or a related public agency with having fulfilled that role as expected.

Another apt illustration can be drawn from the corporate plan. This, in a sense, contains the substantive essence of government control over a public enterprise. But it depends for its success on the controls exercised at the board level over the constituent parts of the enterprise in respect of their respective commitments to the realisation of the plan.

Second, it is well-known that, theory apart, most governments, of developed (23) as well as developing countries, have stepped into areas of internal management of public enterprises by recourse to ad hoc measures of control. Some of these may have an eventual extra-enterprise justification. But these border on details which the boards have to be left free to work out on the basis of appropriate guidelines from the government or a public agency. In some countries governmental interventions have been occasioned by the (alleged) lack of capability on the part of the managements themselves. The most productive way of dealing with the situation consists of strengthening the boards so as to capacitate them in undertaking due control functions efficiently.

Some examples of control items in this context are: targets on shop floor, establishment of profit centres, productivity controls and labour deployment, absenteeism, cost controls, cash management, terms of credit for consumers, incentive schemes, and recruitment, promotion and disciplinary actions.

The argument here is that the government has to give up some of its control excursions and let the boards act in what happen to be their legitimate areas of action. In this sense the boards may be seen as a tool in control decentralisation.

Third, there is a conceptual benefit in considering the enterprise boards as a rung in the ladder of control decentralisation. The government can think in terms of progressively transferring certain powers of control over the enterprise activities to the boards, limiting itself to strategic points of control (24). Incidentally, this tends to incline the boards in the direction of market discipline, within any given extra-enterprise constraints.

However, the efficacy of enterprise boards as a tool in control decentralisation is subject to the following qualifications.

(i) Most boards are not provided with clear objectives or goals. Oftentimes they experience ad hoc pressures on the results to be achieved. Thus, the real levers of their control functions lie outside the enterprise.

(ii) Certain board compositions can defeat the purport of decentralisation. Where a board is predominantly composed of government officials, it is already a vehicle of disguised governmental pressures; and the entrustment of certain control powers to the board does not necessarily guarantee an independent exercise of the powers. There is a tendency today to introduce executive directors and non-official businessmen into the boards so as to enhance the expertise of the boards in businesslike decision making. The more successful this trend, the more purposeful the boards as a step in control decentralisation.

(iii) Governments may not be inclined to part with control powers in favour of enterprise boards if the latter are known to be incompetent (25). Even the competent boards may not derive control powers, since the government tries not to be invidious in the decentralisation measure.

NOTES

1.   Public Corporations Act, Section 5, (Georgetown, 1975).
2.   The budget speech of the Prime Minister and Minister of Finance (Port of Spain, 30 November 1979).
3.   The reference is to the Working Group appointed at the Conference on the Role, Functioning and Pespectives of State Enterprises, July 1979 (Port of Spain), cited by Ramlogan in his paper 'Organisation and Control of Public Enterprises in Trinidad and Tobago' (mimeographed).
4.   Dr. Ferdinando Brunnelli of IRI, at the Rome Seminar (op.cit), pp.54, 55, and 78.
5.   'In effect, control over corporation operations passed from representatives of the national government to the central officers of the holding corporation.'   Of course, there was a price: GIHOC imposed 'stringent controls on almost every aspect of subsidiary operations'.   (Robert C. Pozen, op.cit., p.170).
6.   'Several of the parastatal development and financial intermediaries finance many individual projects.   For such projects, the appraisal of the intermediary itself will be given primary weight and subsequent approval steps will be undertaken expeditiously, particularly to the extent that (i) the project in question requires no direct government financial input; (ii) the intermediary has a history of viable projects; and (iii) the intermediary has a history of being self-financing.' Guidelines for the Preparation, Appraisal and Approval of New Public Sector Investment Projects (Nairobi, 1983), p.5.
7.   See Aubrey Jones's suggestion in First

Report from the Select Committee on Nationalised Industries - Session 1967-68, <u>Ministerial Control of the Nationalised Industries, Vol.1</u> (London, 1969) p.202.

8.   For instance, it is of interest in this context that the majority of the GUYSTAC Board in Guyana are the chief executives of the constituent companies.

9.   The recent episode of the National Enterprise Board (NEB) in the UK and its two major subsidiaries - British Leyland and Rolls Royce - for which they (the latter) and the Government preferred direct relationships, illustrates this point. The two units were transferred from NEB to the Government(direct) - Rolls Royce Ltd. in 1980 and British Leyland Ltd. in 1981.

10.   For example, the Corporacion de Empresas Nacionales of Argentine (now defunct) eventually 'concentrated on the control of the legality of the operations' of the enterprises. See Boneo's observations at the Rome Seminar (op.cit.) p.64.

11.   National Economic Development Office, <u>A Study of UK Nationalised Industries: Their Role in the Economy and Control in the Future</u>, p.46 (London, HMSO, 1976).

12.   Ibid. p.47.

13.   Second Special Report from the Select Committee on Nationalised Industries, Session 1976-77, <u>Comments by Nationalised Industries on the National Economic Development Office Report</u> (London, HMSO, 1977).

14.   Ibid. p.viii (British Airports Authority) and p.ix (British Airways).

15.   Ibid. p.xxxi (National Bus Company).

16.   Ibid. xxi (British Transport Docks Board).

17.   Ibid. p.xxxi (Natinal Coal Board).

18.   Ibid. p.liii (Post Office).

19.   Ibid. p.x (British Airways).

20.   Op.cit. p.xxi (British Transport Docks Board).

21.   Op.cit. p.xviii (British Steel Corporation).

22.   Op.cit. p.xv (British Railways Board).

23.   In the UK, 'the experience of the last thirty years has demonstrated conclusively that if anything was wrong with the nationalised sector, it was that governments were interfering too much rather than too little'.   John Redwood, <u>Public Enterprise in Crisis: The Future of the Nationalised Industries</u> (Oxford, 1980) p.179.

24.   It is interesting to recall the emphasis placed by the Select Committee on Nationalised Industries in the UK on 'rationally determined strategic guidance' by the government 'together with more autonomy for the boards'.   (First Report of the Select Committee, Session 1967-68, <u>Ministerial Control of Nationalised Industries</u>, Vol.1, (London, HMSO, 1969) p.191.

25.   In fact, in some developing countries some boards are so inactive as not even to hold formal meetings, 'sometimes even for more than a year to review and appraise the problems and performance of their organisations'.   Tanzania Audit Corporation <u>12th Annual Report and Accounts for the Year ended 30th June 1980</u>, p.11 (Dar Es Salaam, 1981).

Chapter Twenty

THE MARKET

The concept of the market as a means of control decentralisation calls for an explanation. In most cases of the agencies discussed earlier, the assumption was that control in the sense of a deliberate public intervention was involved; the question was whether it should rest wholly with the government or, to some extent, with some other agency. With the market, on the other hand, the question has a different connotation, namely whether a given issue should at all be the subject of control, or it should be left to be influenced by market forces.

We are up against a paradox at once. The real case for public enterprise arises in a situation of market failure (1), or where the government intends to initiate, in the national interest, a development process that deviates from what the market forces by themselves evolve. To think in terms of the market as a medium of control over public enterprise amounts to an antithesis, viz., remarketisation.

True, but there are circumstances in which some relaxation of public control in favour of market determinations can be fruitful, without harming the purposes for which a public enterprise has been the preferred agency (2).

(i)   The weaknesses attributed to market forces at the time the original decision was taken to set up a public enterprise may have disappeared in course of time. It may no longer be necessary for the government to introduce any deliberate controls in the realisation of the needed investments in a given sector or the needed output results. In

an extreme case, the enterprise may be continuing in
the public sector simply because of inertia on the
part of the government in altering its entrepreneurial status, or because of political problems vitia-
ting such a change, or because of the public exchequer designs on its profits. For example, several
medium and light industries and certain functions
like warehousing, in which private investment interest was lacking at one time, may have gradually
attracted it so noticeably that, in respect of the
public enterprises that continue to exist in such
fields, public controls can be withdrawn in favour
of market controls.   In fact, this would happen
if effective competition from private enterprises
builds up, unless the public enterprises derive
open or disguised advantages by virtue of their
public sector status.

        (ii)   A large number of public enterprises
are so organised as to possess features of monopoly.
A monolithic organisation that covers the total public sector activity in a given field of production,
a holding company structure, and a few multi-plant
giants, are all examples of monopoly elements for
which there may be no justification except for the
government's decision to confer on them such an
organisational status.   It is possible that the
government is not able or willing to break up such
large undertakings so as to make the benefits of
competition possible.   Yet an attempt may be made
to encourage some degree of competition among the
constituent parts of a large enterprise, so that
whatever benefits can emerge from competition in a
given field can be realised and whatever disadvantages or costs exist with monopoly organisation in
that field may be minimised.   True, an effective
monopoly commission can try to take care of the
latter aspect, but to promote competition (3),
positively, is an intrinsically helpful measure.
What this implies, in other words, is not only a
relaxation of any government controls that support
the monopoly elements but an active requirement
that the enterprise should introduce organisational
steps that create conditions of competition within
the single, large apex, as far as possible.

        (iii) There is a tendency on the part of
certain controls to institutionalise themselves in
such a way that they continue long after their
rationale is lost.   In other words, such controls
become a vested interest.   While they have no

positive purpose to achieve, they may be working
against the efficiency of the enterprise by impin-
ging on managerial initiative within the enterprise.

While the logic of marketisation in the above
circumstances is valid, there is a major qualification. The basic purposes of a public enterprise
in the extra enterprise (or social benefits) context
have to be preserved; and controls that are instru-
mental in achieving them have to be maintained.
The enterprise may, therefore, be subjected to certain control disciplines, for example in investment
and pricing. But within the impacts of such controls market forces may be allowed to exercise their
influence on the operations of the enterprise. In
this way we can see some parallelism between the
earlier-mentioned agencies of decentralised control
such as an independent commission and the market.

The government has to lay down the basic criteria, subject to which the commission in one case
and the market in the other are allowed to wield the
rest of the control function. How elaborate or
substantial the basic criteria should be would depend on the activity in question. In the case of
infra-structural activities, these may be very material; whereas at the other end, e.g. in light
industry, these may be of nominal significance.

Interesting illustrations of market as a control agency are available from Italy - in the case
of IRI - and from France - in the case of Renault,
each with a large number of subsidiaries exposed to
market disciplines, subject - in IRI's case - to
investment guidelines in favour of Southern Italy
(4).

The way in which basic public controls can
go along with market controls may be elaborated as
follows. There can be a control on the nature of
regional spread of investments, but within it freedom can exist for the enterprise to go by market
considerations regarding the output mix or even as
regards the exact location. There can be a control
as regards the desired output - e.g. x passenger
train miles, but within this freedom can exist on
the production function and marketing. There can
be a control on the price level in relation to a
financial target and consistent with any physical
indicators of performance set, and within it freedom can remain as regards the price structure and

sales strategy as per market considerations. There
can be a ceiling on investment in a given period,
but within it the actual channels of capital expenditure and terms of procurement may be left to be
regulated by market factors. And so on.

It is necessary to make a comment with reference to the situation in which a public enterprise
may be in competition with private enterprises in a
given area of activity. It is possible that the
government does not leave the former entirely to
market discipline, if it decides to avail of it in
realising certain national objectives. For instance,
it may be required to undertake special responsibilities for technical training, or specialise in the
basic stages of a production activity (such as basic
formulations in the pharmaceutical line) involving
heavy research and development expenditures, or encourage ancillaries by buying certain inputs from
them, even if not very economical, or buy 'national'
inputs rather than cheaper imports, or operate in
rural or underdeveloped areas, or go in for a product-mix that relatively emphasises the less profitable lines. In all such cases the need exists
for the government to introduce some form of public control over the enterprise. What happens in
these cases is that in an apparently competitive
area imperfections are created at government instance in respect of certain sub-markets, output-
wise or factor-wise. The point we should not miss,
however, is that the market should be allowed to
discipline the enterprise in the rest of its operations. The best way of doing this is to treat each
of the extra-enterprise obligations as a contractual
item for which the government offers a payment to
the enterprise, such that these operations do not
complicate the enterprise's market behaviour in
the rest of its operations.

Apparently simple in logic, this method is
not adequately practised by governments. Instead,
various kinds of control relationships are pursued.
The most familiar of these is the control instrument
under which the enterprise has to procure capital
funds from the government (only) and - here the
complication comes in - at artificial below-market
rates of interest. This is the beginning of abridg-
ing the market's influence as an agency of
control.

NOTES

1.   An interesting reference in this context comes from the former Rhodesia. In spite of
its belief 'that the maximum economic growth can
best be attained by maintaining a free enterprise
economy', the Government declared that its 'intervention in production, or in the operation of the
price mechanism, will take place, if, in the
Government's opinion the market mechanism requires
to be regulated in the national interest'. (National
Development Plan, 1965, p.1, Salisbury, 1965).

2.   The World Bank observes that 'both in
socialist countries and within the public sector in
'mixed' economies, reforms based on market mechanisms
have been effective without changes in ownership'.
China has introduced 'a pricing system for medical
services that allows patients to choose'.   World
Development Report 1983 (Washington, 1983), p.53.

3.   Richard Pryke makes an interesting
observation at the end of his recent study on the
nationalised industries in the UK: 'In a number
of industries there is obviously scope for greater
competition and a prima facie case for moving in
this direction.   Where monopoly is inevitable it
would be possible to move away from a unitary form
of organisation and this may well be desirable.'
(The Nationalised Industries, Policies and Performance since 1968, Oxford, 1981) p.266.

4.   For instance 489bn. lire were invested
by IRI in localities 'left to the Group's discretion', as against 676bn.lire in 'locations pre-
scribed by law or the authorities' in 1981.   (IRI,
1981 Annual Report, p.75 (Rome).

Also see Ferdinando Brunell's observations
that, while IRI is under public control, there is
extensive decentralisation of decision making within it and that the relations between the banks
and IRI are the same as those between any private
company and a bank.   The Final Report on the
Seminar on the Management of Public Enterprises in
Latin America and Italy (Rome, 1978).

Chapter Twenty One

CONCLUSION

The purpose of this study is not to minimise the
role of the government in the control of public
enterprises.   It has final authority in the issuance of control instruments; and the constitutional value of parliamentary monitoring over
executive actions can be preserved.

What is suggested here is that the government
can effect a good deal of decentralisation in the
processes of control, such that in some matters an
'empowered' agency concerns itself with most of the
stages leading to final control by the government,
while in certain other matters it may be empowered
to issue a control directive itself.   If properly
devised, such a system can confer on society the
benefits of expertise combined with the compulsions
of macro outlook.   While the preceding chapters
give some idea on the proper devising of the system,
admittedly there can be no uniform model for all
countries.   What is worth emphasising however, is
that the direction towards control decentralisation
is commendable in all countries.

The following pro forma is set up with the
limited purpose of suggesting some detail in the
exercise of control decentralisation.   The issues
in column 1 are illustrative and not exhaustive.
The ticks in the columns-cum-rows constitute the
substance of the exercise; a few ticks are inserted
in the pro forma merely for the purpose of illustration.   From the government at one end to the
market at the other, the ticks represent progres-
sive decentralisation that places premium on the
'actors' nearest to the operations and keeps the
government at an appropriate distance, albeit
equipped with final powers in most matters.   The

more ticks in the 'recommendatory' column under
independent commissions, the greater the reservation of final control powers with the government
itself.

Table 13

An illustrative pro forma of control decentralisation

Aspect	Government	Commissions Recommendatory	Commissions Mandatory	Consumer Council	Holding Company	Board	Market
Investment							
Size	✓						
Location							
Technology							
Procurement of funds							
Surplus							
Overall targets	✓						
Intra-enterprise competiton		✓					
Disposal				✓			
Resources				✓	✓		
Pricing							
Level							
Structure							
Cross-subsidisation							
Quality of output							
Conditions of supply							
Expansion							

Decentralisation of Public Enterprise Control

Table 13 (cont'd.)

Aspect	Government	Commissions Recommendatory	Commissions Mandatory	Consumer Council	Holding Company	Board	Market
Monopoly practices	✓						
Employment							
Size							
Wage levels							
Perquisites							
Recruitment							
Lay-off							
Incentives							
Budget							
Corporate Plan					✓		
Board Appointment etc.						✓	
Purchases							✓
Foreign collaboration and joint ventures							
Establishment of subsidiaries							

APPENDICES

Appendix 1

SOME DEVELOPMENT INDICES

Country	Manufacturing as % of GDP (Below 10)	Energy consumption per capita (kg. of coal equivalent) (Below 50)	Urban population as % of total (Below 10)	Labour force in agriculture % (Above 80)	Adult literacy % (Below 20)
	(2)	(3)	(4)	(5)	(6)
Benin	x	x			x
Chad	x	x	x	x	x
Central African Republic	x	x		x	x
Somalia	x	x		x	x
Rwanda	x		x	x	x
Madagascar	x	x		x	
Niger	x	x	x	x	x
Zambia	x				
Mauritania	x	x	x	x	x
Senegal	x			x	x
Uganda	x	x	x	x	x
Togo	x	x		x	x
Ethiopia	x	x	x		
Tanzania	x	x	x	x	x
Mali	x	x		x	x

(1)

Appendix 1

Appendix 1 (cont'd.)

Country	Manufacturing as % of GDP (Below 10)	Energy consumption per capita (kg. of coal equivalent) (Below 50)	Urban population as % of total (Below 10)	Labour force in agriculture % (Above 80)	Adult literacy % (Below 20)
(1)	(2)	(3)	(4)	(5)	(6)
Malawi	x		x	x	
Upper Volta	x	x	x	x	x
Mozambique	x		x	x	x
Kenya	x		x	x	
Nigeria	x	x			x
Ivory Coast	x				x
Zaire				x	
Guinea				x	x
Sudan				x	x
Sierra Leone		x			x
Liberia				x	x
Cameroon				x	
Burundi			x	x	x
Lesotho			x	x	
Congo, People's Republic					x

Country				
Morocco				X
Bangladesh	X			
Burma	X	X		
Papua New Guinea	X	X		
Indonesia	X	X	X	
Kampuchea		X		
Lao PDR	X	X		
Nepal	X	X		X
Afghanistan	X	X		X
Viet Nam	X	X		X
Yemen Arab Republic				
Thailand	X	X	X	X
Bhutan	X	X	X	
Pakistan			X	X
Haiti	X	X		X

Source : <u>World Development Report 1982</u>, World Bank (Washington, 1982).

253

Appendix 2

UNITED NATIONS MEMBERSHIPS (Accessions)

Year (1)	N. America Europe & Australia (2)	Latin America (3)	Africa (4)	Asia (5)	Total (6)
1945	19	19	4	9	51
1946–50	3			6	9
1950–60	9		5	8	22
1960–65	2	2	25	2	31
1965–70		2	8	3	13
1970–75	2	1	1	7	11
1975–82		6	9	5	20

Source : States Members of the United Nations
DPJ/690 - January 1982 (New York).

Appendix 3

<u>A.I. PUBLIC ENTERPRISES IN INDIA</u>
<u>(CENTRAL GOVERNMENT)</u>

(As covered by the Annual Reports of
Bureau of Public Enterprises, 1981-82)

ENTERPRISES UNDER CONSTRUCTION

      Nagaland Pulp and Paper Co. Ltd.
      National Hydro Electric Power Corp. Ltd.
      National Thermal Power Corp. Ltd.
      North Eastern Electric Power Corp. Ltd.
      India Medicines Pharmaceuticals Corp. Ltd.
      Karnataka Antibiotics & Pharmaceuticals Ltd.
      Maruti Udyog Ltd.
      National Aluminium Co. Ltd.
      Orissa Drugs & Chemicals Ltd.

OPERATING ENTERPRISES

STEEL

      Mishra Dhatu Nigam Ltd.
      India Iron & Steel Co. Ltd.
      Steel Authority of India Ltd.
      IISCO Stanton Pipe & Foundry Co. Ltd.
      Sponge Iron India Ltd.
      Ferro Scrap Nigam Ltd.

MINERALS AND METALS

      Kudremukh Iron Ore Co. Ltd.
      Bharat Aluminium Co. Ltd.
      Bharat Gold Mines Ltd.
      Bharat Refractories Ltd.
      Hindustan Copper Ltd.
      Hindustan Zinc Ltd.
      Indian Rare Earths Ltd.
      India Firebricks & Insulation Co. Ltd.
      Manganese Ore (India) Ltd.
      National Mineral Development Corp. Ltd.
      Pyrites, Phosphates & Chemicals Ltd.
      Uranium Corp. of India Ltd.
      Neyveli Lignite Corp. Ltd.

COAL

      Bharat Coking Coal Ltd.

Central Coalfields Ltd.
Coal India Ltd.
Eastern Coalfields Ltd.
Western Coalfields Ltd.

PETROLEUM

Bongaigaon Refinery & Petrochemicals Ltd.
Bharat Petroleum Corp. Ltd.
Cochin Refineries Ltd.
Hindustan Petroleum Corp. Ltd.
Indian Oil Corp. Ltd.
Indo-Burma Petroleum Co. Ltd.
Lubrizol India Ltd.
Madras Refineries Ltd.
Oil & Natural Gas Commission
Oil India Ltd.
Indian Oil Blending Ltd.
Hydro Carbons India Ltd.

CHEMICALS & PHARMACEUTICALS

National Fertilizers Ltd.
Cement Corp. of India
Fertilizers & Chemicals (T) Ltd.
Fertilizer Corp. of India
Hindustan Antibiotics Ltd.
Hindustan Insecticides Ltd.
Hindustan Salts Ltd.
Hindustan Organic Chemicals Ltd.
IndianDrugs & Pharmaceuticals Ltd.
India Petro-Chemicals Corp. Ltd.
Madras Fertilizers Ltd.
Sambhar Salts Ltd.
Smith Stanistreet Pharmaceuticals Ltd.
Hindustan Fertilizer Corp. Ltd.
Rashtriya Chemicals & Fertilizers Ltd.
Southern Pesticides Corp. Ltd.
Maharastra Antibiotics & Pharmac. Ltd.
Goa Antibiotics & Pharmaceuticals Ltd.
Rajasthan Drugs & Chemicals Ltd.
U.P. Drugs & Pharmaceuticals Ltd.
Bengal Chemicals & Pharmaceuticals Works Ltd.

HEAVY ENGINEERING

Bharat Heavy Electricals Ltd.
Bharat Heavy Plate & Vessels Ltd.
Braithwaite & Co. Ltd.
Bridge & Roof Co. (India) Ltd.
Burn Standard Company Ltd.

Heavy Engineering Corp. Ltd.
Jessop & Co. Ltd.
Mining and Allied Machinery Corp. Ltd.
Triveni Structurals Ltd.
Tungbhadra Steel Products Ltd.
Bharat Wagon & Eng. Co. Ltd.
Lagan Jute Machinery Co. Ltd.
Bharat Process & Mechanical Eng. Ltd.
Weighbird India Ltd.

MEDIUM AND LIGHT ENGINEERING

Balmer Lawrie & Co. Ltd.
Bharat Dynamics Ltd.
Bharat Electronics Ltd.
Bharat Pumps & Compressors Ltd.
Biecco Lawrie Ltd.
Central Electronics Ltd.
Electronic Corp. of India Ltd.
Bharat Brakes & Valves Ltd.
Hindustan Cables Ltd.
Hindustan Machine Tools Ltd.
Hindustan Teleprinters Ltd.
Indian Telephone Industries Ltd.
Instrumentation Ltd.
National Instruments Ltd.
Praga Tools Ltd.
Richardson & Cruddas (1972) Ltd.
Semi Conductor Complex Ltd.
Andrew Yule & Co. Ltd.
HMT Bearings Ltd.

TRANSPORTATION EQUIPMENT

Bharat Earth Movers Ltd.
Central Inland Water Transport Corp. Ltd.
Cochin Shipyard Ltd.
Garden Reach Shipbuilders & Engineers Ltd.
Goa Shipyard Ltd.
Hindustan Aeronautics Ltd.
Hindustan Shipyard Ltd.
Mazagaon Dock Ltd.
Scooters India Ltd.
Cycle Corporation of India Ltd.
National Bicycle Corporation Ltd.

CONSUMER GOODS

Hindustan Paper Corp. Ltd.
Artificial Limbs. Mfg. Corp. of India Ltd.
Bharat Ophthalmic Glass Ltd.

Hindustan Latex Ltd.
Hindustan Photofilms Mfg. Co. Ltd.
Mandya National Paper Mills Ltd.
Modern Bakeries (India) Ltd.
National Newsprint & Paper Mills Ltd.
Rehabilitation Industries Corp. Ltd.
Tannery & Footwear Corp. of India Ltd.
Hooghly Printing Co. Ltd.
Brushware Ltd.

AGRO-BASED ENTERPRISES

Andaman & Nicobar Islands Forest & Plant
Dev. Corp. Ltd.
Banana Fruit Dev. Corp. Ltd.
National Seeds Corp. Ltd.
State Farms Corp. Ltd.
Banarhat Tea Co. Ltd.
Basmatia Tea Co. Ltd.
Hoolungooree Tea Co. Ltd.
Mim Tea Co. Ltd.
Murphulani (Assam) Tea Co. Ltd.
Rajgarh Tea Co.

TEXTILES

National Textile Corp. Ltd.
NTC (Andhra Pradesh, Karnataka, Kerala
& Mahe) Ltd.
NITC (Delhi, Punjab & Rajasthan) Ltd.
NTC (Madhya Pradesh) Ltd.
NTC (Maharashtra North) Ltd.
NTC (South Maharashtra) Ltd.
NTC (Tamilnadu & Pondicherry) Ltd.
NTC (Uttar Pradesh) Ltd.
NTC (West Bengal, Bihar, Assam & Orissa) Ltd.
British India Corporation Ltd.
Elgin Mills Co. Ltd.
NTC (Gujerat) Ltd.

TRADING AND MARKETING SERVICES

Bharat Leather Corp. Ltd.
Central Warehousing Corp.
Computer Maintenance Corp. Ltd.
Cotton Corp. of India Ltd.
Electronics Trade & Technology Dev. Corp. Ltd.
Food Corp. of India
H.M.T. (International) Ltd.
Handicrafts & Handlooms Exports Corp. of
India Ltd.

Jute Corp. of India Ltd.
Metal Scrap Trade Corp. Ltd.
Minerals & Metals Trading Corp. of India Ltd.
North Eastern Handlooms & Handicrafts Dev.
Corp.
Projects & Equipment Corp. Ltd.
State Trading Corp. of India Ltd.
Tea Trading Corp. of India Ltd.
Cashewnut Corp. of India Ltd.
Central Cottage Industries Corp. of India Ltd.
Mica Trading Corp. of India Ltd.

TRANSPORTATION SERVICES

Air India
Indian Airlines
International Airports Authority of India
Dredging Corp. of India
Mogul Line Ltd.
Shipping Corp. of India Ltd.
Delhi Transport Corp.
Vayudoot Ltd.
Air-India Charters Ltd.

CONTRACT & CONSTRUCTION SERVICES

Hindustan Prefab Ltd.
Hindustan Steel Works Constn. Ltd.
Indian Railways Constn. Ltd.
Indian Road Constn. Corp. Ltd.
Mineral Exploration Corp. Ltd.
National Building Constn. Corp. Ltd.
National Projects Constn. Corp. Ltd.
Central Mine Planning & Design Institute Ltd.

INDUSTRIAL DEVELOPMENT & TECHNICAL CONSULTANCY SERVICES

Engineers India Ltd.
Engineering Projects (I) Ltd.
Metallurgical & Eng. Consultants (India) Ltd.
National Industrial Dev. Corp. Ltd.
Rail India Technical & Economic Services Ltd.
Water & Power Consultancy Services (India) Ltd.
Projects & Development (India) Ltd.
Telecommunications Consultants (India) Ltd.

DEVELOPMENT OF SMALL INDUSTRIES

National Small Industries Corp. Ltd.

Appendix 3

TOURIST SERVICES

    India Tourism Dev. Corp. Ltd.
    Hotel Corp. of India Ltd.

FINANCIAL SERVICES

    Housing & Urban Dev. Corp. Ltd.
    Rural Electrification Corp. Ltd.
    National Film Dev. Corp. Ltd.

SECTION 25 COMPANIES

    India Diary Corp.
    National Research Dev. Corp. of India Ltd.
    Trade Fair Authority of India

INSURANCE COMPANIES

    Export Credit & Guarantee Corp. Ltd.
    General Insurance Corp. of India Ltd.
    Life Insurance Corp. of India
    National Insurance Co. Ltd.
    New India Assurance Co. Ltd.
    Oriental Fire & General Insurance Co. Ltd.
    United India Insurance Co. Ltd.

CENTRAL GOVT. INVESTMENT WITHOUT MANAGEMENT

    Orissa Drugs & Chemicals
    Agricultural Refinance & Devel. Corp.
    Industrial Development Bank
    Industrial Finance Corporation
    Visveswaraya Iron & Steel Ltd.
    Wagon India Ltd.
    Damodar Valley Corporation
    Hindustan Diamond Co. Ltd.
    Indian Explosives Ltd.
    Machinery Manufacturing Corp. Ltd.
    Sikkim Mining Corporation
    Sindhu Resettlement Corporation
    Singarani Collieries Ltd.

(Besides there are many Port Trusts, and departmentally organised enterprises like railways, posts and telegraphs, and broadcasting. All major banks are also in the public sector.)

Appendix 3

A.II PUBLIC ENTERPRISES IN THE STATE
OF ANDHRA PRADESH (1) (1982)

INDUSTRY AND COMMERCE

1.   A.P. Industrial Development Corporation
2.   A.P. Industrial Infrastructure Corporation Ltd.
3.   A.P. State Financial Corporation Ltd.
4.   A.P. State Trading Corporation Ltd.
5.   A.P. Mining Corporation Ltd.
6.   A.P. State Textile Development Corporation Ltd.
7.   A.P. Small Scale Industrial Development
     Corporation Ltd.
8.   Leather Industries Development Corporation
     of Andhra Pradesh Ltd.
9.   A.P. Non-Resident Indian Investment Corporation
10. A.P. Handicrafts Development Corporation
11. Nagarjuna Fertilisers & Chemicals Ltd.
12. Godavari Fertilisers & Chemicals Ltd.
13. Hyderabad Allwyns Ltd.
14. Nizam Sugar Factory Ltd.
15. Republic Forge Company Ltd.
16. Andhra Pradesh Steels Ltd.
17. Andhra Pradesh Scooters Ltd.
18. Andhra Pradesh Tyres & Tubes Ltd.
19. Andhra Pradesh Heavy Machinery & Engineering
     Ltd.
20. Andhra Pradesh State Handloom Weavers Coope-
     rative Ltd.
21. A.P. Electronic Development Corporation.

GENERAL

22. A.P. State Police Housing Corporation

GENERAL ADMINISTRATION

23. A.P. State Film Development Corp. Ltd.
24. A.P. Travel and Tourism Development Corpo-
     ration Ltd.

FOOD AND AGRICULTURE

25. Andhra Pradesh State Warehousing Corporation
26. Andhra Pradesh State Seeds Corporation Ltd.
27. Andhra Pradesh State Civil Supplies Corpora-
     tion Ltd.
28. Andhra Pradesh Essential Commodities Corpora-
     tion Ltd.
29. Andhra Pradesh State Cooperative Rural
     Irrigation Corporation

30. Andhra Pradesh State Agro Industries
     Development Corporation Ltd.
31. Hyderabad Chemicals & Fertilizers Ltd.

SOCIAL WELFARE

32. A.P. Scheduled Caste Cooperative Finance
     Corporation Ltd.
33. Andhra Pradesh Scheduled Tribes Cooperative
     Finance Corp. Ltd.
34. Andhra Pradesh Backward Class Cooperative
     Finance Corp. Ltd.
35. Girijan Cooperative Corporation, Visakhapatnam
36. Andhra Pradesh Handicapped Persons Welfare
     Cooperative Finance Corporation

IRRIGATION AND POWER

37. Andhra Pradesh State Irrigation Development
     Corporation Ltd.
38. Andhra Pradesh State Construction Corporation
     Ltd.
39. Andhra Pradesh State Housing Corporation

FOREST AND RURAL DEVELOPMENT

40. Andhra Pradesh Forest Development Corporation
     Ltd.
41. Andhra Pradesh Fisheries Corporation Ltd.
42. Andhra Pradesh State Meat and Poulty Develop-
     ment Corp. Ltd.
43. Andhra Pradesh Dairy Development Corporation

LABOUR EMPLOYMENT & TECHNICAL EDUCATION

44. Ready to Eat Food Factory
45. A.P. Women's Cooperative Finance Corporation

TRANSPORT, ROADS AND BUILDINGS

46. Andhra Pradesh State Road Transport Corporation

ENERGY, ENVIRONMENT, SCIENCE & TECHNOLOGY

47. Andhra Pradesh State Electricity Board
48. Singareni Collieries Company Ltd.

HOUSING MUNICIPAL ADMINISTRATION
& URBAN DEVELOPMENT

49. A.P. Housing Board

Appendix 3

DEPARTMENTAL ENTERPRISES

1. Government Central Press
2. A.P. Government Life Insurance Department
3. Government Power Alcohol Factory, Shakkarnagar
4. Government Distillery – Kimareddy
5. Government Distillery – Narayanguda
6. Government Distillery – Chegallu
7. Government Press, Kurnool
8. A.P. Government Text Book Press
9. Distillery Cell, NSF, Hyderabad
10. Gold Storage Plant, Nizamsagar at Nizamabad
11. Fish Farm, Kadium
12. Ceramic Quality Marketing Scheme, Rajahmundry
13. Ceramic Service Centre, Rajahmundry
14. Saw Mill Division, Rajahmundry
15. Pickle Jars & Bowls Manufacturing Unit, Rajahmundry
16. Bristle Mattresses Fibre Unit, Rajahmundry
17. Low Ceramic Ware Unit for Radio Components, Gudur
18. Ceramic Service Centre Dronachalam
19. Kalamkari Arts Centre, Srikalahasti
20. Industrial Research & Development Fund, Hyderabad
21. Bristle Mattresses Fibre Unit, Baruva
22. Production Wing in Coir Goods School, Baruva
23. Molasses Transactions (Excise) Hyderabad
24. Coir Goods Factory, Narsapur
25. Regl. Pig Breeding Stn cum Bacon Factory, Gannavaram
26. Fish Net Making Unit, Tungrabhadra (TB) Dam
27. Ice cum Cold Storage Plant, TB Dam
28. Fish Farm – TB Dam
29. Tool room cum Composite Servicing Workshop, Hyderabad

NOTE

(1)   One of the States of India

Appendix 3

B. PUBLIC ENTERPRISES IN PAKISTAN (1981)

BANKING

1.   National Bank of Pakistan
2.   Habib Bank Ltd.
3.   United Bank Ltd.
4.   Muslim Commercial Bank Ltd.
5.   Allied Bank of Pakistan Ltd.
6.   Industrial Development Bank of Pakistan
7.   Agricultural Devel. Bank of Pakistan

FINANCIAL INSTITUTIONS

1.   Pakistan Industrial Credit & Invest. Corp.Ltd.
2.   Investment Corporation of Pakistan
3.   National Investment (Unit) Trust
4.   House Building Finance Corporation
5.   Small Business Finance Corporation
6.   Equity Participation Fund
7.   National Development Finance Corp.
8.   Bankers Equity Ltd.

INSURANCE

1.   State Life Insurance Corp. of Pakistan
2.   Pakistan Insurance Corporation
3.   National Insurance Corporation

INDUSTRY

1.   Pakistan Automobile Corp. Ltd.
        Awami Autos Ltd.
        Bela Engineers Ltd.
        Domestic Appliances Ltd.
        Millat Tractors Ltd.
        National Motors Ltd.
        Naya Daur Motors Ltd.
        Pakistan Tractors Corp. Ltd.
        Republic Motors Ltd.
        Sind Engineering Ltd.
        Trailer Development Corp. Ltd.
2.   State Engineering Corp. Ltd.
        Heavy Foundry & Forge Ltd.
        Heavy Mechanical Complex Ltd.
        Karachi Pipe Mills Ltd.
        Metropolitan Steel Corp. Ltd.
        Northern Foundry & Engineering Works Ltd.
        Pakistan Engineering Co. Ltd.
        Pakistan Machine Tool Factory Ltd.
        Pioneer Steel Mills Ltd.

Quality Steel Works Ltd.
State Electrical Corp. of Pakistan, Lahore
Project
Special Steels of Pakistan Ltd.
Textile Machinery Corp. Ltd.
3.   Federal Chemical & Ceramics Corp. Ltd.
     (a)   Antibiotics (Private) Ltd.
     (b)   Ittehad Chemicals
     (c)   Ittehad Pesticides
     (d)   Kurram Chemical Co. Ltd.
     (e)   Nowshera DDT Factory
     (f)   Pakdyes & Chemicals Ltd.
     (g)   Pakistan PVC Ltd.
     (h)   Ravi Rayon Ltd.
     (i)   Ravi Engineering
     (j)   Sind Almalis Ltd.
     (k)   Swat Ceramics Co. Ltd.
     (l)   Swat Elutriation Plant
     (m)   National Fibres Ltd.
4.   National Fertilizer Corp. Ltd.
     (a)   Pak-Arab Fertilizers Ltd.
     (b)   Pak-American Fertilizers Ltd.
     (c)   Pak-Saudi Fertilizers Ltd.
     (d)   Lyalpur Chemicals & Fertilizers Ltd.
     (e)   National Fertilizer Marketing Ltd.
5.   State Cement Corporation of Pakistan
     Zeal Pak Ltd.
     Associated Ltd.
     Gharibwal Ltd.
     Mustehkam Ltd.
     Javedan Ltd.
     Maple Leaf Ltd.
     National Ltd.
     White Cement Ltd.
6.   Pakistan Steel Mills Corporation
7.   Pakistan Industrial Development Corp.
     (a)   Industry Co. Ltd.
     (b)   Banun Sugar Mills
     (c)   Quaidebad Woollen Mills
     (d)   Harnai Woollen Mills Ltd.
     (e)   Larkana Sugar Mills
     (f)   General Refractories Ltd.
     (g)   Karachi Gras Co. Ltd.
8.   Ghee Corporation of Pakistan Ltd.
     Burma Oil Mills Ltd.
     Bengal Vegetable Industries
     E.M. Oil Mills Ltd.
     Associated Industries Ltd.
     Kakakhel Industries Ltd.
     Moreafco Industries Ltd.
     Suraj Chee Industries Ltd.

Appendix 3

United Industries Ltd.
Sh. FAzal Rehman & Sons Ltd.

OIL AND GAS

1. State Petroleum Refining & Petro-Chemical
   Corp. Ltd.
   (a) National Refinery Ltd.
   (b) National Petrocarbon Ltd.
   (c) National Petrocarbon Division
   (d) National Petrospecialities Division
   (e) Enar Petrotechservices Ltd.
2. Pakistan Petroleum Ltd.
3. Oil & Gas Development Corporation
4. Pakistan State Oil Co. Ltd.
5. Paksitan Oil Fields Ltd.
6. Pak-Arab Refinery Ltd.

TRANSPORT AND COMMUNICATIONS

1. Pakistan International Airlines Corp.
2. Pakistan National Shipping Corp.
3. Pakistan Television Corp. Ltd.
4. Pakistan Broadcasting Corp.
5. National Film Devel. Corp. Ltd.
6. Telephone Industries of Paksitan Ltd.
7. Northern Areas Transport Corp. Ltd.

PUBLIC SERVICES

1. Water & Power Development Authority
2. Karachi Electric Supply Corp. Ltd.
3. Rawalpindi Electric Power Co. Ltd.
4. Multan Electric Supply Co. Ltd.
5. Pakistan Agricultural Storage & Services
   Corp. Ltd.
6. National Tubewell Construction Corp. Ltd.
7. Pakistan Tourism Development Corp.
8. Federally Admin. Tribal Areas Devel. Corp.
9. Utility Stores Corp.
10. Investment Advisory Centre of Pakistan

BANKING

National Bank of Pakistan
Habib Bank Ltd.
United Bank Ltd.
Muslim Commercial Bank Ltd.
Allied Bank of Pakistan Ltd.
Agricultural Devel. Bank of Pakistan

Appendix 3

PRINTING AND PUBLICATION

1. Pakistan Security Printing Corp. Ltd.
2. Printing Corporation of Pakistan
3. Security Papers Ltd.
4. National Book Foundation

MINING

1. Pakistan Mineral Development Corp.
2. Resource Development Corp.
3. Gemstone Corporation of Pakistan Ltd.

TRADE AND COMMERCE

1. Trading Corporation of Pakistan Ltd.
2. Rice Export Corp. of Pakistan Ltd.
3. Cotton Export Corp. of Pakistan Ltd.

ENGINEERING AND CONSULTANCY

1. National Construction Ltd.
2. Pakistan Environmental Planning &
    Architectural Consultants Ltd.
3. National Engineering Services (Pakistan) Ltd.
4. National Power Construction Corp. Ltd.
5. Mechanised Construction of Pakistan.

Source : <u>Government Sponsored Corporations 1980-81</u>
         (Islamabad, 1982).

267

Appendix 3

C. PUBLIC ENTERPRISES IN KENYA (1982)

I. DEVELOPMENT INSTITUTIONS

(a) Sectoral Development Corporations

1. Agricultural Development Corporation
2. Industrial & Commercial Development Corp.
3. National Housing Corporation
4. Kenya Tourist Development Corporation
5. Kenya Industrial Estate
6. National Construction Corporation
7. Industrial Development Bank (IDB)
8. Agricultural Finance Corporation
9. Kenya Film Corporation

(b) National Development Corporations

1. Kenya Railways Corporation
2. Kenya Ports Authority
3. Kenya Posts & Telecommunications Corporation

(c) Commodity Development Authorities

1. Cereals & Sugar Finance Corporation
2. Kenya Tea Development Authority (KTDA)
3. Horticultural Crops Development Authority
4. Kenya Meat Commission
5. Uplands Bacon Factory
6. Cotton Lint & Seed Marketing Board
7. Pyrethrum Marketing Board

(d) Regional Development Authorities

1. Tana River Development Authority
2. Lake Basin Development Authority
3. Kerio Valley Development Authority
4. National Irrigation Board

(e) Marketing Boards

1. National Cereals & Produce Board
2. Kenya Sisal Board
3. Kenya Coffee Marketing Board

Appendix 3

II.   FINANCIAL INTERMEDIARIES

(a)   <u>Banks</u>

1.   Central Bank of Kenya (CBK)
2.   Kenya Commercial Bank (KCB)
3.   National Bank of Kenya (NBK)
4.   Kenya Post Office Savings Bank
5.   Grindlays Bank International
6.   E.A. Development Bank

(b)   <u>Financial Institutions</u>

1.   Savings and Loans
2.   Kenya Commercial Finance Corporation
3.   Development Finance Company of Kenya
4.   Kenya National Capital Corporation
5.   United Finance Company

(c)   <u>Insurance Companies</u>

1.   Kenya Re-Insurance
2.   Kenya National Assurance (KNA)
3.   Notcutt Longaroni
4.   Insurance Company of E.A.
5.   Minet ICDC
6.   Kenya Commercial Insurance

(d)   <u>Investment Companies</u>

1.   Dyer & Blair
2.   ICDC Investment Company

III.   COMMERCIAL CONCERNS

(a)   <u>Sugar Companies</u>

1.   Chemelil Sugar Company
2.   E.A. Sugar Industries
3.   Mumias Sugar Company
4.   Nzoia Sugar Company
5.   South Nyanza Sugar Company

(b)   <u>Food and Crop Processing</u>

1.   Milling Corporation
2.   Pan African Vegetables
3.   Kenya Seed Company
4.   Kenya Cashewnuts
5.   Elianto Kenya
6.   E.A. Industries

7. Pano Industries
8. Inter Food Kenya
9. Supa Duka Mombasa
10. Rige Bakery
11. Food Specialities
12. B.A.T. Developments
13. Kenya Peanut Processors
14. Kenya Peanuts
15. Seed Driers
16. Mitchell Cotts Cashews
17. Meru Ginnery

(c) Tea Factories

1. Kangaita Tea Factory
2. Litein Tea Factory
3. Nyokoba Tea Factory
4. Mungania Tea Factory
5. Chinga Tea Factory
6. Chebut Tea Factory
7. Imenti Tea Factory
8. Kambaa Tea Factory
9. Kanyenyaini Tea Factory
10. Kapkoros Tea Factory
11. Nyasiongo Tea Factory
12. Ragati Tea Factory
13. Tegat Tea Factory
14. Thumaita Tea Factory
15. Githongo Tea Factory
16. Githambo Tea Factory
17. Githuthi Tea Factory
18. Mataara Tea Factory
19. Ikumbi Tea Factory
20. Njunu Tea Factory
21. Kimunye Tea Factory
22. Nyamacha Tea Factory
23. Elgon Tea Factory
24. Kenya Tea Packers

(d) Livestock

1. Muus Kenya Limited
2. Galana Game Ranching
3. Kenya Molasses and Livestock
4. Kenya Horse Stud Limited

(e) Textile and Fibre Companies

1. E.A. Fine Spinners
2. Mea Garments
3. E.A. Clothing Company

4. Kenya Toray Mills
5. Raumond Woollen Mills
6. Polysinthetic E.A.
7. Sewing Thread Limited
8. Mt. Kenya Textile Mills
9. Rift Valley Textile Mills
10. Kawan Enterprises
11. Kisumu Cotton Mills
12. Thika Cotton Mills
13. E.A. Bag and Cordage
14. Yuken Textile Limited
15. Kenya Fibre Corporation
16. Unisack Limited
17. African Synthetic
18. Kenya Taitex Mills

(f) Rubber and Plastic Companies

1. Firestone E.A.
2. Tanneries of Kenya Limited
3. Tiger Shoes Company Limited
4. Booth Manufacturers
5. C.P.C. Industrial Plastics
6. Eslon Plastics of Kenya
7. Kenya Industrial Plastics
8. Seracoating

(g) Beverage Industry

1. Rift Valley Bottlers
2. Mount Kenya Bottlers
3. Kenya Wine Agencies

(h) Engineering Companies

1. Kenya Engineering Company
2. Brollo Kenya Limited
3. Metal Box Company
4. Steel Billet Castings
5. Welden Steels Piles
6. Wire Products
7. Kenwest Falls Worlds
8. African Radio Manufacturers
9. Union Carbide
10. Hastings Irrigation
11. Claude Neon Lights
12. Domas Limited
13. African Marine General
    Engineering

(i) Fishing Companies

    1. Kenya Fishing Industries
    2. E.A. Fisheries Ltd.
    3. Lamu Fisheries
    4. Lake Baringo Fisheries Limited

(j) Chemical and Pharmaceutical Companies

    1. Dawa Pharmaceuticals
    2. E.A. Oxygen Limited
    3. Agro-Chemical Food Company
    4. Kenya Furfural Company
    5. Crop Protection Chemicals
    6. Infusion Kenya
    7. N.A. Chemical Fertilizers Co.

(k) Commercial Companies

    1. Uchumi Super Market
    2. African Retail Traders
    3. Sommerset Africa
    4. J.W. Kearsley
    5. Kenya Bowling Centre
    6. Stellascope Printing Company
    7. Kenya National Trading Company

(l) Tourism Sector

    1. Bomas of Kenya
    2. Kenya National Travel Bureau
    3. African Tours and Hotels
    4. Kenya Hotels Properties (Inter Continental Hotel)
    5. Homa Bay Hotel Limited
    6. Mt. Elgon Lodge
    7. Sunset Hotel
    8. Meru Mulika Lodge
    9. Marsabit Lodge
  10. Tea Hotel
  11. The Ark
  12. Emu Hotels
  13. International Hotels
  14. Mountain Lodge
  15. Robinson Hotel
  16. Safari Lodge Properties
  17. Block Hotels
  18. South Coast Hotels
  19. Mnarani Club
  20. Panafric Hotels
  21. Buffalo Spring Lodge

22. Milimani Hotels
23. Lions Hill Camp
24. Maralal Safari Lodge
25. Pollman's Tours and Safari
26. NAS Airport Services
27. Kulia Investments Company
28. Tourism Promotion Services
29. KTDC Utalii Investment
30. Zimmermans (Domant)
31. Kenya Safari Lodge

(m) Mining Companies

1. Kenya Mining Industries
2. African Diatomite Industry
3. Bamburi Portland Cement
4. E.A. Portland Cement
5. Salt Manufacturers
6. Kenya Fluorspar Company
7. Ceramic Industries
8. Nakuru Chrome T. Company

(n) Wood and Paper Companies

1. Pulp and Paper Company
2. Wananchi Saw Mills
3. Sokoro Fibre Boards
4. Pan African Paper Mills
5. Veneers Kenya Limited
6. Madhu Paper International
7. Highlands Paper Mills

(o) Housing and Construction

1. International Construction Company
2. Kabete Housing Limited
3. Loresho Housing Limited
4. Estate Services Limited
5. Own Properties Limited
6. Kenya National Properties
7. Crossroads Development
8. A.A.P. Company
9. Kenya National Properties
10. Lands Limited
11. Kenya Re-properties (KR)
12. Cargo Master International
13. Housing Finance Company of Kenya

(p) Transport and Communications

1. Kenya Airways

2. Kenya Pipelines
3. Kenya Cargo Handling
4. Kenya External Telecommunication
5. Kenya Flamingo Airways
6. Kenya Airfreight Handling
7. Kenatco Transport
8. Kenya Shipping Agency
9. Air Kenya
10. Nakulines

(q) Motor Companies

1. Associated Vehicle Assembly
2. C.M.C. Holdings
3. General Motors
4. Cockar Dynamics Limited
5. Hill Products
6. Associated Battery Manufacturers
7. Leyland Kenya Limited

(r) Energy Companies

1. E.A. Power and Lighting
2. Tana River Development Company
3. Kenya Power Company
4. E.A. Oil Refineries

Source: Report and Recommendations of the Working Party on Government Expenditures (Nairobi, 1982).

Appendix 3

D. PUBLIC ENTERPRISES IN COLOMBIA

TRANSPORT AND OTHER PUBLIC UTILITIES

Post Office
Transport
Shipping
Electricity
Aviation
Telecommunications
Ports
Railways
Radio and Television
24 Regional government enterprises in electricity,
     gas and water
2 Regional government enterprises in transport, etc.
40 Local government enterprises in electricity, gas
     and water
9 Local government enterprises in transport, etc.

INDUSTRY

Aeronautical equipment
Chemicals
Shipbuilding
Arms and explosives
Tannery
Pharmaceuticals
Fats
Frozen food
Concrete
Plastics
Motor vehicles
20 Regional government enterprises in manufacturing
Handicrafts

OIL AND MINERALS

Coal
Mining
Uranium
Salt
Nickel
Petroleum
Oil Pipelines

AGRICULTURE

Farm Products
Agricultural marketing
12 Regional government enterprises, in agriculture,
     hunting, forestry and fishing

Appendix 3

SERVICES

Warehousing (general)
Warehousing – agricultural
Motion pictures
News and documentary films
Food marketing
Hotel
Industrial research
Petroleum distribution
Duty-free areas
7 Regional government enterprises in wholesale or retail trade, etc.
41 Regional government enterprises in sanitary, recreational and cultural or other services
15 Local government enterprises in sanitary etc. services.

FINANCE

Central bank
Coffee bank
Mortgage bank
Cattle bank
Savings and loans institutions
Pension fund
Insurance
Agricultural and export finance
Handicrafts
Transport
Development finance
Public works finance
Electricity finance
Price stabilisation
Agricultural development
Industrial development
Loan guarantees
Private investment finance
Educational finance

HOUSING

24 Regional government financing and insurance institutions
20 Local government financing and insurance institutions

Source : International Monetary Fund, <u>Government Finance Statistics Year Book</u>, Vol.VI, 1982.

Appendix 4

EXCERPTS FROM ANNUAL REPORTS OF PUBLIC
ENTERPRISES IN THAILAND ON OBJECTIVES

The Telephone Organisation of Thailand has the
statutory objectives of 'carrying out and promoting
telephone activities for the benefit of the State
and the public and carrying out the business in connection with telephone activities and other business
incidental, pertaining or beneficial to telephone
activities'. 'In carrying out its objectives, the
Telephone Organisation of Thailand adopts the following principles: 1. To improve and promote the
telephone system with an emphasis on quality, rendering quick, efficient and reliable service to
the public; 2. To expand plants and increase in
quantity in order to meet the demands of the public;
3. To try to minimize hindrances and inconveniences
in telephone usage; and 4. To charge reasonable fees
for services rendered.' And 'the objectives of
financial year 1980' are listed in detail –
concerning installations, maintenance and expansions
– all in physical terms. (1980 Annual Report,
Telephone Organisation of Thailand) p.10.

Thai Airways lists as its objectives the
following:

(1) To undertake business of air transport
domestically, internationally and/or outside the
country, on the routes which have been set or not,
regularly or not, with aircraft or other vehicles
which are the properties of the company or which
have been leased, chartered and acquired by any
other means.

(2) To set up aircraft manufacturing and
maintenance plants and with components, along with
all tools and equipment.

(3) To undertake matters related to airports,
flying stations, aircraft fuelling and lubrication,
runways, hangars, component and service stations,
and all other undertakings related to aviation.

(4) To prescribe regulations concerning the
operating, maintenance, improvement and expansions
of schools of flying training schools, and/or to

provide scholastic specialists, training directors, and trainings for pilots, personnel aboard the aircraft and at the airports, along with personnel in all other sectors.

(5) To lease out properties of the company, or properties which the company has the right to lease out.

(6) To set up branches or to appoint representatives of the company, authorised to undertake business in accordance with the company's objectives in provinces of the country and abroad.

(7) To act as representatives and/or as brokers of other companies.

(8) To be the owner of land which is used for the company's businesses.

(9) To enter into limited partnership with the limited partnerships, or as shareholders in any companies, when it is obvious that the objectives of the limited partnerships or firms are in accordance or similar to the company's objectives.

(10) To export or import goods for commercial purpose.

(11) To carry out any undertakings which promote the company's businesses.

(12) To lend money, and/or giving the limited companies engaged in aeronautical businesses in which the company holds shares to borrow money from the company, including the company's staff who can borrow money as welfare.

(13) To undertake business related to hotels, restaurants and other concerned businesses which promote the company's businesses.

(Annual Report 1980/81, Thai Airways) p.46.

The Provincial Electricity Authority outlines its objectives in the following terms:

(1) To improve the existing system for more efficiency and reliability, and to be adequate for the increasing demand.

278

Appendix 4

(2) To minimise the operating costs. Especially at present time the price of the fuel oil is highly increased, this makes the generating cost by diesel power plant higher accordingly, PEA tries to renounce its own diesel plants by means of extending distribution lines from EGAT's substations to supply power instead.

(3) To extend electricity supply to unelectrified areas as much as possible in due course.

(PEA Annual Report, 1981) p.18.

Appendix 5

A STATEMENT OF PUBLIC ENTERPRISE
PROBLEMS FACED IN ETHIOPIA

(As revealed at a 'high level seminar' under
the chairmanship of Chairman Mengistu Hailmariam
in 1979)

1. Accounts not closed.
2. Asset values as of date of takeover not known.
3. Depreciation not determined.
4. Shortage of qualified manpower, general
    managers, accountants, financial management,
    and auditors.
5. No increase of productivity.   No method of
    costing or quantified planned target of out-
    put.   No way of following up, measuring, or
    evaluating performance on day-to-day or monthly
    basis.   Lack of financial data, or complete
    lack of criteria for measurement of evaluating
    performance.
6. Internal organisational conflict.   No well
    defined lines of responsibility and policy of
    management, labour unions, political discussion
    forums, and Revolutionary guards, corporations,
    state enterprises.
7. External organisational conflict.   No well
    defined policy or clear line of responsibility
    and authority of Ministry, supervising autho-
    rity, mass organisations (AETU, POMA), courts,
    and central government.
8. Managerial
    -   management fear
    -   lack of managerial know-how
    -   lack of independence in respon-
        sibility and authority
    -   management's limited power over
        money, material, manpower.
9. Lack of scientific and technical methods for
    production control, inventory control, re-
    placement and maintenance technic and policy.
10. Labour
    -   strong labour demand
    -   strong labour negotiation
    -   increase in work force (employment)
    -   weakness and strength of labour law.
11. No clear-cut plan on management's administra-
    tive responsibility over funds and resources,
    allocation of accumulated fund to
    a.   management

      b.   employee incentive
      c.   expansion and contraction
      d.   contribution to central treasury

(J. Lannes Kinfu, 'Towards better understanding of the development and performance of state corporation and state enterprise – with reference to Ethiopian experience' in <u>The Role of Public Enterprises in Development in Eastern Africa</u>, Institute for Development Studies, Nairobi, 1980).

Appendix 6 PRICE DISTORTION AND GROWTH RATE (1970s)

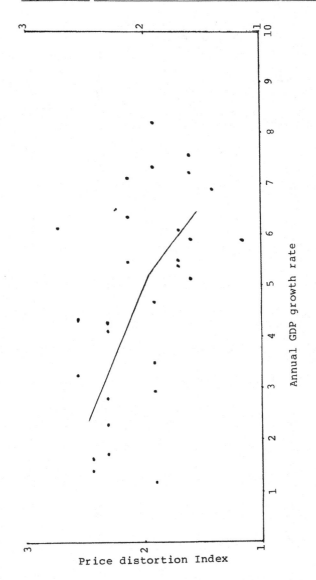

Annual GDP growth rate

Price distortion Index

Appendix 7

GOVERNMENT CAPITAL EXPENDITURE IN PUBLIC
ENTERPRISES IN SRI LANKA (1982)

(In Rs. million)

Ministry (1)	In public enterprises (2)
Agricultural Development & Research	276
Plantation Industries	54
State Plantations	–
Coconut Industries	50
Fisheries	37
Industries and Scientific Affairs	1,007
Textile Industries	48
Rural Industrial Development	51
Lands and Land Development	12
Local Government, Housing and Construction	1,657
Highways	–
Power and Energy	564
Transport	294
Trade and Shipping	749
Posts and Telecommunications	321
Education	–
Higher Education	–
Health	2
Defence	127
	5,249
Mahaweli etc. projects	6,716
	11,965

Source : The figures are compiled from the detailed
data available in Performance 1982, Ministry of Plan Implementation, Colombo, 1983.

The total of capital expenditures of the government
during 1982 was (provisionally) Rs.16,258 million.
Central Bank of Ceylon, Annual Report for the year
1982 (Colombo, 1983) p.31.

Appendix 8

PLANNED SHARE OF PUBLIC AUTHORITIES IN
TOTAL GROSS INVESTMENT (percentages)

Percentage (1)		Countries (2)	
Above 70	Togo	Iraq Nepal Syrian Arab Republic	
50 - 70	Cameroon Mauritius Nigeria Zambia	Iran	
30 - 50	Ivory Coast	Khmer Republic Malaysia Rep. of Korea Sri Lanka Thailand	Dominican Republic Paraguay Peru Venezuela
Below 30		Lebanon Philippines	Colombia Costa Rica Guetemala

Source : Journal of Development Planning, No.6.
p.136 (UN, New York, 1973).

(The data refer to plans of early 1970s)

284

Appendix 9

PUBLIC INVESTMENTS IN MANUFACTURING

Country	Year	Public investment in manufacturing (%)
(1)	(2)	(3)
Egypt	1975	90
Ivory Coast	1971-75	19
Nigeria	1970-74	18
Somalia	1973	80
Tunisia	1977-81	54
Yemen	1975-76	76
Turkey	1966-76	55
India	1975-76	61
Iran	1974	33
Iraq	1975	98
Pakistan	1975-80	76
Republic of Korea	1972-76	10
Sri Lanka	1972-76	55
El Salvador	1973-77	41
Guatemala	1976-79	16
Haiti	1976-81	10
Mexico	1976	35
Peru	1971-75	25
Venezuela	1976-80	50

Source : UNIDO, World Industry since 1960: Progress and Prospects (New York, 1979) p.325.

CLASSIFICATION OF COUNTRIES
BY DEVELOPMENT INDICES

Column   (1) Country

Column   (2) Average annual growth (%) 1960-80

Column   (3) Population (mill.) mid-1980

Column   (4) Manufacturing as % of GDP 1980

Column   (5) % of labour force in agriculture 1980

Column   (6) Average annual growth of labour force
             (%) 1980-2000

Column   (7) Urban as % of total population 1980

Column   (8) Enrolment in higher education as % of
             population aged 20-24

Column   (9) Energy consumption per capita (Kg. of
             coal equivalent) 1979

Column (10) External public debt as % of GNP 1980

Low income economies (1)	(2)	(3)	(4)	(5)	(6)	(7)	(8)	(9)	(10)
Kampuchea		C	C					A	
Lao PDR		B		A	B			A	
Bhutan	A	A		A	C	A			
Chad	A	B	A	A	B	A		A	B
Bangladesh		E	A	A	A	A	B	A	B
Ethiopia	B	E	B	A	B	A		A	C
Nepal	A	D	A	A	B	A	B	A	D
Somalia		B	A	A	B	C	A	A	B
Burma	B	E	B	B	B	B	B	A	C
Afghanistan		D		A	A	A	A	A	
Viet Nam		E		A	A	A		B	
Mali	B	C	A	A	A	B		A	B
Burundi	C	B	A	A	B	A	B	A	C
Rwanda	B	C	C	A	A	A	A	A	C
Upper Volta	A	C	B	A	B	A	A	A	C
Zaire	A	D	A	A	B	C	A	B	A
Malawi	C	C	B	A	A	A		A	B
Mozambique	A	D	A	B	B	A		B	
India	B	E	C	B	B	B	C	B	D
Haiti	A	C	B	A	B	B	A	A	D
Sri Lanka	C	D	C	B	B	B	A	B	B
Sierra Leone		B	A	B	B	B	A	A	B
Tanzania	B	D	A	A	A	A		A	C
China		E	A	A	D	A	A	D	
Guinea	A	C	A	A	B	A	C	A	A

Low income economies (1)	(2)	(3)	(4)	(5)	(6)	(7)	(8)	(9)	(10)
Central African Rep.	A	A		A	B	D	A	A	C
Paksitan	C	E	C	B	A	B	B	B	B
Uganda	A	D	A	A	A	A	A	A	D
Benin	A	B	A	C	B	A	A	A	C
Niger	A	C	A	A	A	A		A	C
Madagascar	A	C	C	A	B	A	B	A	B
Sudan	A	D	A	A	A	B	B	B	B
Togo	D	A	A	B	A	B	B	B	A

Appendix 10

Middle income economies (1)	(2)	(3)	(4)	(5)	(6)	(7)	(8)	(9)	(10)
Ghana	A	D	B	B	A	C		C	D
Kenya	C	D	B	A	A	A	A	B	C
Lesotho	E	A	A	A	B	A	B		D
Yemen, PDR	E	A	B	C	A	C	B	D	A
Indonesia	E	E	A	B	C	B	B	B	C
Yemen Arab Republic	E	C	A	A	B	A		A	C
Mauritania	B	A	A	A	A	B	B	B	A
Senegal	A	C	C	A	B	B		C	B
Angola	A	C	A	B	B	B	B	B	B
Liberia	B	A	A	A	A	C		C	A
Honduras	B	B	C	B	A	C	C	B	B
Zambia	A	C	C	B	A	D	B	D	A
Bolivia	C	C	B	B	A	C	D	C	B
Egypt	D	E	E	B	B	D	D	D	A
Zimbabwe	A	C	E	B	A	B		D	D
El Salvador	B	B	C	B	A	D	C	C	C
Cameroon	C	C	A	A	C	C	A	B	B
Thailand	E	E	D	A	B	A	C	C	D
Philippines	C	E	E	C	A	C	E	C	D
Nicaragua	A	A	E	C	A	D		C	A
Papua New Guinea	C	B	A	A	B	A		C	C
Congo, People's Rep.	A	A	A	C	A	D	B	B	A
Morocco	C	D	C	B	A	D	B	C	B
Mongolia		A		B	A	D		D	
Albania		A		B	B	C		D	

Middle income Economies (1)	(2)	(3)	(4)	(5)	(6)	(7)	(8)	(9)	(10)
Peru	B	D	E	C	A	E	D	D	B
Nigeria	E	E	A	B	A	B	A	A	D
Jamaica	A	A	C	D	A	D		D	A
Guatemala	C	C	D	B	A	C	C	B	D
Ivory Coast	C	C	B	A	B	D	B	B	B
Dominican Republic	D	C	C	C	A	D		C	C
Colombia	D	D	D	D	A	E	D	D	D
Ecuador	E	C	A	B	A	D	E	D	C
Paraguay	D	B	C	C	A	C	C	B	D
Tunisia	E	C	B	C	A	D	C	D	B
Korea, Dem. Rep.					A	E		E	
Syrian Arab Rep.	D	C	D	C	A	D	D	D	C
Jordan	E	B	C	D	A	D		D	B
Lebanon		A		E	A	E	E	D	
Turkey	D	E	D	B	B	D	C	D	C
Cuba	E	C	E	D	B	E	D	D	C
Korea Rep. of	E	E	D	C	B	D	D	D	D
Malaysia	D	D	D	B	A	B	B	B	D
Costa Rica	D	A	D	D	A	D	E	D	B
Panama	D	A	B	D	A	D	E	D	A
Algeria	D	D	B	D	A	D	B	D	B
Brazil	E	E	D	C	A	E	D	D	C
Mexico	C	E	D	C	A	E	D	E	C
Chile	B	D	D	D	B	E	D	D	C
South Africa	C	D	D	C	A	D		E	C

Romania	E	D	E	D	E	D	D	E	C
Portugal	E	C	D	D	E	C	D	D	D
Argentina	C	D	E	E	D	E	E	E	D
Yugoslavia	E	D	E	D	E	D	E	E	D
Uruguay	B	A	B	E	D	E	D	D	
Iran		E	A	C	A	D	C	D	
Iraq	E	D	C	C	A	E	C	D	
Venezuela	C	D		D	A	E	E	E	
Hong Kong	E	C	E	E	D	E	D	D	C
Trinidad & Tobago	D	A	B	D	B	B		E	D
Greece	E	C	C	C	E	E	D	E	D
Singapore	E	A	E	E	D	E	C	E	D
Israel	D	B	D	E	B	E	E	E	A

Appendix 10

(1)	(2)	(3)	(4)	(5)	(6)	(7)	(8)	(9)	(10)
High income oil exporters									
Libya	E	B	A	D	A	D	C	E	E
Saudi Arabia	E	C	A	B	A	E	C	E	E
Kuwait	A	A	A	E	A	E	D	E	E
United Arab Emirates	E	A	A			E		E	E
Industrial market economies									
Ireland	D	B		D	C	D	D	E	E
Spain	E	E		D	E	E	E	E	E
Italy	D	E	E	E	E	E	E	E	E
New Zealand	B	B	D	E	D	E	E	E	E
United Kingdom	C	E	D	E	E	E	E	E	E
Finland	E	B	E	E	E	E	E	E	E
Australia	C	D	E	E	E	E	E	E	E
Japan	E	E	E	E	E	E	E	E	E
Canada	D	D	C	E	E	E	E	E	E
Austria	E	C	E	E	E	D	E	E	E
U.S.A.	C	E	D	E	E	E	E	E	E
Netherlands	E	D	E	E	E	E	E	E	E
France	D	E	E	E	E	E	E	E	E
Belgium	D	C	E	E	E	E	E	E	E
Norway	D	C	C	E	E	D	E	E	E

Denmark	D	C	D	E	E	E	E	E	E
Sweden	C	C	D	E	E	E	E	E	E
Germany, Fed.Rep.	D	E	E	E		E	E	E	E
Switzerland	B	C		E	E	D	E	E	E
Non-market industrial economies									
Poland	E	E	E	C	E	D	D	E	E
Bulgaria	E	C	E	C	E	E	D	E	E
Hungary	E	D	E	D	E	D	D	E	E
U.S.S.R.	E	E	E	E	E	E	E	E	E
Czechoslovakia	E	D	E	E	E	E	D	E	E
German Dep. Rep.	E	D	E	E	E	E	E	E	E

Printed in the United States
by Baker & Taylor Publisher Services